14—

④

THE LATEST COUNTRY HOUSES

THE LATEST
COUNTRY HOUSES

John Martin Robinson

THE BODLEY HEAD
LONDON   SYDNEY
TORONTO

ACKNOWLEDGEMENTS

The book would not have been possible without the generous co-operation of most of the owners and architects, and I am most grateful to them. In addition, several people have helped with the research and photographs, especially Martin Andrews, Stephen Croad, Miss Catherine Cruft, Robert Innes-Smith, Mrs Anthony Richardson, Gavin Stamp, David Walker and Robin Wyatt. Peter Reid as well as helping with the initial research has read my text and made many necessary corrections and improvements.

It should be explained that plans have been omitted for reasons of security.

John Martin Robinson,
Flookburgh,
Christmas 1983.

Frontispiece: The drawing-room at Freechase, Warninglid, Sussex. A Modern interior.

British Library Cataloguing
In Publication Data
Robinson, John Martin
The Latest Country Houses
I. Title

728.8'3'0941 NA 7620
ISBN 0 370 305620

© Text copyright John Martin Robinson 1984
Printed in Great Britain for
The Bodley Head Ltd,
9 Bow Street, London WC2E 7AL
by William Clowes Ltd, Beccles
First published in 1984

CONTENTS

INTRODUCTION

An explanation may be necessary for inflicting yet another book about country houses on the long-suffering public (a friend suggested that I should call it *Positively the Last Country Houses*), but so much that has been written on the subject, including the reviews and publicity surrounding the 'Destruction of the Country House' Exhibition in 1974, seems to me so wrongheaded that I have felt impelled to produce an antidote and to show that the country house tradition in Britain is far from dead. Anybody who compares the gazetteer at the end of this book with the lists of demolished houses in the catalogue of the 'Destruction of the Country House' Exhibition will find that a surprisingly large number of the houses listed there, which are not situated in industrial deserts, have been replaced by new houses. I have wanted to write this book since I was a schoolboy in the 1960s and first noted the dichotomy between the architectural activity I could see all around in the country and the doom-gloom I could read in the newspapers. The immediate impetus to get down to the job came with the recent publication of a book called *The Last Country Houses*, which ended in 1939!

My book is intended in an informal and general way to follow the country house series begun by Christopher Hussey in the 1950s, which so far covers from the early seventeenth century to the mid-twentieth century. The previous seven volumes (by John Cornforth and Oliver Hill, James Lees-Milne, Christopher Hussey, Mark Girouard and Clive Aslet) were published by Country Life, Oxford University Press and Yale University Press respectively. The aim of my book is to draw attention to the country houses built since the Second World War, largely by old-established landowners wishing to continue a traditional way of life on their estates. These houses are architecturally interesting because the majority of them are Neo-Georgian; it was the patronage of country landowners which kept alive the Classical tradition in English architecture after the Second World War. While the Modern Movement monopolised public architectural patronage, the owners of country houses for various reasons stuck to Neo-Georgian. Nobody would claim that all the country houses built in Great Britain and Ireland in the 1950s, 1960s and 1970s were of artistic merit, but they do represent a significant corpus of buildings. Now that Classicism is once again fashionable, it may be that these houses will come to seem at least as significant an aspect of post-war architecture as the once greatly admired prefabricated primary schools in Hertfordshire. They will certainly last longer.

In historical terms they are interesting because they bridge the gap between the Arts and Crafts response to the Georgian style at the beginning of this century and the more rigorous and scholarly approach of the New Palladians like Quinlan Terry, and some of the current generation of architectural students.

These houses are generally unknown, the majority never having been published in the architectural press and hardly recorded in Nikolaus Pevsner's *Buildings of England* series. The subject could almost be subtitled 'furtive house-building' as the owners have not been particularly keen to draw attention to their enterprise in this field. It is not just a policy of discretion on the part of the rich, however, which has kept their houses out of the limelight, but a positive lack of interest on the part of the architectural intelligentsia; for instance, in 1983, the leading architectural magazine, the *Architectural Review*, refused to publish Quinlan Terry's pavilion at Thenford in Northamptonshire because it is a Classical building. Nevertheless the present seems a good time to tackle the subject, not least because several designers, like Claud Phillimore, whose post-war architectural practices were devoted to country houses, can be studied in some detail following the deposit of their drawings in the RIBA Drawings Collection. There are, of course, difficulties in writing about buildings where the client and the architect may still be alive. At least when dealing with eighteenth- or nineteenth-century architectural history one is not faced with the difficult task of combining objectivity with courtesy. In the following chapters I have tried to be as frank as the circumstances will allow without, I hope, being rude about anybody living.

A few words about the scope of the subject may be in order. A country house is, of course, the capital of a functioning agricultural estate, an estate being anything from a few hundred acres upwards. Most of the houses described in this book occupy estates of between 1000 and 3000 acres, but some are considerably larger: Snaigow, for instance, is the centre of 7000 acres, Dupplin 12,000 acres, Arundel 14,000 acres, Gannochy 18,000 acres and Glen Tanar 27,000 acres. I have applied this definition rigorously. But it does pose a problem in that there are a lot of architecturally interesting new houses which are not the centres of estates while some which are, especially in Scotland, are little better than bungalows. A further problem had to be faced in deciding how far to cast the net in defining a 'new' house. Should this just include houses built completely afresh from the foundations upwards, or should it include reconstructions? I had no doubt about including the latter. Not only are some of the best new houses formed since the war reconstructions rather than new-builds, but previous country house volumes have followed similar criteria. Thus Christopher Hussey included Burton Constable as Georgian, Mark Girouard Carlton Towers as Victorian, and Clive Aslet Lindisfarne Castle as Edwardian. The real problem is knowing where to draw the line between

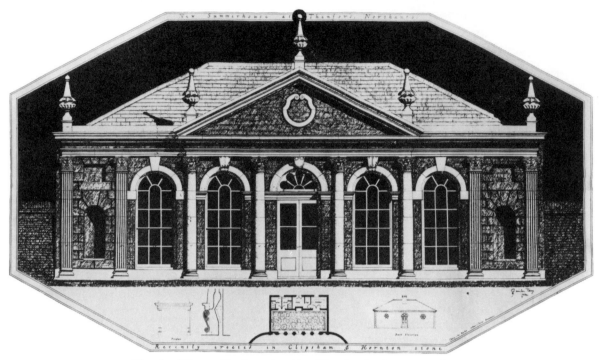

Thenford House, Northamptonshire. Elevation for the summer house
for Michael Heseltine by Quinlan Terry.

'reconstruction' and 'restoration'. In this I have simply followed my own taste
and other people may not agree with me. Thus I have included Scottish tower
houses—'new castles for old'—Francis Johnson's Yorkshire houses or Roger
Hesketh's Meols Hall because I believe that in all these cases the post-war work
has added a significant new dimension to the architectural appeal of the
building, but I have excluded jobs like Ian Lindsay's restorations of The Hirsel
or Mertoun, Philip Jebb's Cornbury Park or Woolbeding and much of Donald
Insall's work, because though ambitious and expensive they are consciously
self-effacing and intended to perpetuate the existing form of the buildings.

One last point on geography: I have covered England, Scotland, Wales and,
to a lesser extent, Ireland, but have not really got to grips with British country
houses overseas though the reader will encounter the odd reference to houses
in former colonies or in America. There are many interesting British-designed
houses abroad, including palaces for Arab potentates or holiday homes in the
West Indies, such as Oliver Messell's Classical confections on Mustique. These,
however, do not feature in the following pages.

I
THE ARCHITECTURAL
BACKGROUND

A few years ago I was taken to a 'new country house', Sevenhampton Place, in Wiltshire. It was a fine summer's day and we had drinks in the garden, before stepping through a French window into the dining-room for lunch. Any defects of internal planning therefore were not immediately apparent and the house seemed a most agreeable eighteenth-century-style *trianon* with a romantic garden, lake and prettily decorated rooms. In reply to some conventional compliments the owner said that the best description of her house could be found in Evelyn Waugh's *Diary*. Looking up the relevant pages later, the following emerged: 'A two-day visit to see what Ann has been up to. Laura and I arrived after dark by the wrong road over a cart track. The full horror of her edifice did not appear until the next day. That evening we were ushered by a butler, who had arrived only a few minutes before us, through a little dining-room (the only means of access) into a lofty drawing-room with a good carpet, otherwise sparsely furnished. A log fire (the only one in the house), a mean chimneypiece, a good fire-back, the sole surviving feature of the demolished house . . . No curtains. Appalling echoes everywhere much magnified by Maurice Bowra's voice . . . A narrow staircase (the only one) led to a few minute rooms and bathrooms; a plethora of beds. No chairs or writing materials. Narrow little built-in cupboards. The walls so thin as to admit every sound. Next morning . . . we were able to inspect the property—a strip of swamp 100 yards wide and $\frac{3}{4}$ mile long, which she is attempting to drain and level with imported soil. Of the house only one Caroline wing survives, the dining- and drawing-rooms; at right angles a low stone edifice, the bedrooms. On this Ann has spent twice the price of any of the most beautiful houses in the kingdom.'[1]

The contrast between these, not entirely flattering, words and my own

Sevenhampton Place, Wiltshire.

fleeting impression highlights the chief problem to be faced in writing about post-war country houses—how to assess their architectural quality. What seems attractive on a short visit on a sunny afternoon may not stand up to more rigorous analysis. While it might be accepted that many new houses are compact, convenient and comfortable for their owners, can it also be claimed that they are possessed of architectural merit? Many people probably wonder whether there have been enough country houses built since the war to form the subject of a book. The answer is that a surprisingly large number have been built; well over two hundred country houses by authentic landowners on traditional estates. They have not been paid for out of agriculture, but then neither were the great houses of the past. Edward III's Windsor Castle was financed by loot from the Hundred Years War, Hatfield House by Robert Cecil's exploitation of his public offices, Harewood by a West Indian sugar fortune and Arundel Castle by Sheffield ground rents.

The period since 1945 has in some ways been the most interesting in the history of the English country house. It has seen not just its survival against the odds, but its revival as a significant force in national life. The most important large houses have been painstakingly restored and opened to the public. The domestic side has been revolutionized to cope with the sudden disappearance of live-in servants. There has been a series of extraordinary redecoration schemes by a group of decorators who have created in the process a style known, on both sides of the Atlantic, as the 'English Country House Style'. Apart from the many old houses adapted for continued use there have been other cases where the owner has decided to build a new house. Sometimes this was because the old house had been burnt by troops during the war, or had been given to the National Trust by a jittery uncle under Attlee's government, or was just too big and uncomfortable or riddled with dry rot to carry on. It is these houses which form the subject of this book. It cannot be claimed that all of them are of great artistic merit; some of them are little better than grandiose bungalows. There are, however, a substantial number of architecturally interesting new country houses, or reconstructions, and they represent a significant aspect of post-war architecture. They include a large series of tower house reconstructions in Scotland, which cannot be paralleled before the last war; a substantial group of Neo-Georgian houses which continue the country house tradition firmly established in the first decades of this century; and even a number of interesting country houses in the Modern style though, on the whole, Modern architecture has not found much favour with traditional landowners and the best English Modern houses are to be found not in the country but on a smaller scale in suburbs like Hampstead or outer Cambridge.

One reason why post-war country houses are interesting is that they are largely unknown. They represent an aspect of British architectural patronage which has been deliberately ignored by the architectural press. The reason for this is simple; they do not fit into any 'acceptable' version of English social or architectural history. Private patronage by country landowners is difficult to reconcile with the one-sided emphasis on the development of a 'socially relevant' architecture—schools and community centres—in Welfare State Britain. Another factor which has led to the disparagement of these houses is that most of them are Neo-Georgian, built of brick or stone or stucco with small-paned sash windows. The general run of upper-class taste has been Georgian for the last fifty or sixty years. Landowners prefer well-proportioned rooms with high ceilings and cornices, long windows overlooking fine views—'Yes, it all belongs to us, as far as the eye can see. Indeed, a good deal further'—wall space for hanging family portraits, and marble chimneypieces with log fires. The development of this particular architectural taste goes back to the early twentieth century, and an abrupt change in the country house tradition. From at least the 1820s, for nearly a hundred years the standard dish for country houses had been some version of Tudorbethan harking back to 'ye Mansions of England in Olden Tyme'; it encompassed the products of Salvin, Blore and Burn, and the softer more sensitive work of Devey and his followers in the late nineteenth century. From the 1890s and increasingly by 1900, the leaders of the architectural profession had rediscovered Classicism, with results like Norman Shaw's Bryanston in Dorset or Chesters in Northumberland. After 1900 new houses were often Neo-Georgian and by the 1920s and 1930s it had become the dominant mode, just as Tudorbethan had been earlier.

The development of Neo-Georgian taste went hand in hand with a growing concern for real eighteenth-century architecture. This is marked by protests against the demolition of fine Georgian buildings in London and culminated in the founding of the Georgian Group in 1937. Its early meetings were held round a mirror on the floor of the Baroness d'Erlanger's house in Piccadilly and the members included many who were to be closely involved with country houses after the war and whose attitudes were to be important in forming the country house ethos of the 1950s, including Lord Gerald Wellesley, later 7th Duke of Wellington, whose taste in furniture and objects was greatly admired, Christopher Hussey, the architectural editor of *Country Life* whose articles in the 1950s did much to mould the outlook of his readers, Claud Phillimore, the most prolific designer of country houses in the post-war period, and James Lees-Milne, the organizer of the National Trust country houses scheme in the 1940s and 1950s.

In the 1920s, it was thought that an enthusiasm for Georgian things was just one of many passing fads, it was not foreseen that it would become permanent. Valentine Lawford recalls being shown by a Cambridge friend a design for a Classical memorial tablet in 1928: 'I remembered that the eighteenth-century design for his [grandfather's] tombstone that Tony showed me at the time marked the dawning of my realisation that so far as the English upper classes were concerned the "Georgian" style was "in" again, though naturally I could

not have guessed that its vogue would be quite so everlasting.'[2]

There were many reasons for the success and longevity of Georgian taste. A factor not to be underestimated is that the finest family portraits and furniture in most people's possession are largely Georgian. Such things look best in properly proportioned Georgian-style rooms. Most landowners building a new house wished to keep their family things and show them to advantage —indeed this was often the *raison d'être* for building a new house. Many architects working in the Modern style either did not appreciate this, or did not care. Sir Martyn Beckett recalls that he got the job to design the new house at Herriard Park in Hampshire for the Jervoises because, of twenty architects interviewed, he was the only one who was prepared to incorporate in his design the eighteenth-century furniture, chimneypieces and paintings from the old house.[3] As well as providing a sympathetic setting for the family heirlooms, the Classical style is in many ways the most practical for a late-twentieth-century house. It is a style 'infinitely manageable, economic, discreet, dignified and beautiful'. Its proportions suit well the arrangement of tall principal rooms on the ground floor with less lofty bedrooms above. A variation on the Palladian villa plan with a main block and flanking wings is in many ways ideal. It provides spacious rooms for entertaining and living, and humbler ranges for garages, the central heating boiler and other twentieth-century appendages. In addition to its practical advantages, it may also be that the Palladian manner is appropriate because of the historical parallels between late-sixteenth-century Venice and late-twentieth-century England, and the active engagement in agriculture of their respective aristocracies as an antidote to the decline of mercantile wealth and overseas possessions built up over previous centuries.

The role of the English country house during the Second World War is a subject which would well repay detailed study. The great majority of houses were requisitioned for emergency use, in some cases to store antiquities and works of art (the 'Hittite Horrors') from London museums, or for occupation by schools evacuated from the cities, or more usually by the military for hospitals, barracks or administrative headquarters. In some ways the war was the country house's finest hour. The D-Day Landings were planned from the Double Cube Room at Wilton. MI5 had its headquarters at Blenheim. Occupation by the armed forces was the worst fate that could befall a house and several were burnt down, while others were so maltreated as to be incapable of repair. When the army left Egginton Hall in Derbyshire, for instance, at the end of the war, all the taps were left running and the interior was so damaged by water flowing through the ceilings that it had to be demolished. Apart from casual damage and general hard use, very little routine maintenance was possible for five or six years after 1939, so that in 1945 the country house presented a huge, seemingly

13

Mrs Fleming's drawing-room at Sevenhampton Place.
An example of interior decorator John Fowler's influence.

insoluble problem to its owners. In the immediate post-war years there was a feeling that nobody would ever live in style in a big house again, but this soon gave way to a determination to restore at least a partial semblance of traditional order as people rethought their position and made decisions for the future of their estates and families. In many cases there seemed no alternative to demolition of the old house and in the next ten years a considerable number were demolished. But, contrary to the gloomy prognostications of many commentators, this was not the end for the country house, and in fact during the 1950s and 1960s new houses were built on many estates where the old house had been demolished or sold.

Work started immediately after the war on repairs, reconstruction and new building, but at first was seriously hampered by the rationing of building materials, through government licences rigorously enforced by the regional offices of the Ministry of Works. Building licences had been introduced at the beginning of the war under Defence Regulation 56A and were designed to conserve scarce materials for use on essential work only. The controls were considerably tightened in 1941, and extended to cover all repairs in addition to new construction. They restricted the amount which could be spent on any one property within twelve months to £100 unless a special licence was first obtained from the regional office of the Ministry of Works. The aim of the original regulations had been primarily to establish an order of priority. The aim of the revised regulations was to restrict all civil building to the absolute minimum. In this they were successful. Any infringement of the regulations could lead to the client, architect and contractor being prosecuted and fined or imprisoned.[4]

At the end of the war it might have been assumed that this type of defence measure would have been relaxed, but on the contrary building licences were enforced with renewed vigour, partly with the intention of restricting 'luxury building' as part of the general austerity cultivated by the Attlee government. When the Conservatives won the election in 1951, Harold Macmillan found himself responsible for building licences as Minister of Housing and determined to abolish them as soon as the shortage of building materials could be overcome. To this end he worked with the Minister of Works, Sir David (now Viscount) Eccles, and licences were gradually phased out in 1952 and 1953 by raising the general limit for unlicensed work first to £500 and then £1000, and for 'designated buildings' (which included anything to do with agriculture) to £2000 and then £25,000.[5] They were totally abolished in 1954. This was an important step in clearing the way for the revival of country house building in the mid-1950s.

The extent to which licences were enforced varied, but several post-war schemes for new houses had to be abandoned because licences were not

14

Plas Brondanw as restored after the fire.

forthcoming, including Claud Phillimore's design for a new house at Lockinge Park in Berkshire and Marshall Sisson's design for Uffington House in Lincolnshire. But in cases where a house was being reconstructed as a result of wartime damage or destruction by fire, licences could usually be obtained though they could still be restrictive, as in the case of Newton Ferrers in Cornwall where the shell had to be gradually reinstated in stages as licences were forthcoming, or Plas Brondanw where Clough Williams-Ellis got a licence to reconstruct the house but was forced to perform feats of frugal ingenuity to do it within the sum permitted. Working within licences could be a great strain for architects. Philip Tilden grumbled about the lengths to which he was forced to go in his post-war work, reusing every scrap of second-hand timber and substituting asphalt for lead on flat roofs. Doing as cheap a job as possible was not his particular forte.[6] Clough was even more critical: 'some obstructive body has temporarily intervened to cast its shadow' on British architecture, and he objected strongly to the 'penny-wise pound-foolishness of the government building programmes'.

Some people ignored licences and went ahead regardless. When they had their own building yards, with carefully stored materials for estate work, it was especially galling to be told they could not use any of it on their own buildings. In some cases they got away with ignoring the regulations, especially with black-market decorating, or in remote areas. But a number of landowners came

15

well-publicised croppers. Earl Peel in Lancashire embarked on a scheme of enlarging and embellishing Hyning Hall without the necessary licences. The work included the addition of a new drawing-room with a handsome marble chimneypiece and was planned to make the house more worthy of his role as Lord Lieutenant. Unfortunately the cost of these embellishments greatly exceeded the amount permitted and led to him being prosecuted, fined and forced to resign as Lord Lieutenant. At Woburn the 12th Duke of Bedford, who as a pacifist had little time for the war effort and had already refused to allow the eighteenth-century iron railings from Bedford Square to be taken for scrap, went ahead with an ambitious scheme of truncation and remodelling at the Abbey under the direction of a London surveyor called W. Cunningham. In March 1953 a summons was issued against him. The Duke's factotum at Woburn, Mrs Osborne Samuel, and Mr Cunningham were both sent for trial. She was fined £50, Mr Cunningham was ordered to pay £100 costs and the Bedford family company, the London and Devon Estates Company, was fined £5000 and ordered to pay £300 costs.[7]

At Belsay in Northumberland Sir Stephen Middleton and his agent Captain Thomas Atkinson got into trouble twice. On the second occasion, which involved unlicensed work to one of the farmhouses, the agent was sentenced to six months' imprisonment at Newcastle Assizes.[8] The first time, in 1951, the Bench had taken a more lenient view: 'There are mitigating and unfortunate circumstances in this case. It is perfectly obvious to the Bench that none of these people would wish deliberately to flout the law, and that at any rate a great part of their fault had been the sin of omission rather than commission; because we have no doubt that if proper steps had been taken they would have been able to get supplementary licences to complete this house.' Sir Stephen on inheriting the family estate after the war had decided to close the large and unwieldy Neo-Grecian Belsay Castle and to rebuild for his own occupation Swanstead, a smaller house on the edge of the park which was to be renamed Belsay House. The architect employed was Claud Phillimore whose first executed country house this was, and an inauspicious opening to his career. Licences for £7000 had been granted for the work, but they were exceeded by 100%. When completed the house was described by the Ministry of Works inspector as 'a beautiful building with no austerity finish about it', and praised by Christopher Hussey in *Country Life* for its ingenious plan combining a feeling of spaciousness with compact arrangement. In the event, because of the trouble over building licences, two small flanking pavilions, which had formed part of the original design, were never completed. As Christopher Hussey put it, it was 'sad that the original proposals had to be curtailed'. Sir Stephen, Claud Phillimore, the agent and the builders were fined £500 each.[9]

This austerity was the unprepossessing introduction to the architectural story

16

of post-war country house building. Clough Williams-Ellis spoke for many when he wrote that he feared that the war and socialism had greatly reduced or even 'permanently killed off the species, wealthy patron of architectural taste', but later admitted that he was 'too pessimistic, but soon after the war little could be done'.[10] By the mid-1950s, the situation had eased considerably. For well over a decade, inexpensive high-quality building materials were to be available on a scale perhaps never to be repeated. Copper, for instance, was particularly cheap and plentiful before the independence of Rhodesia, and this tempted many people in the 1950s to use it as a roofing material in preference to lead. With the general expansion of the economy, the late 1950s and 1960s saw a building boom throughout the country, the effects of which for better or worse (mainly the latter) transformed the centre of most British towns and cities. It is also reflected, on the whole with less deplorable results, in country houses though not all the schemes proposed then materialized. Many people who had no real need to move out of an old house seriously considered building a new one on their estate. At Mentmore, for example, Lady Rosebery, following the lead of her daughter the Duchess of Norfolk at Arundel, was keen to give up the Victorian pile and to build a new house to the design of Claud Phillimore, but her husband refused. One of the most ambitious abortive projects of this sort was San-dringham where it was intended in the 1960s to demolish Edward VII's house and to build an equally large new one 'in the style of our time' to the design of David Roberts of Cambridge. In this case the proponent was Prince Philip and it was the Queen who turned the scheme down. Instead Sir Hugh Casson was employed to modernize and refurbish the existing house.[11]

The Coach House, Haseley, Oxfordshire. Converted into a house by Mrs Nancy Lancaster.

Bathroom designed by Roderick Gradidge
at Tancreds Ford, Surrey.

The stables, Studley Royal, Yorkshire. Converted into a house
after the old house burnt down in 1947.

As well as completely new houses, there was a fashion for converting stable blocks. This was a rural reflection of the pre-war craze for smart mews conversions in London when people moved out of their large houses in Mayfair to the groom's cottage at the back. Though the inspiration for stable conversions is therefore metropolitan, there was one notable country precedent —Penicuik in Midlothian where, when the big house was gutted by fire in 1899, the Clerk family transferred to the quadrangular stable court. It was converted for them by Lessels and Taylor to the wishes of Aymée, Lady Clerk, the work being completed in 1902 and incorporating fittings rescued from the big house and other old buildings in the locality. This was a formula repeated many times after the Second World War. When Studley Royal burnt down in 1945, for example, the Vyners converted the stable block into a new house for themselves. Often the stables have been used as the basis of a new house when an estate has been bought by a new owner, as at Edenhall in Cumberland where Webster's stables have been made into a house of some grandeur to the design of Michael Bottomley of Kendal for the Hindleys, or the Clock House, Sawrey, in Lancashire where the Naylors have carried out a good conversion of the stable block of the demolished Victorian house to the design of Captain Gordon Thompson of the Liverpool School of Architecture. Stables have the advantage usually of having an exterior of considerable architectural presence. Indeed, in the case of many English country houses the stables are more monumental than the house itself, so they provide a handsome façade for a new house. Their drawback is that the ranges of buildings are rather narrow, usually not more than fourteen feet, which makes it difficult to plan the interior, and more or less dictates a series of interconnecting narrow rooms.

18

Bowood, Wiltshire. The grandest
stables conversion in England.

The grandest stable conversion is Bowood in Wiltshire where the Marquess of Lansdowne demolished the Big House in 1955 and adapted the two stable courts, including the so-called Little House, to form a new country seat. This was completed in 1957. Bowood had been occupied by Westonbirt School, then used as an RAF hostel during the war. As early as 1947 Lord Lansdowne decided to demolish the Big House and to concentrate on the stables but the implementation of work was delayed till after the end of building licences. Preliminary steps were taken in the early 1950s when F. Sortain Samuels (who also advised Lord Derby on the remodelling of Knowsley) was commissioned to adapt the Little House, stable courts and Adam greenhouse to form the house that exists today. A vital consideration was to provide a setting for the family collection, the remains of the contents of three houses. Adam's greenhouse, along the front, was ideal for this purpose and was converted into a picture gallery which could also be used as a more formal approach to the main rooms, as occasion required. The principal library, by Cockerell, was retained and repaired and an Adam chimneypiece from the Big House installed. The second library was converted into the drawing-room, and a dining-room formed out of the Green Hall in the north wing, adjacent to the new kitchen. It is a comparatively low room, so rich fittings were avoided and a carved and painted wooden chimneypiece from one of the demolished bedrooms used instead of a marble one. Throughout the new work the 'temptation to enrich and aggrandise' was firmly resisted and the simplest alternative chosen in every case. The entrance hall and staircase, designed by Sir Martyn Beckett, in the centre of the east range are particularly successful. The new iron staircase balustrade, copied from an eighteenth-century Irish design, was made by a local craftsman in Frome. An advantage of the quadrangular plan at Bowood is

Bowood. The staircase.

Below: Bowood. The dining-room with an Adam chimneypiece from one of the bedrooms in the Big House.

Opposite page: Castle Gyrn, designed by the architect John Taylor for himself and completed in 1977.

that it is easily adaptable according to the numbers staying in the house, and those available to run it. For large house parties, the grand rooms in the southeast corner can be opened up, but if the family are on their own they can retreat to the North Wing and shut the rest. From the outside Bowood is handsome enough and there is no sense of imbalance in the composition despite the demolition of the Big House. A defect of the design, however, is the lack of an approach or entrance on the scale of the house or consonant with the formality of the architecture.[12]

Another type of country house for which there has been a considerable vogue since the war is restricted to Scotland. This is the enthusiastic restoration of ancient tower houses, either from ruin or from the midst of Victorian accretions. In many cases, work of this type is so sweeping that the result counts as a new house rather than simple restoration. These tower jobs are the nearest in the post-war world to the late-nineteenth- and early-twentieth-century craze for castle building, though there has been one completely new castle, Castle Gyrn in Wales, the second stage of which has recently been completed (1977) to his own design by the architect John Taylor of Chapman, Taylor and Partners as a country retreat. It forms a pleasant, asymmetrical composition and is solidly built in rubble stone with carved keystones by Nicholas Wood.

Since 1960 tower houses have been the subject of more major restorations and reconstructions than any other type of country house in Scotland. They have the appeal of being manageable in size and distinctively Scottish in character. Not all of them are strictly speaking country houses, some of them being very grand holiday cottages, but several have been restored by landowners as the chief houses on their estates, notably Druminnor Castle in Aberdeenshire, restored by Ian Lindsay for the Honourable Margaret Forbes Sempill; Abergeldie, Aberdeenshire, restored in 1963 by John Lamb for John Gordon; Udny Castle, Aberdeenshire, by John Lamb for the Honourable Margaret Udny-Hamilton, 1962–4; and most recently Aboyne Castle for Lord Aboyne, son of the Marquess of Huntly, which won an RIBA award in 1983.

The idea of restoring a ruined tower house as a gentleman's residence without adding to it is by no means recent. There are a number of late-Victorian examples including the Marquess of Bute's refitting of the Old Place of Mochram or the Earl of Rosebery's rebuilding of Barnbougle. These jobs aimed at a high degree of modern comfort within the old walls and an authentically ancient-looking exterior. But the fashion for tower houses lapsed between the wars and it is only since the 1950s that it has become a conspicuous architectural phenomenon, latterly with the help of North Sea oil prosperity. Ian Lindsay's restoration of Aldie *circa* 1950 set the standard and the last twenty years have seen the resurrection of at least sixty of them. In some cases all four walls survived and in a few even the roof, though dilapidated, but in many others there was little but a heap of stone and the results are in the way of being miniature Pierrefonds, the interiors at least being complete rebuilds. As a part of these restorations the opportunity is usually taken to reinstate traditional harling (Scottish for roughcast) on the external walls in place of the exposed rubble stonework beloved of the Victorians. The result is to give the buildings a smoother and more cheerful appearance. The harling is often brightly painted —pink at Udny, or terracotta at Abergeldie. One of the most spectacular recent re-emergences of a harled tower house, in this case out of a pile of varied Victorian buildings, is Aboyne Castle, where it is almost impossible to recognize the result as in any way related to the previous building.

Apart from stable conversions and 'new castles for old', another architectural development which is distinctively a post-war phenomenon in country houses is the swimming pool, as a focus for a relaxed out-of-door life in the summer and al fresco meals. There are examples from before the war, notably Philip Tilden's Roman 'bathing tank' for Sir Philip Sassoon at Port Lympne; but it is only since 1945 that a pool has become a ubiquitous adjunct to the country house. In some cases, there are *two*, as at Nantclwyd in Wales or Eaton Hall, which has one indoors and one out. Country house swimming pools can be holes in the ground painted a nasty shade of blue like most suburban ones, but

22

Top: New castles for old: Aboyne Castle, Aberdeenshire, before.

Bottom: Aboyne Castle after.

there have been a number which are architecturally distinguished. Hugh Casson's firm, for instance, has designed one or two: notably at Ashden, Kent, for Lord Sainsbury and another, more Classical, with a tented changing pavilion and trellis balustrades for Peter Cazalet at Fairlawne, Kent. Three of the most exciting new country house pools are Peter Foster's enclosed Pompeian pool for Lord de Ramsay at Abbot's Ripton, Huntingdonshire, Philip Jebb's for Simon Sainsbury at Woolbeding House, Sussex, and Charles Worthington's very grand Classical pool with fifty-six Tuscan columns round it, designed by himself at Kingston Russell in Dorset. A frequent variation on the new-built swimming pool is the conversion of a former orangery, like Wyatville's (Gothick) at Windsor Castle, or the varied Wyatt Classical ones at Wynyard, County Durham, Capel Manor, Kent, and Stratfield Saye, Hampshire. The latter is surrounded by marble columns bought at the Fesch sale in Paris by the 1st Duke of Wellington for his never-executed Waterloo Palace; they were found still in crates after the last war. Swimming pools give scope for architectural features in the form of pavilions containing changing rooms, saunas, or outdoor sitting rooms. A notable Classical example is Quinlan Terry's at Thenford, Northamptonshire, for Michael Heseltine. There has also been a distinct taste for Gothick ones such as Roderick Gradidge's, complete with fibreglass fan vaulting, for the Marquess of Cholmondeley at Cholmondeley Castle in Cheshire.

From swimming pools it is a temptation to go on to discuss the post-war garden and the work of a whole series of talented landscape designers: Geoffrey Jellicoe, Brenda Colvin, Silvia Crow, James Russell, Lanning Roper and Russell Page. It could be argued that since 1945 the English garden has enjoyed one of the most enterprising and exciting phases in its whole history. The subject, however, is big enough to fill a book on its own and the urge to discuss pleached lime walks, grey borders, old shrub roses and white painted Gothick trellis must be resisted here for lack of space.

NOTES

1 Michael Davie, Ed., *The Diaries of Evelyn Waugh* (1976), p. 791, 25 October 1963.
2 Valentine Lawford, *Bound for Diplomacy* (1963), p. 114.
3 Ex info Sir Martyn Beckett.
4 *Architect's Journal*, 25 December 1941, p. 409.
5 Ex info Viscount Eccles; Circular 95/52, 31 December 1952 from the Ministry of Housing and Local Government; *The Builder*, 25 July 1952, 9 January 1953.
6 Philip Tilden, *True Remembrances* (1954), pp.

168–70; Clough Williams-Ellis, *Around the World in Ninety Years* (1978) pp. 2–5, 13.
7 Duke of Bedford, *A Silver-Plated Spoon* (1959), p. 184.
8 *The Builder*, 16 January 1953, p. 141.
9 Ibid, 5 October 1951, p. 459; 16 January 1953, p. 141; *Country Life*, 2 April 1959, 724–6.
10 Clough Williams-Ellis, op. cit. p. 3.
11 Ex info Casson and Conder Partnership.
12 *Country Life*, 8 June 1972.

Swimming pool in the shell of the conservatory at Capel Manor, Kent.

II
SOCIAL CHANGE AND CONTINUITY

In 1890 Gladstone predicted that in a hundred years' time England would be a country in which the great landed estates would still be intact. In 1984 it looks as if he was right. Of the twenty-five non-royal dukes, nineteen still own estates of more than 10,000 acres, and in the case of Buccleuch, Westminster and Atholl of more than 100,000 acres. A recent study[1] has shown that of the great estates listed by Bateman in his *Great Landowners of Great Britain and Ireland* in 1878 there is not one example where an original family retains its estate heartland (house, gardens and park) with less than a thousand acres, and in the 'greater gentry group' only four per cent. They have either kept a fully-fledged estate with home farm, tenant farms, and tied cottages or disappeared entirely, usually to be replaced by another family. Several of the greatest landowners today, for instance, are post-Bateman, including the Cowdrays, the Wills, the Leverhulmes, the Mantons and the Vesteys.

The great majority of new country houses since 1945 have been built by traditional landowners. This is a striking departure from the pattern established earlier this century when new houses were built mainly with new money often from overseas investments, South African gold mines or Brazilian railways. In the last forty years the pattern has been reversed and country houses have been built chiefly by authentic landowners, including the inner circle of 'Court' and 'ruling' families like the Derbys, Halifaxes and Norfolks, and established eighteenth- and nineteenth-century dynasties like the Rothschilds, Hambros and Barings. There have of course been houses built, or substantially remodelled, by the new rich, but most new houses have been built by families established for at least three generations.[2] The reasons for this are simple. It is more expensive to build a new house of quality than to buy a good old one. Somebody wishing to set himself up in the country therefore will

26

get better value by buying an estate with an attractive old house than by building a new one, and as a result there have been many elaborate restorations of old houses. Those who build new houses must have a strong reason for living in a particular place. In practice this usually means they have inherited an estate which they wish to keep going and to live on. It requires a strong traditional impetus and sense of responsibility to the past and the future to do this.

This revival of the old-established gentry has to be set against the general view of the decline of the traditional landowner. It is true that at least four hundred historic houses have been demolished since 1945. But many of these were delayed war losses, victims of requisitioning, and as this book demonstrates they have in many instances been replaced by new houses. It is also true that the size of many, but by no means all, traditional landed estates has decreased in this century and there has been a constant background chorus shouting ruin as each new tax has been proposed or passed—the 1949 Finance Act, the introduction of Capital Gains in 1965 and, under the last Labour government, the threat of a wealth tax intended to squeeze 'the rich till the pips squeak', according to Mr Healey. Nearly every book on the country house begins or ends with a jeremiad: 'The English country house is as archaic as the osprey,' and goes on to relate a catalogue of disaster, demolition, bankruptcy and death duties. But without wishing to minimize the problems faced by the landowner in the twentieth century, it has to be pointed out that there is a difference between transitional difficulties surmounted and final catastrophe. Compared to other once flourishing British institutions—national newspapers, the docks, provincial cities, heavy manufacturing industries, grammar schools and the Church of England, for instance—the country house has struggled to the end of the twentieth century in a state far from pitiable.

In many ways, the worst period in recent history for the landowner was the last decade of the nineteenth and first decade of the twentieth century. At that time his political power, landed wealth and social status were all undermined by the reform of local government, the extension of the franchise, the introduction of industrialists into the peerage, the imposition of death duties and the Liberal attack on the House of Lords. The agricultural depression from the 1870s wrecked the economic viability of his estate and led to a dramatic fall in the value of land. The institution of county councils took away many of the immemorial rights and duties of the squire as the traditional focus of local government. The 1882 Militia Act removed the great landowner's control of military affairs in his county. The imposition of death duties was followed by a threat of a land tax in 1909. Finally, disproportionate losses were suffered by the landed élite in the First World War. All this is well known, and most commentators assume that the graph continues downwards thereafter. But does it?

27

Surely the remarkable development in the twentieth century has been the way in which the landowners have rallied. All the vestigial powers, prestige and privileges which remained with them in 1910 remain with them still. The aristocracy of the United Kingdom, unlike its confrères in Europe, remains a peerage and not a mere nobility. The House of Lords has performed efficiently and responsibly in its reformed role as a chamber of check rather than veto, and its hereditary element remains its strongest active component. The Court, too, and all its outworks, from the officers of the Royal Enclosure at Ascot to the Crown Estate Commissioners, has since 1945 been almost exclusively a preserve of the traditional upper classes, very different from the *nouveaux riches* who surrounded Edward VII and the café society cultivated by Edward VIII.

Though his absolute power in the county was dissipated a hundred years ago, the traditional landowner has maintained a surprisingly active role in local life and fulfils a function not dissimilar from that of the constitutional monarch in national life, still acting as the focus of social, ceremonial and charitable activities in his area. Above all his estates have survived as viable economic and social units. Usually the portions which have been sold have been the least profitable, often outlying properties brought in by later marriages and not forming part of the historic heartland or financial base of the estate. As the Duke of Devonshire has pointed out at Chatsworth, having to find £8,000,000 in death duties had the beneficial side effect of causing a reassessment of the working of the whole family estate, and it was the least essential bits which were sold to meet the tax bill. The Eastbourne ground rents and the Derbyshire mineral rights were retained, together with the three major estates round the family seats at Chatsworth in Derbyshire, Bolton Abbey in Yorkshire and Lismore Castle in County Waterford, amounting in all to about 70,000 acres. The Duke of Bedford, who faced a similarly high death duty bill, tells the same story. The nucleus of Bloomsbury, the financial base of the family fortune, was kept, together with Woburn Abbey and the 12,000-acre Bedfordshire estate,

while outlying properties in Devon and Buckinghamshire were sold. These amputations, though unpleasant, have led to a more realistic management policy for the estate as a whole. The effect of death duties on the Duke of Westminster's estate was even more spectacular. Having to find nearly £20,000,000 to pay the Treasury on the death of the 2nd Duke in 1957 proved the spur to adopting more dynamic and expansionist policies which transformed the estate into a worldwide property empire and reaped more like £200 million than £20 million.

The same story can be repeated, on a smaller scale, on many other estates. Departments which had been losing money for a generation, such as the shoot or building yard, have been turned into commercial ventures which at least break even and in some cases actually make a profit. Farming itself, of course, has in general been highly profitable since the war and most landowners have taken in hand as large an area of home farm as possible. Land values have also consistently risen since the mid-1950s; indeed, a graph of the rise through the 1950s, 1960s and 1970s looks just like a perpendicular line. Another not inconsiderable source of income to the traditional landowner has been the spectacular increase in the value of works of art. By selling one inherited chattel it is possible to earn as much in five minutes at Christie's or Sotheby's as a Victorian businessman's lifetime of trading in guano or ostrich feathers, or manufacturing brass bedsteads. At least three of the new country houses described in this book (the reader must guess which) were paid for largely out of the proceeds of a private treaty sale of a painting to the National Gallery. The Duke of Devonshire has raised two and a half million pounds (invested largely in America) as an endowment for the Chatsworth House Trust by the sale of one or two paintings from his 'second eleven' and some duplicates from his library.

Many landowners have also been able to tap new sources of income, most notably tourism. Opening to the public is not a factor that can be taken into account in a discussion of new houses, but many estates are kept ticking over by a discreetly placed caravan site, and at Lulworth in Dorset it was partly the profits from caravans which encouraged the building of a new house. Being constantly on their toes in order to meet the threats of new fiscal measures is not necessarily a bad thing for landowners, and it is certainly one of the factors which has led to a more forward-looking and efficient pattern of estate management, farming and forestry in the country as a whole. Socialist policies which might have been thought of as a threat but in fact have proved a positive boon include the nationalization of the coal mines in 1947. At a stroke this relieved landowners of a decaying and embarrassing asset; they were paid out at the top of the market. Those who invested the proceeds wisely can congratulate themselves on being well out of it.

The problem in talking about landed estates is that there is no national

29

Parties: family occasion. The Duke of Norfolk's celebration
of the quincentenary of the dukedom attended by 200 Howards
and one or two clergy, heralds, etc., 28 June 1983.

inventory of who owns the land and never has been, apart from the Domesday Survey in 1085 and the Census of Returns of land in 1873 on which Bateman based his book, and so most of what is written on the subject is guesswork[3] or sample statistics which, of course, can be used to prove whatever the author wants. The situation is further complicated in that most estates do not in legal terms belong to an individual at all, but are vested in a series of elaborate settlements and trusts. When it is said that the Duke of Omnium owns 25,000 acres, in fact he probably owns only the clothes he stands up in, while all the rest is vested in trustees as part of a 'charitable trust', or a 'marriage settlement', or is held for 'younger beneficiaries', or is a limited company, or has been handed over to the dowager, or is let on a long lease to the Forestry Commission. This seemingly chaotic pattern of property-holding enshrines the loopholes in fifty years of financial legislation by successive governments.

If it is accepted that on the whole the landed wealth of the upper classes has survived, and in some cases increased, since 1945 there is still the problem of the social revolution after the Second World War—the creation of the Welfare State, the expansion of university education, the growth of a large new lower middle class owning its own houses and cars, the contraction of the traditional working class, and the rise in the general standard of living whereby somebody on the dole in the 1980s is better off than the average labourer in the 1930s; not to mention the cultural revolution in the 1960s with the apotheosis of pop stars, smart photographers and property developers. Surely all this has had some impact on the traditional upper classes? The answer is, not much. The widespread prosperity enjoyed in the late 1950s and 1960s was achieved as a result of general economic growth and not by any one class at the expense of another. The upper classes have maintained their own independent culture alongside the Welfare State. They are the permanent cast which continues regardless, with its own social life based on field sports, family occasions like coming-of-age parties, and the patronage of local events like parish fêtes, its

own financial base, and its own distinctive outlook in general.

The late 1950s and 1960s in fact saw a great revival of country house life. In the days of Macmillan's 'cousinhood government', Chatsworth and Hatfield were still the powerhouses they had been in the nineteenth century. 1955 is the key year; it saw the numbers of demolitions of country houses reach their peak (seventy-six losses in that year) and then fall abruptly (twenty-six in 1957) and gradually tail away to nothing, while the building of new houses which forms the subject of this book gathered force. The decision of the Devonshires to move back into Chatsworth, taken in 1955 and completed in 1959, marks the turning point in the post-war history of the English country house. Chatsworth had not been lived in since the death of the 9th Duke in 1938. During the war it was occupied by a girls' school. The 10th Duke never lived there and his death in 1950, three months too soon to save his estate from death duties, threatened the whole place with extinction. But in the event the duty was paid, the estate saved and the house refurbished. The Duchess explains: 'We were living in a house in the village then and nobody thought we would ever live here because of these awful death duties. So six, seven, eight years went by and the agent, Hugo Reid, said to Andrew, "Somebody's got to live in the house," and he thought it had better be us. Slowly the idea sunk in. Uncle Harold [Macmillan] was against it. He said, "You can never say you haven't got a bed." He meant for boring relations.' Much of the redecoration was completed for the Marquess of Hartington's coming of age in 1965 with gold plate in the dining-room and dancing in the 6th Duke's state rooms. Outside, mazes, serpentine hedges, an architectural parterre of box and ornamental hens rejuvenated the gardens; not to mention a large conservatory of the most advanced design full of bananas, orchids and the re-planted Victoria Regia water lily which had first flowered at Chatsworth for Paxton. Today the Devonshires spend April at Lismore (salmon), August at Bolton (grouse) and the rest of the year at Chatsworth with short stays in London.[4]

The sense of well-being in the late 1950s and early 1960s was partly nourished by capital gains, and also the steady rise in the stock market. This formed the background to a short-lived boom summed up in *Vogue* as 'The new dash. The extravagance of England.' In this context it is worth quoting from an article in that magazine on the Marquess of Londonderry: 'Young and noble. Involved. Unique.' It captures a now forgotten mood of optimism: 'Perhaps for the first time since World War I, there is a feeling of affluence about in England. Men had money before now, but it was a brute piling up; suddenly wealth is making arabesques . . . By the same token there is a resurgence of the aristocracy; that institution which ten years ago seemed in certain decline is reviving. Peers are definitely a social force again, compromising between the self-conscious egalitarianism of the post-war years and the awful grandeur of the Victorian

31

Far left: Parties: local event. The crowning of the Churchtown Rose Queen at Meols Hall, 9 July 1983.

Left: Parties: a shoot. The Duke of Devonshire's grouse shoot at Bolton Abbey, 12 August 1983.

Dukes, who were mostly mad north-north-west with sheer power and dreadfully whiskered.'[5] Lord Londonderry himself, 'dressed modestly in well-cut black corduroy', had architectural tastes which while not immediately spectacular were not insubstantial. 'He runs to solid luxuries like bull-dozers, crawler cranes, dredging gangs. He has had the vast Grecian front of Wynyard scaffolded and shot-blasted, a quarter of an acre of derelict outbuildings cleared, and the site grassed. When he came into the property nine years ago, the house was a ruin. His grandfather, an eccentric gentleman, had lived in one room with about thirty dogs, sharing the rest of the house with an academy for young ladies.' At one end of Wynyard Lord Londonderry created a new house with its own entrance porch and a smartly decorated interior: 'warm, with crisp enfolding colours, rich patterns and well-hung pictures, a world that sets off the solemnities of the outside, preserves the splendour of the old house, and still is scaled to humanity'. The visitors' book, we were assured, was filled with the names of 'the young and ingenious from London'. But the Londonderries nevertheless fulfilled their 'county obligations' with traditional pheasant shoots, speeches to local organizations, and Lady Londonderry opening fêtes 'with great aplomb in specially selected floppy pink hats'.[6] This restoration was paid for by the sale of the run-down harbour at Seaham, developed as a coal port by the 3rd Marquess and his formidable wife, Frances Anne, and Londonderry House in Park Lane, London, for half a million pounds before the introduction of Capital Gains tax.

The sudden freeze in the 1970s with the oil crisis, the three-day week and a national mood of frugality and conservation found country house owners in their element. They all love frugality and conservation; they are manic savers of bits of string and switchers-off of lights. At the time of the three-day week when the nation was abjured to economize, one family was heard to say, 'We have always been so mean there is absolutely nothing we can do in the way of further retrenchment.' Then they hit on a new idea, always leaving the curtains drawn so that any heat there might be (not much) in the rooms would have more difficulty escaping. Strict housekeeping and making-do are essential ingredients in a country house owner's outlook and it is quite normal to buy a job lot of silk and store it for fifty years to save money when the drawing-room chair covers finally wear out, or to make new curtains by dying army surplus blankets. So in the 1970s house owners suddenly found themselves in the national mainstream and their post-war style of interior decoration, making the most of old fabrics and inherited furniture (see next chapter), has filtered down and influenced popular taste. Indeed, for the first time for over a century they have found themselves in the vanguard of national taste as a popular version of the English Country House Style has been marketed successfully by firms like Laura Ashley.

32

Dressing-room designed by Roderick
Gradidge at Tancreds Ford.

Shooting is the foundation of country house social life, much more so now than hunting because it is easier to finance. By making the shoot a commercial syndicate and letting off days to rich Germans or Eastern potentates for large sums of money it is possible for a landowner to subsidize the rest of the shoots for his family and friends. Grouse captures the public imagination because of the 'Glorious Twelfth' and the annual race on the part of London hotels, clubs and restaurants to serve the first birds shot that day. But grouse is restricted to the moors of the North and it is pheasants, and to a lesser extent, partridges, which are the *raison d'être* for the shooting season proper from October to January. This is demonstrated by the statistics. According to the Game Conservancy Council on average two million grouse are shot annually (less recently, due to disease and falling numbers) compared to six million pheasants. In most country houses the shooting season, culminating in Christmas, is the time when the house comes into its own with constant house parties but the business of rearing pheasants is a year-round occupation. The eggs are hatched in April in electric incubators (no longer under broody hens; modern hybrid hens have had broodiness bred out of them); the chicks are then transferred to pens before being released fully-grown into the woods in the summer. English pheasants, unlike Asiatic ones, live in trees because of foxes.[7] At houses where the owner is quite young, or he has sons interested in shooting, it is often quite common now for the keeper to be helped in this work by the family and for there to be 'press-gang' house parties in the early summer to help build the pheasant pens, the inducement being that those who do not help then do not get invited to shoot in the autumn. This is one reflection of the way in which houses are becoming more and more self-contained and independent in a different way from the past; in fact they are run 'by the upper classes for the upper classes'. Cooks hired for the weekend, or nannies, for instance, are now more likely to be 'Sloane Ranger' girls than traditional domestics.

Since the war upper-class social life has tended to concentrate in the country. All the large houses in London have gone and hotels are horrible places. Coming-of-age dances and other celebrations therefore are now usually held in country houses in the early summer rather than in London. The Scottish season is later than the English, beginning in August and early September and taking in the grouse and the Edinburgh Festival before moving on in the late autumn and early winter to the Highland meetings, 'the Alcatraz of the British social circuit'. Of course there are local exceptions to this general pattern dictated by particular events. Goodwood week in June, for instance, is the high point in the social year in Sussex with many large parties, and in the 1950s and 1960s the Queen staying in alternate years at Arundel and Goodwood. Other areas have similar high spots, Doncaster Races in Yorkshire or the Grand National in

Top: The Manor House, Hambleden, Oxfordshire, with bathing pavilion by Sir Martyn Beckett on the left.

Bottom: The library at The Cottage, Badminton, decorated by Colefax and Fowler.

Lancashire and north Cheshire. This type of entertaining has affected the planning of new houses, many of which are still provided with gun rooms and a reasonable number of spare bedrooms so that people can be put up for shoots or family parties. The new house at Knowsley, for instance, has eight principal bedrooms, as have Hinton Ampner and Dalton, Meols has eleven, Eaton and Garrowby twelve. Latterly there has been a tendency in some houses to make do with fewer bedrooms, especially near London, and just to have people for a day's shooting or for dinner rather than staying the night. Cars make it much easier to have a busy social life in the country without the effort of having people to stay in the house. In the North or Scotland it is thought nothing to drive fifty miles there and back for dinner.

In addition to their private social life, most authentic landowners still play a role in the public life of their county. Though some are, of course, national political figures and many sit on county councils, it is the ceremonial local role left them by the late-nineteenth-century reforms which is their most distinctive characteristic. The offices of Lord-Lieutenant, Custos Rotulorum, and High Sheriff are automatically theirs, and many also serve as commissioners for income tax, magistrates, and officers in the Territorial Army. Just as constitutional monarchy retains many of the trappings and functions of the medieval kings, so the present-day landowner perpetuates many of the forms of feudalism. In any county which has not been totally industrialized or suburbanized he can expect to preside at the head of many local organizations and to fill a number of picturesque posts, including those of the High Stewards of Cathedrals, Constables of Royal Castles, Hereditary Keepers and the Royal Company of Archers in Scotland. The filling of the three ancient county offices of Lord-Lieutenant, Custos Rotulorum and High Sheriff (not the latter in Scotland, Scottish law being different) still reflects the division of the landed classes into great magnates and ordinary landed gentry as the former tends to go to peers and baronets and the latter to younger sons and untitled landowners. Neither Labour governments nor the 1972 Local Government Reform Act have affected any of this. In 1945 it was feared that Attlee might recommend the King to appoint 'a different sort of person' as Lords Lieutenant, but in the event he continued to appoint traditional landowners, as also, on the whole, did Harold Wilson. The 1972 Act merely adapted the whole set-up to the new county boundaries but otherwise left it alone, apart from a regrettable tidiness of mind which led the civil servants who drafted the Bill to iron out some delightful variations and antique anomalies in the wording of commissions.

The office of Her Majesty's Lord-Lieutenant is the most prestigious of county posts. The builders of new houses since the war who have held it include the Earl of Derby (Knowsley), Sir Ian Walker-Okeover (Okeover), Sir Joseph Weld (Lulworth), the Duke of Norfolk (Arundel), Captain John Hamilton-Stubber

34

(Aughentaire). In some ways the post has become even more splendid since 1945 with a smart new uniform designed under George VI's direct supervision. 'No, it will not do,' he said from the other end of a long corridor at Buckingham Palace, on being shown the preliminary model, 'not enough room for decorations and orders.' It is dark blue with silver shoulder cords, red stripes down the 'overalls', boots with spurs, a 'forage cap' with gold Lord-Lieutenant's badge, a crimson and silver sash and a 'scimitar 1831 pattern' sword developed from that worn by the Duke of Wellington at Waterloo. More recently a special Lord-Lieutenant's flag has made its appearance to fly over his house and on the bonnet of his car when representing his sovereign: a Union Jack with a sword and crown on it, the 'Union Flag charged with a sword fess-wise or, and ensigned with the Imperial Crown proper'. The office of Lord-Lieutenant (only hyphenated since 1972) dates back to the sixteenth century and was an invention of the Tudors—its date of origin is usually taken to be about 1547. It was at first a short-term military commission to deal with local tumults or the threat of foreign invasion but under Elizabeth I became the appointment of a peer for life to represent the Crown in a county, with other duties as well as military. The military importance of the Lieutenancy was abolished by the Militia Act of 1882 but a shadow of the past is preserved in that the Lord-Lieutenant is automatically president of the Territorials, the home defence force set up in 1908 to replace the various yeomanry and volunteer units which in turn were the successors to the Anglo-Saxon *fyrd* or general military levy.

The Lord-Lieutenant is the Sovereign's representative in the county and takes precedence as such. He (or she) is responsible for organising, hosting and accompanying royal visits, and for standing in for the Queen at various ceremonies such as presenting colours to local regiments, giving out medals or the Queen's Award for Industry, etc. Lord-Lieutenants are nearly always Custodes Rotulorum in their counties, but need not be and there have been two cases since the war of non-Lord-Lieutenants holding the latter post, including Lord Denning in the City of London. This ancient post (its greater antiquity is attested by the fact that the appointment is made by Royal Sign Manual rather than Letters Patent) is a legal office and gives its holder the responsibility for the custody of county records relating to the peace. He also advises the Lord Chancellor (Chancellor of the Duchy of Lancaster in the County Palatine of Lancashire) on the appointment of Justices of the Peace in a particular county.

The Lord-Lieutenant is assisted by Deputy Lord-Lieutenants whom he can appoint himself, and also a Vice Lord-Lieutenant to stand in for him when he is out of the county. The Deputy Lord-Lieutenants are largely honorary, and again confined to the ranks of traditional landowners, but might very occasionally be expected to stand in for their Lord-Lieutenant at short notice. They too have their own uniform, but can wear service dress if they are entitled to it. The

Lord-Lieutenant of Sussex, going down with flu the day before he was due to meet 'some very important Frenchmen' at Newhaven, *circa* 1970, telephoned his Deputy Lord-Lieutenant nearest to Newhaven, an elderly colonel, and asked him to stand in for him. The elderly colonel explained that his uniform was a bit out of date. 'Oh, never mind. Get on with it,' was the reply. The French visitors were somewhat surprised to find themselves greeted on behalf of the Queen by an elderly gentleman dressed in Boer War uniform, complete with puttees, bandolier and slouch hat.[8]

The High Sheriff is the oldest secular dignitary under the Crown and was created by the Saxon kings as their principal county officer responsible for raising the *fyrd* (local military levies), collecting the revenues of the royal estates and the administration of the King's Law. It is with this last duty that the Sheriff has, over the centuries, become most conspicuously associated. For those who talk in isolation about the decline of the political power of landowners in the twentieth century, it is perhaps worth pointing out that the heyday of the Sheriff was the twelfth century and that he lost his military functions in the sixteenth. The High Sheriff is appointed for one year beginning after the Hilary term. The Queen makes the appointment in the traditional manner by 'pricking the name' on a roll of 'eligible gentlemen in the county' on the 'morrow of All Souls'. His function is to look after the circuit judge. He is no longer personally responsible for the day-to-day organization of the courts or security but for the judge's general well-being while he is in the county and for entertaining him—'Mrs High Sheriff' often does the flowers in the Judges' Lodgings. The High Sheriff accompanies the judge on certain occasions and can wear military uniform but most prefer to wear eighteenth-century court dress with lace ruffles, a silver-buttoned black coat, knee breeches and an épée sword.

These types of occupation impose a semi-official role on the landowner which in turn is reflected in the architecture of his house. It would, for instance, be rather incongruous to fly the Union Jack 'ensigned with the Crown Imperial' over a tiny bungalow. A certain formality is required in the exterior. Public entertaining, such as High Sheriff's tea parties, requires at least one large room, sometimes the hall but more usually a formal drawing-room. This latter requirement is reinforced by the fact that most landowners preside over a series of local charities, societies and institutions; opening fêtes, chairing or serving on committees and generally behaving as 'constitutional monarchs' within their own county.

It goes without saying that a country house is *per se* the administrative centre of an agricultural estate, and many new houses incorporate a purpose-built estate office, often with its own external access so that it can be reached directly from the farm without going through the main house. The Palladian plan of centre block and flanking wings or pavilions lends itself well to an arrangement

36

A traditional kitchen. Kings Walden Bury, Hertfordshire. By Raymond Erith and Quinlan Terry.

whereby the estate office and gun room can occupy one of the wings, the kitchen offices the other, with the family living in the main block.

Whereas the social and public sides of a landowner's life have hardly changed in this century and the main rooms in his house—drawing-room, dining-room and library—would not be that different from those designed for his grandfather, there has been a dramatic change on the domestic side. This has two aspects: the almost complete disappearance of live-in servants, and its concomitant, the disappearance of the green baize door and the elevation of the kitchen to main-room status. Much has already been written about the disappearance of domestic servants in England, due partly to rising wages, the social stigma felt to be attached to working in somebody else's house and the introduction of electric labour-saving gadgets, so it is not necessary to say more here about the reasons for the current state of affairs. It is now exceptional to come across a country house with a large staff. The most that can be expected is perhaps a live-in couple acting as general caretakers, the man doubling as butler and the wife as cook-housekeeper, with dailies to do the dusting and perhaps one man doing the garden helped out in off-periods by the farm workers. But there are exceptions. At Chatsworth, seventy people are employed in the house, including three nightwatchmen, a silver steward and a

man to wind the clocks, and there are eighteen gardeners. Some great landowners like the Marquess of Salisbury and the Duke of Norfolk run to gentleman-retainers like chaplains and librarians.

On the whole, though, traditional household staffs have disappeared. It is often said that this happened in 1939 when there were still over a million domestic servants in England. All the young people went off to war and never came back again. In fact the date that servants disappeared from country houses is later than that, and *circa* 1960 would be more accurate. While many younger people may not have come back to the Big House in 1945 the older members of staff carried on to the end of their lives and there were enough servants around in the 1950s for those planning new houses to make lavish provision for domestic staff, including butlers' pantries, housekeepers' rooms, and even servants' halls and the odd back staircase. But after 1960 this suddenly ceased and the long tail of domestic offices to one side of a house, which had grown longer and longer in the nineteenth century, could at last be done away with, to the undoubted advantage of the overall architectural composition in the case of symmetrical Classical designs. In the 1960s properly trained servants gave way to temporary Portuguese and Eastern couples, and now it is rare for there to be any regular live-in staff at all. At most, there is a hired cook or butler from an agency for a shooting lunch or other big event. For the house-owner, this may impose something of a strain but for the house guest it is an unmitigated boon as it is much more relaxing staying in a house without servants, especially for the mean tipper.

It is difficult to be precise about the exact number of servants in England at any time since 1945. The census figures in 1951, 1961, 1971 and 1981 which one might have hoped would have recorded the decline of servants in graphic detail are in fact no real help, as all 'employees engaged in service occupations caring for food, drink, clothing and other personal needs' are lumped together, whether hotel staff, waiters in restaurants or even window-cleaners, as part of 'Socio-Economic Group 7 (Personal Service Workers)'. From architects' designs and personal accounts, however, it is quite clear that servants were still taken for granted in larger houses in the 1950s, even if they were not as plentiful as before the war. For example, when the Duke of Bedford moved back into Woburn Abbey in 1955, his 'small staff' comprised six nightwatchmen, fourteen dailies, and seven live-in servants including a chef and a butler.[9] But from the 1960s servants had become more than a problem, they had more or less ceased to exist. Many houses built in the late 1960s and 1970s were designed to operate, if necessary, without any servants at all, so that the family could retreat to one or two easily manageable rooms or open up greater or lesser portions of the house, depending on the time of year, number of visitors and amount of domestic help available. Both Meols Hall in Lancashire and Gar-

38

A Modern kitchen. Capel Manor, Kent. By Michael Manser.

rowby Hall in Yorkshire are particularly good examples of well thought out flexible plans. The transitional period in the country house produced many amusing anomalies. Jane, Lady Abdy recalls that when she was first married, Nanny used to have her meals in the dining-room with Sir Robert and herself at Newton Ferrers because there was no longer a footman to take food up to the nursery on a tray and Nanny could not eat in the kitchen with the cook.[10]

The rise in importance of the kitchen is perhaps the most striking innovation in the post-war country house. It is now one of the main rooms: symmetrical plans reflect this, with the library, drawing-room, dining-room and kitchen filling the four corners, as for example at Arundel Park or Kings Walden Bury. Before the war the kitchen was tucked away far from the dining-room—one of the improvements planned for Chatsworth in the 1930s was an underground

railway or conveyor connecting the dining-room and kitchen. The owner, of course, never went near the kitchen. Just before the sale at Mentmore in 1976, a house in which she had lived for fifty years, Eva, Lady Rosebery was asked the whereabouts of the kitchen and replied that she had no idea as she had never been there. In all the houses described in this book, at least from the late 1950s, the kitchen is placed immediately adjoining the dining-room, or connected to it by a pantry, and is used by the family at least as a breakfast room. In many of Claud Phillimore's houses the kitchen has a special breakfast alcove, often with a bay window to catch the morning sun. In many new houses, especially where there is a young family, the kitchen is now used as an all-purpose day living-room or family dining-room, as at Dalton in Westmorland or Lulworth in Dorset. In architectural terms this has had the result that the new country house kitchen is often a large well-proportioned room with large windows overlooking attractive views and all the stoves, cupboards, sinks and other fittings carefully designed, often in the style of the house. The kitchen at Garrowby is on the site formerly occupied by Lord Halifax's study, enjoys handsome views to the south and east over the park, new lake and new temple, and is cheerfully decorated in red and white. In Modern-style kitchens, designed down to the last detail including the knives (which makes it difficult for left-handed people to use them), there is a self-conscious resemblance to geometrical still-life paintings. Great attention needs to be paid to easing the visual transition from a formal dining-room with mahogany furniture and family portraits to a 'mod-con' kitchen. The solution at Meols is especially successful, with the intervening pantry treated as a china room with Gothick glazed wall cabinets containing the best family china, and the sinks concealed, when not in use, by shelves which pull over them. Architecturally as well as socially there is nothing to regret about the abolition of the green baize door.

NOTES

1 Heather Climenson, *English Country Houses and Landed Estates* (1982).
2 The rough comparative statistics, which can be checked against my gazetteer, are: old money, 3; new money, 1.
3 An entertaining example of inspired guesswork in the form of a Fabian tract is John McEwan's *Who Owns Scotland?* (Edinburgh 1978).
4 The Duchess of Devonshire, *The House: A Portrait of Chatsworth* (1982), and surrounding publicity.
5 Peter Laurie, 'The Londonderries', *Vogue*, 1 August 1964, p. 115.
6 Ibid.
7 For an accurate description of a pheasant shoot and the gamekeeper's year, I would recommend Barry Hine's *The Game Keeper* (1975); it is a novel but based on the late Lord Fitzwilliam's shoot at Wentworth Woodhouse.
8 C. Neville Packett, *The County Lieutenancy in the United Kingdom (1547–1975)* (1975); Ex info Sir Richard Cave.
9 The Duke of Bedford, *A Silver-Plated Spoon* (1959).
10 Ex info Jane, Lady Abdy.

III
MODS AND
BAROQUERS

One of the more striking aspects of the English country house in the late twentieth century is the extent to which its interior is the work of professional decorators. Even in the 1920s and 1930s it was comparatively rare for a country house to be professionally decorated in the way that a Mayfair drawing-room might have been. Old houses were full of the accumulated possessions of the centuries, and new houses tended to have interiors designed by their architects. Lutyens, for instance, chose his own colours for the walls, patterns for floor coverings, and was personally responsible for details like light fittings and quite a bit of the furniture. Grand people took their inherited possessions for granted and would refer to the Reisener commode from Marie Antoinette's boudoir at Versailles as 'that old chest of drawers where I keep my hunting stockings'. The idea of displaying furniture and pictures to advantage would have been considered rather suspect. This is demonstrated by Lord Derby's grandfather's remark after being complimented on some pieces of 'Chippendale' at Knowsley: 'Damn cheek, that fella noticing my chairs.' Now all is changed. There is hardly an old house in England which has not been professionally redecorated and all the furniture expertly rearranged. In the case of new houses it is almost a matter of course for the interior to be decorated by a designer other than the architect, and for this to form part of a separate contract. Houses as unselfconsciously jumbled as Brocklesby or Badminton are now the exception rather than the rule.

The emergence of the expert approach to decoration and contents is due to two factors, both of foreign origin. The first is the development of art history as an accepted academic discipline following the influx of refugee German scholars into English universities in the 1930s. The fruits of art-historical research have slowly filtered into the consciousness of average house-owners, so that most now know far more about their possessions than their grand-parents did. This has been achieved partly through death duties (now Capital Transfer Tax) which have had one beneficial side effect in that works of art of 'national importance' have always been exempted. Over the years the defini-tion of 'importance' has been widened to cover historical interest as well as high artistic merit. As a result, when an owner dies, a detailed inventory of the contents of his house is drawn up for probate purposes, usually by Sotheby's or Christie's, with recommendations for exemption. These in turn are vetted by experts from the national museums on behalf of the Treasury, and they contest or confirm the attributions and valuations in the light of their own knowledge. By now, therefore, most country house owners have a reasonably authoritative inventory of the contents of their houses, telling them exactly what is what. If the chairs in the former housemaids' bedrooms are valued at £30,000 while the Edwardian copies in the drawing-room (which Granny thought so pretty) are only valued at £300, it is not necessary to be a very knowledgeable art connoisseur to consider doing a swap. Possibly less lasting in its impact is the advice of visiting experts, for their comments tend not to be written down and bound neatly in brown card covers tied with green ribbon. Their opinions also tend to be contradictory. Nevertheless, most owners of important possessions are constantly besieged with requests to inspect this or that by knowledgeable professionals from museums, the National Trust, the great auction houses, American universities and earnest researchers in general who produce hitherto unknown facts about 'the kit' in country houses. This increase in knowledge has led to a much more professional, even scholarly, approach to the display and arrangement of family pictures and furniture than prevailed before the war.

Even more pervasive in its impact on the country house than the influence of the art expert is that of the interior decorator. Interior decoration in its modern professional form was invented in America in the late nineteenth century, and passed to England from the States in the early years of this century. It gradually took root in London drawing-rooms and mews cottages between the wars before hitting the country house scene with full force after 1945. Perhaps at this stage it is worth defining 'interior decoration', and the words of the Australian-born American decorator Rose Cumming, written in 1929, immediately present themselves for the purpose: 'Interior decoration is a frivolous sister of the architectural profession. It requires primarily that one be an expert in color, design, period and placing furniture [and that] one can intelligently interpret the original design of the architect. The decorator should, in addition, be blessed with a sixth sense—a kind of artistic alchemy which endows the articles of furniture with that elusive [quality] of liveableness which transforms houses into homes.'[1] While the advice of the art-history expert aims at transforming a house into a museum, the job of the decorator is to make it a 'home' with lots of cushions, curtains and carpets. The cross-fertilization of these two approaches has led to the evolution of a distinctive mode known, especially in America, as the English Country House Style. Its hallmark is an effortless blend of museum-quality furniture, chintzy sofas and bottles of gin regimented on marble-topped side tables.

The evolution of modern interior decoration in New York in the 1880s and 1890s was partly due to the fusion of American and European experience as rich Americans travelled on the Continent and succumbed to the charm of crumbling Italian *palazzi* and French *châteaux*. On their return home, armed with all the antiques that dollars could buy, they aimed at creating a bigger and better effect on Fifth Avenue. This was the culmination of a late-nineteenth-century campaign against native 'bad taste' in magazines like *Godfrey's Lady's Book*, *Harper's New Monthly Magazine* and *Harper's Bazaar*. Catherine Beecher and her sister Harriet Beecher Stowe had contributed to this campaign in the chapters on the 'decorating of homes' in their books on household management. Edward Bok, the influential editor of the *Ladies' Home Journal*, had run a series in the 1890s of double-page spreads showing houses 'in good taste' on one side and houses 'in bad taste' on the other. Much of this campaign was directed at ordinary housewives, but out of it came the idea that women could actually work as decorators. Candice Wheeler published an article in *Outlook* in 1895 called 'Interior Decoration as a Profession for Women' in which she pointed out that there were very few professions which a woman could practise without 'offending respectability' and suggested decorating because it would use a woman's 'instinctive knowledge of textiles and intimate knowledge of the convenience of domestic life'. In 1897, Edith Wharton, in collaboration with Ogden Codman, wrote *The Decoration of Houses* which was the first serious study of house decoration as a branch of architecture to have been published for fifty years. And a few years later in New York Elsie de Wolfe (Lady Mendl) set up as 'America's first woman decorator'. Her reputation was made when Stanford White (with Lutyens, the greatest of twentieth-century Classical architects) persuaded a committee of ladies to engage her services to do the interior of the Colony Club on Madison Avenue. Her fortune was made when Henry Clay Frick gave her the job of furnishing the residential floor of his palatial house/museum on the corner of Fifth Avenue and 70th Street. He paid her ten per cent commission on every stick of furniture she bought for him and she bought him millions of dollars' worth. Her influence was all-pervasive on early-twentieth-century Anglo-American taste. Though an innovator she was not an original philosopher of design. She pounced on Edith Wharton's word 'suitability' as her keynote—'The essence of taste is suitability'—and was largely responsible for the creation of the 'Period Room' look with appropriate 'antique furniture' disposed around rooms painted in tasteful shades of mushroom, cream and 'celadon green'.[2]

The 'Period Room' arrived in London in the early 1900s as part of the baggage of American heiress-wives. The American-born Lady Randolph Churchill, for instance, was one of the first women in England to interest herself in interior decoration. But it was only after the First World War that the big firms of fashionable decorators such as Lenygon and Morant, Thornton Smith, Keebles and White Allom took off and swept through Mayfair and Belgravia in a wave of Period style. Even in the 1930s, however, it was rare for these firms to undertake large-scale work in the country. Alongside the big and (rather boringly) grand firms there were also several influential individuals such as Syrie Maugham with her famous all-white look. Her work, however, was entirely metropolitan and of no importance in the world of country houses. It is significant, for example, that Evelyn Waugh in a *Handful of Dust* treats a Syrie Maugham-type scheme as a temporary aberration wholly inimical to the spirit of the house when Tony Last allows his wife Brenda to employ the horrible Mrs Beaver to destroy the Victorian morning-room at Hetton Abbey and replace it with a horror of chrome plate and white sheepskin. Before disappearing up the Amazon he gives orders for it to be restored to its original glory.

Another woman decorator in the 1930s who did have an important effect, and did prepare the ground for a particular type of country house taste in the post-war period, was Mrs Guy Bethell. She had a highly personal shop called Eldon in Duke Street, Mayfair, and helped various leaders of fashion with their

houses including Mrs Ronald Tree (now Mrs Nancy Lancaster) when she was decorating Kelmarsh in Northamptonshire, *circa 1927–30*. Mrs Lancaster, also an American by birth, is of course a key figure in the creation of the mid-twentieth-century country house interior in England. She was brought up at Mirador in Virginia, the Langhorne family house—the beautiful Langhorne sisters, Nancy Astor and Phyllis Brand, were her aunts. This old Southern house had a great influence on her architectural taste which later she expressed in the series of houses she decorated for herself—Kelmarsh, Ditchley, and Haseley—as well as the houses she decorated for relations such as Eydon Hall in Northamptonshire for the Brands. Mrs Lancaster, together with Lady Colefax and John Fowler, was largely responsible for the evolution of the sophisticated and romantic English Country House Style with its air of effortless ease and atmosphere of 'unruffled continuity and nostalgia for Augustan order'.[3]

Lady Colefax, the wife of Sir Arthur Colefax, a lawyer, was a leading hostess and turned to decoration after her husband lost money in the 1929 slump in order to finance her entertaining. She started the business, which still bears her name, in 1933 and was joined in 1938 by John Fowler who was to become 'without doubt, the most important figure amongst the post-war decorators of the upper-class world'.[4] The outbreak of war in 1939 brought all decorating to a halt for the best part of ten years and it was only in the late 1940s and early 1950s when owners were tackling the problem of restoring or replacing houses damaged by wartime requisitioning that Colefax and Fowler and all the other decorating firms came into their own. The fact that most people were starting from scratch, getting their furniture out of store and repainting rooms that had been occupied by the army or evacuated school-children meant that there was enormous scope for decorating. Economic conditions also had an effect. Many people had little money to spend, and the rationing of materials limited the amount that could be done. Interior decoration was a comparatively cheap way of bringing life back to ravaged old rooms, or plainly designed new ones. And as Mrs King, one of a group of smart women decorators who operated from the purlieus of Mount Street, announced in 1951: 'Austerity makes people more determined to cling on to what elegances they can.'[5]

Decorating was all about making do with flair and limited resources, as Lady Diana Abdy triumphantly demonstrated at Newton Ferrers in Cornwall. The house had been burnt in 1940 and only the shell remained. It was rebuilt after the war in stages as building licences permitted. Because of the restrictions it was not possible to do anything internally apart from plainly plastering the walls and ceilings. All the impact of the new rooms had to be created through surface decoration. Thus the drawing-room was painted in *trompe l'oeil* with porphyry columns, and blackamoors were cut out of paper and stuck on the

John Fowler's full-blown decorative style:
Mrs John Dennis's drawing-room.

walls between the windows. The dining-room walls were also painted in *trompe* to look like fabric, while the elaborate curtains were a '*tour de force* of make-do-and-mend', being dyed parachutes lined with dyed dust sheets and hung from gilded drain pipes doing duty as curtain poles. The parlour curtains were also made of parachute silk. The hall and ante-room were both painted to represent marble. Much of this work was done by Lady Diana Abdy herself, a daughter of the Earl of Bradford and 'a talented amateur artist'.[6] Other cases of aristocratic do-it-yourself were Bulbridge House near Wilton, where Lady Juliet Duff worked all the rugs in *gros point* from designs made by Rex Whistler before his death, and Send Grove, Surrey, where Loelia, Duchess of Westminster made the stair-carpet out of her own needlework. Her articles on house decorating in the late 1940s and 1950s in *House and Garden* capture the atmosphere of the period beautifully.

The most important feature of post-war interior decoration was the rise and rise of John Fowler, 'Prince of Decorators' as the Duchess of Devonshire has called him. John Fowler, who died in 1977, was at school at Felsted in Essex when the Reverend Conrad Noel was rector of Thaxted, and Noel's Arts and Crafts and High Church fittings there probably formed his introduction to interior design. His early life was overshadowed by the death of his father when he was only six, leaving his mother in straitened circumstances and meaning that he had to leave school and start work at the age of sixteen. After a series of uncongenial jobs his lucky break came when, through a friend of his mother's, he was taken on by Thornton Smith in Soho Square to paint Chinese wallpaper for fifteen shillings a week. There he learnt many of the tricks of the

decorating trade while teaching himself about historical styles in his spare time at the Victoria and Albert Museum. In 1930 he was employed to manage the newly established studio of painted furniture at Peter Jones, and also did work for Mrs Bethell at Eldon. In the 1930s too he came under the influence of fashion designers like Chanel and Schiaparelli, and it was from them that he learnt to be daring in the use of colour and selective about materials. He strongly disliked the no-colour craze in pre-war decoration and in retrospect can be seen as a quiet revolutionary preparing the way for the post-war breakthrough into colour and pattern. Though he worked entirely in the Classical manner, he was an innovator who brought a new sense of vitality and harmony to the world of decoration. The eighteenth century, both English and French, for he was strongly francophile, was his first love and the source of inspiration for all his work. It is the combination of detailed historical knowledge together with his feeling for colour, pattern and materials which gives his work an aesthetic reality quite different from 'Reproduction' and miles apart from run-of-the-mill 'Knightsbridge Good Taste'. The secret of his style is an expensive simplicity, a calculated down-playing of effect, but using only the very best ingredients. As he put it himself, 'I like things that look simple but cost a mint.' Characteristic components of a Fowlerized room are painted furniture, glazed chintzes, needlework rugs, and an overall sense of comfort. He eschewed gilded chairs, elaborate brocades and oriental carpets. He had a distinctive sense of colour with a preference for pondy shades, 'the muds and greens of England', or bright clear yellows, blues and pinks. A particular apricot, or smoked salmon, is a *leitmotif* of his style and found many imitators. But none of them has the feel of the original, which depends on the mix and the tone and application of the paint as well as the colour. In the cloisters at Wilton, for instance, which he redecorated for Lord Pembroke in 1963, each face of the vaulting was painted a slightly different shade dictated by the fall of light from the windows.[7]

John Fowler was a great perfectionist, and an awesome task-master for those who worked under him. At the new house at Arundel, Lavinia, Duchess of Norfolk remembers how the painters spent all day mixing and re-mixing the paint for the hall until he considered the colour to be exactly right. People dreaded the moment when he said, 'The dado rail needs to come down six inches—no, eight.' He could be equally frightening to prospective clients who were made to feel that they had to pass rigorous tests of taste before being considered worthy of the privilege of employing him. To one unfortunate person who dared to move some china he had just placed on the chimneypiece he exploded, 'Young man, if you think you can decorate this house better than I can, I am leaving right now!' In Mrs Dennis's new London drawing-room he had all the frieze taken down after execution and put back three inches higher. This room, made by removing the floor above and raising the ceiling, he

Far left: John Fowler's francophile mood.

Left: The hall table with the visitors' book at Arundel Park.

considered to be almost perfect, and it shows many of the features of his mature style in the 1950s. It is painted in an almost diagrammatic scheme of different shades of white and blue; and has elaborately ruched curtains, comfortably upholstered chairs and odd eccentric touches such as Baroque urns on console brackets. He liked objects of character, and not just things that were pretty. When faced with a choice between prettiness and 'personality' he always let personality win, as Mrs Lancaster's bedroom at Haseley demonstrated. The big attraction of his rooms, however, was not just that the detail was aesthetically satisfying but that they looked, and could be, lived in. They do, in fact, look best when they are worn and faded; when the chair covers are full of dogs' hairs, the carpets slightly threadbare and the paintwork darkened by wood smoke from the fire. Then their romantic, nostalgic, poetic quality of 'comfort and pleasing decay' comes to the fore. In many ways his was a painter's approach, with an artist's feel for light, colour and the massing of objects. Added to this he combined, in John Cornforth's words, 'the approaches of the craftsman and the historian'; and this is perhaps why he was seen as one of the chief representatives of the Romantic Classical tradition in England.[8]

In 1945 Colefax and Fowler moved to its present address at 39 Brook Street (Wyatville's old house) and Lady Colefax sold out to Mrs Lancaster. In many ways the post-war country house practice was a partnership between John Fowler and Mrs Lancaster. In the late 1940s and 1950s they visited houses together and she was responsible for introducing him to many of his major clients, including the Astor connection which runs like a thread through his career from Bruern to Grimsthorpe. They learnt a great deal from each other and enjoyed a stimulating partnership with strongly expressed differences of opinion, for there is nothing like the details of taste for provoking quarrels. Lady Astor described them as 'frankly, the unhappiest unmarried couple I have ever met'. At Haseley Court, Mrs Lancaster's house in Oxfordshire, they worked together to create one of the most sumptuously decorated interiors in post-war England. It was a work which brought out the best in both, with John Fowler doing Mrs Lancaster's bedroom in a fantastic *trompe l'oeil* Gothick and painting a Chinese wallpaper for the Palladio Room, while Mrs Lancaster hunted down excellent pieces of furniture and interesting objects for the rooms.

John Fowler's first important country house was Ramsbury Manor in Wiltshire for Lord Wilton in 1950 and it was the first of a vast series that included most of the major houses of England, and not just in England—two of his best works were Château Latour in France and the Mellon town house in New York. A great coup was the commission to do the 'Mill Over the Water' for the Duke and Duchess of Windsor in 1953, the most sought-after job of the day. Official work included Chequers for the Prime Minister and the Queen's Audience

Top: John Fowler's Gothick.

Bottom: The drawing-room at Arundel Park.
All the hallmarks of 'the English Country House Style'.

A detail of Mrs Dennis's drawing-room: John Fowler comfort.

Room at Buckingham Palace. He was directly responsible for the decoration of many of the new houses described in this book and worked with a number of traditional architects on several different occasions, including Claud Phillimore at Arundel, Betterton and Knowsley; Philip Jebb at Cornbury and several other houses; Raymond Erith at Hunton Manor and Gatley Folly; and with Sir Martyn Beckett at Bruern Abbey. Perhaps even more important than the houses where he was directly employed was his general impact on the interiors of the great majority of new houses built since the war. He, and Mrs Lancaster, promoted a particular type of upper-class style which is ubiquitous in a certain kind of interior and has an instantly recognizable vocabulary—three-tone colours, rush matting, scumbled, dragged or antiqued paintwork, plain card lampshades, fringed curtains and French tablecloths. It has become the basis of a country house vernacular. As the *New York Times* magazine put it in 1979, John Fowler did not invent the English country house interior but was 'responsible for the way we perceive that sort of decorating today'. His style became one of 'the most enduring of our time' with a large following in both England and America, and latterly has filtered down to become part of popular taste in just the way that the design fashions of the eighteenth century passed down through society.

Towards the end of his life John Fowler became something of a controversial figure through his work for the National Trust. His often sweeping schemes of redecoration were compared by some to Victorian cathedral restorations where much of later interest was swept away in an attempt to get back to a hypothetical state of original perfection. It was considered that an organization like the National Trust, whose purpose was to preserve houses as museums, should not in any case have employed a fashionable decorator. It has to be admitted that these critics were probably right, but this need not undermine an assessment of John Fowler's work for private clients and in new houses where the aim was to create an agreeable and stylish backdrop to suit the needs and taste of a particular client. As new houses form the subject of this book it is fortunately not necessary to get involved further in the controversy over the 'authentic' decoration of historic houses.

By the 1960s a younger generation of designers was evolving a different kind of balance in interior decoration to John Fowler's. They had a stronger predilection for visual stimulation and diversity of experience; they liked very bright colours, over-scaled objects and vivid geometrical patterns. Their taste was affected by a renewed sympathy for the Victorians on one hand and the Baroque on the other. This led to a liking for crowded rooms, cluttered 'table-scapes' and the perverse juxtaposition of objects of different kinds, for example, gilt Louis Quinze chairs and modern stainless steel furniture. This approach involved a partial rejection of the 'good Georgian taste' exemplified by John Fowler and the cultivation of a bolder, more restless 'Mannerist' style. These designers were romantic in a more progressive way and their interpretation of the past, while less understated and informed than John Fowler's, has a certain zip and full-blooded spirit which is lacking in his work. The doyen of the younger generation of decorators was David Hicks who made his debut in *House and Garden* in 1954 at the age of twenty-four with his own flat 'near Eaton Square'. After a period in partnership with Tom Parr, who later transferred to Colefax and Fowler, he emerged as the most publicized designer of the 1960s. His style was most completely expressed in his own house at Britwell Salome in Oxfordshire which he bought at the age of thirty in 1960 and entirely redecorated to create a remarkable blend of eighteenth-century proportions, modern pictures and objects of all periods and nationalities, but nevertheless with a formal and tailored appearance. His own bathroom was stippled black and white and filled with Gothic furniture, marble obelisks and eighteenth-century architectural drawings. The drawing-room was entirely beige and cream except for the strident primary colours of the modern paintings on the walls and the matching flowers in vases on tables beneath them. Britwell was described by Gervase Jackson-Stops as 'the epitome of the 1960s' response to the past, a response that is in large part of David Hicks's own creation'.[9]

David Hicks's marriage into the royal family made decorating a smart occupation for enterprising young men, rather as Lord Snowdon's had raised photography into the pantheon of respectable professions. Added to this, David Hicks combines his role of decorator with that of landowner, and takes an almost eighteenth-century virtuoso's interest in the embellishment of his estate. He himself designed the Octagon House in the village at Britwell Salome and commissioned Raymond Erith to design a pair of farm workers' cottages and the farm manager's house for the home farm at Britwell. He was also partly responsible for the design of the neighbouring Swyncombe House in Oxfordshire. Work in other people's country houses includes the decoration of the new library designed in the Hawksmoor manner by Roderick Gradidge at Easton Neston for Lady Hesketh, an extensive scheme of redecoration in the family wing at Belvoir Castle for the Duke of Rutland and an ambitious replanning and redecorating of the interior of Barons Court, County Tyrone, for the Duke of Abercorn. One of his major country house jobs was the conversion of the former office wing at Wynyard Park, County Durham, into a house for the Marquess of Londonderry in the 1960s. Wynyard, a Neo-Classical palace designed by Philip Wyatt, had not been lived in properly since the war. When Lord Londonderry decided to move back, the enormous rooms in the main block were not considered suitable for family life and it was decided instead to demolish part of the complex of office buildings at the east end of the house and to remodel the remainder to make a new house which also incorporated the smaller private rooms at that end of the main block. David Hicks evolved a scheme which would give these rooms, some of which were an awkward shape, colour, style and a sense of *luxe*. The hall and staircase were painted a strong orange, while the principal drawing-room, an octagon in plan, was given a yellow colour scheme as a background to the famous Londonderry portraits by Lawrence. David Hicks also designed a special geometrical patterned carpet reflecting the form of the room. As illustrated in *Vogue* in 1964 with Beatles record covers lying on a table in the foreground it was the quintessence of the grand 'Mod' style of the decade.[10] Unlike John Fowler who would not allow his work to be photographed, as he thought photography an intrusion into the privacy of his clients, and who therefore relied entirely on personal recommendations for jobs, David Hicks has been a great self-publicist. As well as innumerable features in the illustrated 'glossies' he has himself published several books on his work with titles like *David Hicks on Living with Taste*.

Just as John Fowler was the key figure in the 1950s and David Hicks in the 1960s, so the 1970s too had a particular leading decorator in the country house field. This was David Mlinaric. Unlike his precursors, Mlinaric had trained as an architect, having attended the Bartlett School of Architecture at London

Top: The Palladio Room at Haseley Court.
The wallpaper was painted by John Fowler.
Note the properly furnished writing table.

Bottom: Mrs Lancaster's bedroom at Haseley Court,
painted by John Fowler in *trompe l'oeil*.

University for three years and then spent two years with Michael Inchbald and Dennis Lennon before going to Rome for a time. He set up on his own at the age of twenty-four and by the time he was thirty he had completed over 150 commissions. He is strongly of the view that men make the best decorators: 'Men have good judgement or no judgment at all. Women tend to dabble. Also they rarely have any idea of scale—they seem to get things out of proportion. Women usually hate living in big houses or buying large objects for a room. It frightens them. It's a sort of doll's house complex, I suppose.'[11] Words which would make the American women pioneers of the profession turn in their graves, could they hear them!

In many ways Mlinaric's style is a stronger version of John Fowler's with a similar romantic combination of apricot and mud colours, rush matting and plain linen upholstery. One of his earliest and most successful country house jobs is the interior of the family wing at Shugborough for the Earl of Lichfield, and among completely new houses Llanstephan in Wales is particularly good. It is symptomatic that he should have succeeded John Fowler as adviser on decoration to the National Trust. As he has become more successful he has slowed down and now concentrates on very few very grand jobs. *Harpers and Queen* wrote of him in September 1983: 'If you have a fine building then this is the decorator you need; though you may have to wait as he only does two jobs a year. He was trained as an architect and has sensitivity and feeling for a building, and he exercises great patience to see that the right materials are used for restorations. As the adviser to the National Trust, he is the natural and

worthy successor to John Fowler.'

In addition to the impact of individual decorators on the interiors of post-war country houses, the period has also seen the enthusiastic revival of a number of eighteenth-century modes of decoration such as print rooms, decorated with stuck-on prints, or large-scale wall-paintings in the grand manner. The print room is essentially an amateur activity and is an occupation on winter evenings for those with a steady hand, armed with a pot of paste and pair of scissors. Such schemes are inspired by the splendid authentic eighteenth-century print decoration at Woodhall Park in Hertfordshire or at Castletown in Ireland. Convincing recent creations are the print rooms done for Sir William Rees-Mogg at Ston Easton, near Bath, with prints of various shapes against a pale blue ground, that at Leixlip Castle for Desmond Guinness, and most recently Reresby Sitwell's sitting-room at Renishaw decorated with eighteenth-century Italian prints found in the attic, pasted on a yellow ground.

The late-twentieth-century taste for grandiose wall-painting owes much to Rex Whistler whose work in the 1930s, such as the splendid dining-room with Italianate scenes at Plas Newydd or the *trompe l'oeil* Gothick drawing-room at Mottisfont Abbey, captured the imagination of his clients and their friends. As a result, having a painted room in the house has become the *sine qua non* for anyone with aspirations towards being an aristocratic patron of the arts. At their best these painted rooms are among the most attractive products of the nostalgic Romantic Classicism which forms the principal thread in the late-twentieth-century country house aesthetic. Since the war, a series of artists

55

Left: The drawing-room at Kings Walden Bury decorated by Isobel Monckton, the epitome of '*le Grand Style Anglais*'.

Above: Painted bedroom at Meols Hall, Lancashire, by Richard Willis. A dream northern landscape.

have done work of this type with greater or lesser success and varying degrees of technical competence. Some of it, one feels, is closer to Covent Garden scenery than Tiepolo. Roland Pym's murals in the saloon at Woburn, for instance, can only be described as regrettable. On the other hand, Felix Kelly's witty and evocative views of buildings which Vanbrugh never designed, in the re-created Garden Hall at Castle Howard, are a worthy addition to the house and show the genre at its best. They strike just the right note of poetic nostalgia. The most ambitious project of the type and the largest undertaken since the early eighteenth century, is in an historic interior rather than a new room or a new house, but nevertheless as a large-scale post-war commission it deserves a mention here. This is the staircase at Ragley in Warwickshire where Graham Rust created a vast scheme of mural decoration between 1969 and 1983. He was commissioned to do this by Lord Hertford after they had met in Virginia in 1967. The theme is 'The Temptation'. On the ceiling Christ and the Devil are seen through an open-topped dome surrounded by a dramatic perspective of cleverly foreshortened Baroque architecture. Round the upper part of the walls is a colonnaded balcony with portraits of the Hertford family, their friends (and dogs) looking down into an idyllic tropical landscape below. The work is carried out in strikingly bright colours and is an astonishingly successful piece of decoration. This is Graham Rust's largest and finest work but he has done a number of smaller murals in other country houses including Duncombe Park, Yorkshire (1966), Basildon Park, Berkshire (1969), Arthington Hall, Yorkshire (1973) and Mawley Hall, Shropshire (1979–80). A number of new houses have been embellished with work of this kind. At Arundel Park, Lawrence Toynbee painted views of the castle on the back wall of the loggia leading to the west pavilion. At Meols Hall in Lancashire Roger Hesketh employed Richard Willis to decorate the principal bedroom with romantic Northern landscapes; a personal note is struck in one of them by the appearance on a rocky eminence of Lumley Castle, Lady Mary Hesketh's childhood home.

NOTES

1 Katherine Tweed, Ed., *The Finest Rooms* (New York 1964), p. 44.
2 Ibid, pp. 19–22; *The Old House Journal* (New York 1976–83), various articles on the nineteenth-century American interior.
3 John Fowler and John Cornforth, *English Decoration in the Eighteenth Century* (1974), pp. 17–20.
4 *House and Garden*, March 1960, p. 50.
5 Ibid, May 1951, p. 46.
6 Ibid, August 1952, p. 34.
7 Colefax and Fowler office files. I am most grateful to Mr Stanley Falconer for allowing me access to these.
8 *Country Life*, 28 April, 1982, p. 1092.
9 Ibid, 12 October 1972, pp. 883–7.
10 *Vogue*, 1 August 1964, pp. 115–22.
11 *House and Garden*, July/August 1969, p. 37.

IV
OLD GEORGIANS

There are several ways of writing about the architecture of individual country houses built since 1945 and different possibilities of grouping the material; for example, according to geography, or the family connections of clients, or the type and size of the house. But on consideration it seemed that the best way of approaching the problem was to divide the houses into a series of clearly identifiable categories according to their architects; and it seems as well to start with the group of designers whom I have labelled 'Old Georgians'. These are the architects whom one might have thought were dead, or at least retired, by 1945. In fact a surprisingly large number of architects who had trained and even begun practice before the First World War and might be thought of as essentially inter-war architects, were still actively designing houses in the 1950s and 1960s. They include Oswald P. Milne (died 1968), A. S. G. Butler (died 1968), Philip Tilden (died 1956), Vincent Harris (died 1971), Darcy Braddell (died 1970), Sir Albert Richardson (died 1964), Marshall Sisson (died 1978) and Trenwith Wills (died 1972), as well as several old architectural firms who continued to do the occasional country house job, sometimes under another name, such as Bostock and Wilkins (originally Unsworth, Son and Triggs).[1]

Despite the lure of more profitable public and commercial work, they continued to design the type of country house for which they had been trained in the palmy days of Edwardian England and, unlike a lot of younger architects, they had no qualms about giving their clients the houses they wanted; that is, ones which combined modern standards of convenience with a traditional, mainly Georgian, appearance. Most of them had trained in the old articled pupil system whereby a young man was placed in the office of an established architect for a number of years and was introduced there into the mysteries of

57

Sir Edwin Lutyens's The Salutation, Sandwich, Kent. The ideal
and main inspiration for the 'Old Georgians'.

measured drawing, surveying on site, and the traditional ways of building.
This type of education turned out an entirely different kind of designer from the
more cerebral product of the big architectural schools where the training
tended to induce an over-emphasis on international theory (whether Beaux
Arts or Modern), arbitrary aesthetic standards and contempt for local tradition.
The architects who trained as articled pupils in the years around 1910 absorbed
the full inheritance of the Arts and Crafts Movement, and as a result had an
enthusiasm for local building methods and materials, a strong love of England
and things English, and a desire to foster traditional craftsmanship. The Arts
and Crafts, originally a vernacular-inspired reaction against the elaborate
revival of historical styles, had by about 1905, in the wake of Lutyens's
discovery of the 'Great Game', turned increasingly to Classicism. There evolved
thereby a type of house which, though rooted in the vernacular and drawing
heavily on traditional building crafts and materials in its construction, was
stylistically inspired by the glories of English domestic design from the reigns of
Charles II to George IV, especially the simpler houses of the seventeenth-
century 'artisan mannerists', or the provincial builders of eighteenth-century
England, or the primly elegant rectories and villas of the Regency, but not the
more Continental Baroque or Palladian splendours of Chatsworth or Holkham.
This house-type achieved its most perfect manifestation in Lutyens's The
Salutation at Sandwich, Kent, and formed the model for several generations of
twentieth-century English country houses. The Old Georgians had in general a
great reverence for Lutyens and many of them, though not all, had at some
stage worked in his office or attended his lectures at the Royal Academy.

58

Lutyens's chief surviving pupil after the Second World War was Oswald Milne, who had been articled originally to Sir Arthur Blomfield and Son but had transferred to Lutyens's office in the years before the First World War. He is perhaps best known for his inter-war alterations to Claridge's, but in 1954 he designed one last country house. This was for Lord and Lady Churston at Lupton Park in Devon, to replace their former family seat which had been let to a prep school. The new house was built on a virgin site in the park with a splendid panoramic view out across Tor Bay. The exterior was stuccoed and painted white, in the traditional Devon manner, while the roof was covered with grey Delabole slates. The main accommodation comprised a drawing-room (28′ × 16′), dining-room and study, four principal bedrooms, two dressing-rooms and three bathrooms. The latter were fitted out with every manifestation of luxury including walls lined with marble and mosaic. The house was designed specially to contain the principal family portraits and furniture from the old house and, with its old parkland setting, gave *Country Life* reason to think that it felt 'important', despite its relatively small size.[2]

The most enthusiastic of Lutyens fans, Andrew Butler, had somewhat ironically never been a pupil of the great man but of E. J. May. May, who is remembered chiefly for his work at Bedford Park, had himself been articled to Decimus Burton and Norman Shaw, but was a contemporary, friend and admirer of Lutyens, responsible for encouraging him to join the Art Workers' Guild. This enthusiasm he relayed to Butler and it is enshrined in Butler's monumental three-volume monograph, *The Architecture of Sir Edwin Lutyens*, published in 1950, and also in much of Butler's own architectural designing. During the First World War Butler had fought in Flanders, and was wounded on two occasions, at Ypres and Arras. In 1919 he began his own country house practice and acquired some interesting jobs between the wars, including the modernization of Kedleston for Lord Curzon in 1924–6 and the reconstruction of Schloss Samek Rondnice in Czechoslovakia for Prince Lobkowicz, a scheme halted and never completed because of the Nazi invasion. During the Second World War he spent his time in London recording bomb-damaged buildings and was one of the original members of St Paul's Watch. In 1945 he started again on country houses by rebuilding Lessingham Manor in Norfolk for W. Neave and extending Hungerhill House in Sussex, together with several new estate cottages there, for the Earl of Cottenham between 1947 and 1955. The existing house at Hungerhill was Neo-Tudor and of little interest, but Butler's additions are pure Lutyens. He contrived an impressive square forecourt with stone walls and gateways entered from a formal avenue. The large additions to the house itself have windows with Classical architraves and entablatures but a vernacular stone-flagged roof and tall chimneys like Lutyens's Tigbourne Court. The real give-away is the treatment of the materials of the walls. These are built of mixed red and yellow bricks with square stones interspersed to form an irregular chequer and diaper pattern. It is quintessential Lutyens, and the homage from an admirer to the master could not be more clearly expressed.

Other houses where Butler designed substantial alterations or additions from the late 1940s onwards include Knights Farm at Colne Engaine, Essex, where a new entrance front and forecourt was added to an older house for George Courtauld; Wormington Grange in Gloucestershire, a Regency house reduced and replanned for Lord Ismay; and Wakefield Lodge in Northampton-shire, where the stables were converted into staff flats and the house substan-tially remodelled for Norman Gee. Today Wakefield Lodge is generally assumed to be entirely the work of William Kent and Pevsner's description in *The Buildings of England*, for instance, makes no reference to Butler's contribu-tion. In fact one of the principal elevations and nearly all the interior, apart from the two-storeyed hall, is by him. The house had been greatly enlarged and altered in the nineteenth century, and in 1947 Butler demolished all the Victorian extensions, designed a new garden façade to hide the scars, and remodelled the principal rooms in a simplified Lutyens style with high coved ceilings, moulded cornices and plaster wall panels.

One of his most successful country houses is Pennyholme in the North Riding of Yorkshire for the 3rd Earl of Feversham. This was done in stages, as building licences permitted, between 1949 and 1951, and is a charmingly played-down exercise in rustic Georgian set in a Lutyens-type architectural garden planned as an integral part of the overall scheme. The house was developed out of a simple moorland cottage and this explains the informal plan, with bits at angles to each other as if the product of centuries of organic growth. It is a model of how to do this type of job without creating an effect of incongruous or embarrassing grandeur. Pennyholme is situated at one end of the great Helmsley estate, ten miles from the principal family seat at Duncombe Park. It was intended as a branch estate office for the administration of the moorland and as an occasional residence for shooting, though latterly occupied

as a dower house by the 3rd Earl's widow. It is built of local sandstone with a roof of red pantiles and white-painted sash windows; despite its modesty of character it is definitely a 'gentleman's house'. The main rooms have decent eighteenth-century chimneypieces and the men's lavatory downstairs has marble surrounds to the wash basins. Likewise, the inside, though compact, has a feeling of spaciousness thanks to a quite large drawing-room (26'6" × 17'9") overlooking the formal garden with terrace, little cascade, stone-lined basin and a vast view over Sleightholmedale. When writing about Pennyholme in *Country Life* in 1958 Christopher Hussey described it as the latest in the diminishing succession of seats on the Helmsley estate, following the feudal castle (ruined), the Baroque palace of Duncombe Park (girls' school) and the Victorian mansion of Nawton Tower. Since then the process has been reversed and, at the time of writing, Pennyholme has been put on the market and the present Lord Feversham is preparing to move from Nawton Tower back into Duncombe Park.[3]

An entirely new house, not even incorporating part of an old cottage (often necessary at that time in order to get planning permission), was Bourne Wood at Hurstbourne Priors in Hampshire, Andrew Butler's last work, designed in 1956 for Colonel and Mrs Kingslake Tower. This was more a dower house for an elderly couple than a proper country house, and occupied a site on a corner of a friend's estate. The Towers had hitherto lived in a sprawling Scottish castle replete with dining-room, drawing-room, morning-room, study, library, billiards room and dozens of bedrooms, so they approached the problem of living in a small house with all the enthusiasm of novelty. Bourne Wood was built of sand-faced bricks, had windows with glazing bars and a low-swept roof of hand-made tiles; it was deliberately designed to look 'rather 1906' so is a fascinatingly late, though authentic, specimen of the Arts and Crafts Movement. It was planned as compactly as possible with the drawing-room as the only room of any size, and only five bedrooms and two bathrooms. The Towers wished to run the house without servants, no longer having any old ones of their own, and did not feel that they wanted a separate dining-room; on the other hand they could not picture themselves actually eating in the kitchen; they compromised and dined in the library instead. Using the library as a dining-room seems to have been the Victorian equivalent of eating off a tray in front of the television. Queen Victoria and Prince Albert, for example, often ate in the library at Balmoral as part of the cult of the simple life in their informal Highland retreat. The origin of the habit does not seem to be recorded; it may have been simply that libraries were rooms containing a number of convenient tables.[4]

Another architect whom one is surprised to find still around in the years after the war is Philip Tilden, the doyen of fashionable 1920s designers, much

Far left: Hungerhill House, Sussex. Addition by Andrew Butler showing strong Lutyens influence.

Left: Hungerhill House. Detail of forecourt wall by Andrew Butler.

Pennyholme, Yorkshire. House and garden by Andrew Butler.

employed by Sir Philip Sassoon, among others, to give Port Lympe an overdose of Hollywood grandeur. Despite his smart veneer, Tilden too was Arts and Crafts at heart. His extraordinary autobiography, *True Remembrances*, published in 1954, fails to mention that he was born and brought up in Birmingham but goes on at length about his Kentish yeomen ancestors—'All through the centuries the family had possessed many Kentish manors'—and manages to obfuscate reality with a cloud of hops, half-timber and half-ruined castles. His role in the post-war country house scene, alas, does not do him much credit. He became the advocate *par excellence* of ruthless schemes of truncation of historic houses. It was Tilden, for instance, who first suggested to Lord Lansdowne pulling down the Big House at Bowood and retreating to the Little House and stables. He spoilt Luton Hoo by closing the main portico, selling the lead from the roof and converting the public part of the house into a lifeless museum. His worst mistake was the irreparable mutilation of Cortachy Castle in Angus by demolishing Bryce's wing. In order to understand the attitude of mind behind this type of job it is perhaps best to quote Tilden's own words: 'Towards the end of the war, and for several years after it, I had plenty to do in the role of plastic surgeon, repairing the ravages of time and war, removing growths, rejuvenating and reducing great houses built in more prodigal times.' And to be fair to him, some of the more florid Victorian bits which he lopped off were so incongruous that his surgery did improve the appearance of a house as well as making it more conveniently manageable.

63

Top: Wakefield Lodge, Northamptonshire.
Dining-room by Andrew Butler.

Bottom: Wakefield Lodge.
Drawing-room by Andrew Butler.

Antony House in Cornwall is a case in point, where he removed a huge asymmetrical red-brick wing and restored the house to the original 1720s composition: 'It was a pleasure to organize the amputation of this disfigurement and restore the house to its former symmetry. The red bricks from the demolition I had buried in a quarry lest anyone should be tempted to re-use them in this district of greystone and granite. I also replanned the kitchens and simplified the gardens so that both could be run with less labour, and converted the service wings into self-contained flats for employees and relatives.' Similarly at Whitfield, in Herefordshire, he successfully extracted and partly re-faced the 'Georgian pearl' from a 'Victorian Gothic oyster', though he found that doing this as cheaply as possible so as not to exceed the building licence was 'very exhausting'. As well as truncations and remodellings he designed one completely new house in the 1950s: Blackhall in County Kildare, with nine bedrooms and walls built of concrete, for Sir Harold Wernher and Lord Astor.[5]

Sir Albert Richardson, the 'Professor', was another survivor from the Edwardian period. By this stage in his career he had developed into a larger-than-life eccentric, with a passionate love for everything Georgian, often wearing a wig, being carried around in a sedan chair and reading 1790s copies of *The Times* in his club. A deeply conservative President of the Royal Academy, urbane and courtly yet mischievous and jolly, a self-conscious maestro in the tradition of Burlington, Soane and Henry Holland, he stuck to his own distinctive version of the Grand Manner in direct and deliberate opposition to the accepted Modernist ethos of the architectural establishment. But unlike many of the other traditionalist architects described in this book, he neverthe-less ran a very large and profitable architectural practice ranging from council cottages to whisky distilleries, and including the Jockey Club at Newmarket, a score of office blocks—most notably the excellent *Financial Times* building in the City—and over sixty church restorations, as well as country houses. He was more than a professional architect, at least in the narrow sense; he was also a lecturer, writer, conservationist, painter and avid collector. His eighteenth-century house at Ampthill, Bedfordshire, was a kind of latter-day Soane Museum, lit by candles and oil lamps, the gas having been taken out as too modern and electricity never having been installed. One ungrateful guest advised a friend not to stay there because all 'the mattresses are stuffed with Georgian wigs'.[6]

Sir Albert's country houses included the restoration of several houses after fire damage, for example, Florence Court, County Fermanagh, and Melford Hall, Suffolk, where a wing gutted by the army in the war was reconstructed as the family residence for the Hyde Parkers when the main rooms were opened to the public by the National Trust. He was also responsible for a number of alterations and additions to existing buildings such as the large new drawing-

64

room at Barnwell Manor, Northamptonshire, for HRH the Duke of Gloucester. This was specially designed with eighteenth-century style panelling to display a series of large sporting paintings on canvas of the Duke of Rutland hunting. At Woburn Abbey Sir Albert was called in after the building licence fiasco (see page 16) to design handsome new stone elevations to the truncated wings and a balustraded stone staircase down into the courtyard, an exercise which successfully captures the quality of Henry Holland's work at the Abbey and is some compensation for the 12th Duke's vandalistic demolition of Holland's entrance front and riding school. Less attractive is the new wing containing a double-decker picture gallery added to Anglesey Abbey for Lord Fairhaven in 1955–6. The upper gallery was intended for Lord Fairhaven's hundreds of views of Windsor Castle, a collection reminiscent of a stamp album, while the lower was for the Altieri Claudes which had once belonged to William Beckford. The style is a somewhat bleak version of Hollywood Tudor that is meant to reflect the style of the old house. Lord Fairhaven's own work in the garden was more satisfactory. It included a circular temple or colonnade of ten Corinthian columns (rescued from the demolition of Chesterfield House in London) erected in 1953 to commemorate the coronation of Queen Elizabeth II. This displays an excellently managed sense of scale absent from the house itself. Anglesey is altogether an uneven creation and it seems a pity that the money expended on its grandiose embellishment was not spent instead on rescuing one of the important eighteenth-century houses at that time threatened with demolition. The transatlantic atmosphere which it exuded amidst the austerities of post-war Britain is beautifully captured in James Lees-Milne's recently published diary: 'Got to Anglesey Abbey for tea. Wonderfully appointed house, soft-treading carpets; full of semi-works of art, overheated, over-flowered, and I do not covet it or anything in it. We had a frugal tea but sumptuous dinner prefaced by whisky and epilogued by port. Lord F. is precise, complacent, dogmatic. But hospitable and kind, although aloof and pleased with his noble position. Who is he anyway? The son of an American oil magnate.' It might be added that he still had his bootlaces ironed in the 1950s and 1960s.[7]

Sir Albert, after the war, worked in partnership with his son-in-law Eric Houfe, and it was the latter who was responsible for several of the completely new houses undertaken by the firm in the 1960s, including a stable block for Baron Schroder, the financier, at Ascot in 1961, Kenwick Hall, Lincolnshire, for Captain Oscar Dixon, the paper manufacturer, in 1960, and Merryfield, Sussex, for Ribton Crampton, the Canadian millionaire, in 1963. Sir Albert was enthusiastic about these buildings and said, 'I couldn't have done better myself.' The Kenwick estate was bought by the Dixons from Lord Allenby. The old house (eighteenth-century with additions) had been bombed in the war and

Graham Rust's ceiling painting of 'the Temptation of Christ' over the staircase at Ragley Hall, Warwickshire.

Kenwick Hall, Lincolnshire.

badly restored by the War Damages Commission at a cost of £40,000. The Dixons demolished it and started again on the same site and incorporating the old cellars. They came to Richardson and Houfe because their son had already employed them to do £70,000 worth of work at his own house, Abbey House, including a cast-iron Chinese bridge. Kenwick has a pair of segmental bays and a 'Trafalgar' verandah on the garden front, and on the entrance front a porch displaying the characteristic thin columns to be found in all Richardson and Houfe's work, and derived from Georgian four-poster beds, rather than Vitruvius. The materials and craftsmanship are excellent. The house is built of fawn Stamford bricks, those for the gauged arches of the windows being specially manufactured for the job; all the glazing bars are of mahogany, painted; and inside, the elegant staircase and other joinery, including the fitted sideboard and cupboards in the dining-room, are of Agba wood, an exotic substitute for mahogany. Merryfield is a smaller version of Kenwick, and was built on a house-less estate. A small cottage on the site was demolished and the new house built from scratch. It is stuccoed, with a porch of 'four-poster' Tuscan columns. The best room is the five-bay library. The staircase is semi-circular and of concrete with a slender timber balustrade.[8]

Of the houses by 'Bankers' Georgian' architects in the 1950s, perhaps the most notable is Newsells in Hertfordshire designed by Victor Heal in 1954 for Sir Humphrey de Trafford, Bt. The de Traffords, one of Lancashire's ancient

66

recusant families, had moved to Hertfordshire from Trafford Park, Manchester, following the destruction of the amenities of their estate by industry and especially the construction of the Manchester Ship Canal, the water in which was seventy per cent sewage. The new house was built on the site of a seventeenth-century one, burnt down during the war; Sir Humphrey wished to stay at Newsells and to replace the house because of the successful stud which he had started there in 1926 with his trainer Marcus Marsh, the son of Edward VII's principal trainer.

At the Doncaster Sales in 1948 he had bought a mare called Chenille for 3000 guineas and in 1950 Chenille had produced a bay filly called Lightning which won at Ascot in the autumn of that year and in 1955 produced Alcide, which went on to win the Chester Vase, the Lingfield Derby Trial Stakes, the St Leger at Doncaster and the Voltigeur Stakes at York. Obviously, in the light of this success, Sir Humphrey was keen to keep Newsells a going concern.

Victor Heal's house is eleven bays wide and one of the largest built in England in the 1950s. It was somewhat austere externally, though it is less so now because a subsequent owner added a giant portico on the garden front *circa* 1973. It is built of hand-made sand-faced brick with stone dressings including the surround to the front door, which has a semi-circular pediment containing a carved shield of the de Trafford arms. The generally traditional appearance conceals a steel-framed structure to the roof and an ingenious oil-fired heating system of water-radiant panels embedded in concrete in the floors and ceilings. The accommodation is spacious and includes a two-storeyed hall,

large drawing-room (41′ × 35′), dining-room, library, sitting-room, study, breakfast room, kitchen, silver room, service lift, larder, store-room, butler's pantry and housekeeper's room. The lower ground floor and basement contain further staff rooms and the central heating as well as a billiard room. There are eleven main bedrooms and eight principal bathrooms. The rooms generally are decorated in 'Mayfair Georgian'. The drawing-room is the most handsome and has stripped pine panelling, carved doorcases and a Grinling Gibbons-type overmantel, all brought from 32 Grosvenor Square (demolished in 1957), but said to be by Wren and to have come originally from the 'Old Rectory in Charterhouse Square'.[9]

Nearly as large as Newsells and arguably the finest house built in England in the 1950s is Okeover Hall in Staffordshire, the work of Marshall Sisson, an architect who is much under-rated. His training was unusually scholarly and international by twentieth-century standards, and is curiously reminiscent of Sir John Soane's in the late eighteenth century, beginning with apprenticeship to a country builder and culminating in a scholarship to study in Rome. He served in the Ambulance Brigade on the Western Front in the First World War, then from 1919–20 worked under a local builder, W. T. Nicholls, and an architect called William Chambers in Gloucester before entering the Bartlett School at London University. From 1924–6 he was a scholar at the British School in Rome and then went as Duveen Scholar to New York where he worked for a year in the office of the last of the great American Classicists, Henry Russell Pope, architect of the National Gallery in Washington and the Elgin Room at the British Museum, whose immaculate and scholarly style made a great impact on his pupil; echoes of Pope's cool understated Classicism can be discerned in much of his work, including the otherwise very English Okeover. This was a job which was both a restoration or a new house, depending on how you look at it. Restoration in that it incorporates a genuine eighteenth-century wing freed from later accretions; a new house in that two thirds was designed completely afresh. That Okeover repeats the shape of the previous house, demolished in the early nineteenth century, is a coincidence dictated by the site. The drawing showing the full extent of the eighteenth-century house only emerged from the archives after Marshall Sisson had completed his own designs, as he explained in a letter to Arthur Oswald: 'I deduced that some such layout had been intended, but assumed until Potter's plan turned up, that it had never been completed. It was a surprise to find that the whole scheme had existed until curtailed by Potter, and I was interested to find that I had arrived at a similar result, possibly for the same basic reasons.'[10]

Okeover was Marshall Sisson's major new house though he had done quite a number of alterations to historic houses including work to Ditchley, Oxfordshire, and then to Ramsbury Manor, Wiltshire, for the Earl of Wilton, and

68

Top: Okeover Hall, Staffordshire. The Victorianized house before reconstruction.

Bottom: Okeover Hall, after reconstruction by Marshall Sisson.

Hinchingbrooke Castle, Huntingdon, for the Earl of Sandwich, not to mention an ambitious scheme for building a new house for Lady Muriel Barclay-Harvey at Uffington House, Lincolnshire, where the seventeenth-century house had been burnt in 1904. But this latter project came to nothing because of trouble over obtaining the necessary building licences.[11]

The Okeover estate is situated on the Staffordshire-Derbyshire border at the entrance to Dovedale, and has the distinction of having passed down in the same family for eight hundred years. On the death of Mr Haughton Ealdred Okeover in 1955 it was inherited by his nephew Sir Ian Walker, Bt., grandson of the donor of the Walker Art Gallery in Liverpool, who at that time lived in a large Victorian house, Osmaston Manor, near Derby. He had no hesitation in making up his mind about which house to keep. He added Okeover to his name, demolished Osmaston and moved to Okeover in order to perpetuate the exceptional continuity of the family and estate. The existing house at Okeover was a hotchpotch of Victorian buildings stuck on to the back of a mutilated wing built *circa* 1750 by Joseph Sanderson for Leake Okeover. This peculiar plan was the result of a drastic reduction of the house in the early nineteenth century followed by piecemeal enlargement later. Sir Ian Walker-Okeover thought of demolishing the lot and starting again, but Marshall Sisson could discern beneath the asymmetrical bay windows, plate glass and ugly dormers the bones of a good Georgian building and evolved a plan whereby it could be retained as one wing of a new U-shaped house with the entrance centred on a pedimented temple in the garden to the north.[12] This plan was adopted and the reconstruction was begun in 1957, being completed in 1960.

All the 1860 additions were demolished and the 1750 east wing was cleared of excrescences, re-glazed with proper sashes and generally put back to its original appearance. This wing was balanced on the west by a new office wing duplicating its design and re-using materials from the demolished bits. The main block in between was given a principal façade facing south over the park. This was made symmetrical by re-using half the stone dressings from the east pavilion to form a matching pavilion on the west, while the central three bays were given prominence by making them a semi-circular bow. The new entrance front facing north was treated in a simpler, more Vanbrughian, manner with square staircase towers in either corner and a central projecting porch the full height of the house with a pediment and giant lead statues on top from the garden at Osmaston. A subtle unifying feature of this façade is the broken string course which is carried right across in the form of simple 'capitals' to the pilasters of the porch and towers, and the entablatures of the upper windows. One of the reasons for the success of Okeover is the lucid economy of the design which relies on simple clean details in the new work or cleverly reused features salvaged from the demolished parts. There is also a sense of inevitability about

70

Top: Marshall Sisson's design
for the entrance front.

Bottom: Okeover. The entrance front.

the way the house fills the site between a steep hillside and existing old buildings such as the medieval parish church and the eighteenth-century stables. It has a feeling of 'rightness' not often encountered in a new building.

The interior is equally successful. The entrance porch gives on to a transverse corridor or gallery the length of the centre block; its generous width is dictated by the eighteenth-century staircase at one end. This impressive space is given an appropriately monumental appearance by a segmental plaster tunnel vault. The main rooms open off to the south, facing the park and ancient oak trees, the predecessors of which gave the place its name. The drawing-room and boudoir at the east end survive from the eighteenth century, and have exceptionally fine plasterwork and joinery, but the garden hall in the centre, behind the bow, is entirely Marshall Sisson's. It has a late rather than mid-eighteenth-century character thanks to the Ionic columns and excellent mahogany doors salvaged from James Wyatt's Henham Hall in Suffolk, demolished in the early 1950s. The dining-room is also Sisson's but has a heavier Victorian quality due to the furniture and tapestry brought from Osmaston. More of the tapestry is displayed on the upper flight of the secondary staircase in the east tower where the pleasingly simple iron balustrade was designed by Sisson and made by a local blacksmith. The interior decoration was done by Barbara Oakley and is nicely understated so as to let the architecture and contents, amalgamated from two large houses, speak for themselves. [13]

Another architect whose training was partly in an architectural school and whose work, like Sisson's, is perhaps closer to inter-war American Classical architecture than the typical English Arts and Crafts product is Trenwith Wills. He had been in practice for twenty years before the war in partnership with Lord Gerald Wellesley, but on the latter's succession as 7th Duke of Wellington in 1943 he continued the firm first on his own then in partnership with Simonne Jinsenn from 1949: they married in 1951. Mrs Wills completed several jobs after his death in 1972 and continued the practice till 1983. Trenwith Wills trained in the Liverpool School of Architecture in its Edwardian Beaux Arts phase under Professor C. H. Reilly, the most American of English twentieth-century Classicists. During the First World War he took part in the Gallipoli campaign, the effects of which damaged his health for the rest of his life. After leaving the army he joined the office of Detmar Blow and Billeray one of the leading firms of the day engaged in traditional country house work, and also attended the Royal Academy School of Architecture for five years as a student under Sir Aston Webb and Sir Edwin Lutyens. During this period he won the RIBA Tite Prize. Both before and after the Second World War he was engaged almost exclusively on restoration work to important historic buildings, or new and remodelled country houses together with associated structures, including gate lodges and memorial tablets. Of the latter, perhaps the most distinguished is the hand-

Top: Okeover. The gallery.
Bottom: Okeover. Staircase.

some Classical monument at Stratfield Saye to his old partner, which was designed in the Duke's lifetime. (The Duke, who always paid great attention to detail, was most insistent that the central feature of the memorial, an antique porphyry urn, should be lined with metal to prevent it being cracked by his ashes should they still be hot when placed inside.) Over the years Trenwith Wills did several alterations to Stratfield Saye including the central cupola, built in 1965, which was an inspired solution to the problem of relieving the long low lines of the house. Following the death of both the 7th Duke and Trenwith Wills, their scheme for the Jubilee Lodges was carried out by Mrs Wills in 1974 for the present Duke of Wellington.

Other work to famous historic buildings encompassed the repair of the four eighteenth-century temples at Rievaulx and Duncombe for the Earl of Feversham, the restoration of Wimpole for Mrs Bambridge, the daughter of Rudyard Kipling, and work for the National Trust at Clivedon and Petworth, but Trenwith Wills's major restoration job was the initial reinstatement of Castle Howard for George Howard in 1951 after the gutting of the central block in a disastrous fire thought to have been started by a home-sick girl while the house was occupied by an evacuated school during the war. He rebuilt the dome as closely as possible to Vanbrugh's design, modernized the east wing for the family's occupation and restored the Temple of the Four Winds in the park. The reinstatement of the interior still continues at Castle Howard and George Howard (created Lord Howard of Henderskelfe in 1983) is currently remaking the state rooms on the south front to the design of Julian Bicknell, in a Vanbrugh-inspired manner, and with romantic wall paintings in the new Garden Hall by Felix Kelly. Some of this recent work has been paid for out of the proceeds of the ITV serial of *Brideshead Revisited*, which was largely filmed in the house.

Houses remodelled by Trenwith Wills include The Holt, Upham, Hampshire, for Commander and Mrs E. A. Leavett-Shenley in 1962. This commission ran to a garden pavilion and garden layout as well as the internal reconstruction of the main house. At Bridgham Manor near Thetford, Norfolk, the old house was largely demolished and rebuilt in 1962 to form a Georgian-style country house of colour-washed flintwork with a Tuscan porch. A contemporary job was the addition of two large wings more than doubling the size of Great Hundridge Manor, near Chesham in Buckinghamshire, for Viscount Ednam (now Earl of Dudley). The work there also included a new stable block. All these brick-built additions were cleverly designed to blend in style with the original quite modest seventeenth-century house which remained at the front. At Jenkyn Place, Bentley, Hampshire, substantial internal remodelling as well as garden work and a new swimming pool with changing pavilion was carried out for Lieutenant Colonel Gerald Coke in 1963–

Castle Howard. Model for rebuilding the dome by Trenwith Wills, to achieve the right silhouette. Note the bust raised on pennies.

Bridgham Manor, Norfolk.

Stratfield Saye, Hampshire, Jubilee Lodge.

67, and at Pentillie Castle, Cornwall, the early-nineteenth-century Gothic house was demolished and a late-seventeenth-century wing retained and restored as the nucleus of a new house in 1968–70.

Trenwith Wills made something of a speciality of adding one room to an existing house. At Parracombe, Devon, he built a tactful one-storeyed Regency-style ballroom, paraphrasing the elevation of the old house, for Major Lindsay; at Upton, in Warwickshire, he converted a former squash court into a top-lit picture gallery for Lord Bearsted; and at Biddick in County Durham he was responsible for the Neo-Georgian remodelling of the dining-room for Lord Lambton; this was one of a series of improvements made to this medium-sized early-Georgian house by Lord Lambton when he made it his seat in preference to the truncated Victorian Lambton Castle.

The best completely new house built by Trenwith Wills after the war was Buckminster Park in Leicestershire to replace an old house for Major Tollemache. Buckminster is a very handsome, rather American-looking Neo-Georgian house of red brick with stone quoins and other dressings, rectangular in plan with a hipped roof rising behind a blank panelled parapet with urns. The garden and entrance fronts are both seven-bay compositions divided 2:3:2, but on the garden front the central three bays project and have a pediment, whereas on the entrance front they are recessed and without a pediment. The entrance porch has Tuscan columns with fluted neck bands, and on the end of the house there is a loggia also with four Tuscan columns.

Another new house similar in scale to Buckminster is Fonthill House in Wiltshire designed for Lord Margadale. This is the seventh house to be built on this historic estate in the last three and a half centuries, and at twice a century gives Fonthill the record for the most replaced country house in England. The present house succeeds the seventeenth-century Fonthill, scene of one of England's most sordid sex scandals, Alderman Beckford's Fonthill Splendens, James Wyatt's Fonthill Abbey, T. H. Wyatt's Fonthill House, William Burn's Fonthill Abbey and Detmar Blow's Fonthill House. All these previous houses have been demolished except for fragments. Trenwith Wills's house is on the site of Detmar Blow's, in whose office he had worked as a young man. It is plain Neo-Georgian and was built between 1972 and 1974. At the time of his death Trenwith Wills had prepared only sketch elevations and it was left to his wife, Simonne, to polish these into detailed plans for execution. She had worked closely with her husband on many of his houses since joining him in 1949.

Perhaps their finest joint work, and certainly one of the most splendid country house interiors to have been created since the war, is the reconstruction of Hinton Ampner, Hampshire, in 1962–4, following a devastating fire, for the collector and writer Ralph Dutton, now the 8th Lord Sherborne.[14]

The story of Hinton Ampner is a twentieth-century country house classic.

Parracombe, Devon, showing the ballroom added to the design of Trenwith Wills.

Ralph Dutton inherited the estate, with a carefully accumulated capital sum, from his father in 1935 and immediately set about remodelling the ugly Victorianized house into the semblance of a Georgian one with sashes and a parapet rather than mullions and gables. He employed as architects his friends Lord Gerald Wellesley and Trenwith Wills. They all formed part of a group of writers, architects and collectors—Christopher Hussey of *Country Life* was another—who were interested in Georgian things and cultivated a precocious taste for Neo-Classicism and especially brass-mounted Regency furniture, porphyry urns and lapis lazuli obelisks. The work at Hinton Ampner was structurally complete by 1938 but the interior decoration was delayed by the outbreak of war—though an Adam ceiling from Berkeley Square was installed in the dining-room in 1940—and was only completed in 1945–9, using black market decorators and doing the work after dark so as to get round the problem of building licences. The game was given away somewhat by the blaze of light night after night from the uncurtained windows; but fortunately none of the neighbours complained to the authorities. By the 1950s, Hinton Ampner, with its collections and gardens, was complete and rapidly became celebrated as one of the most perfect houses in England; it was even the envy of French visitors. Christopher Hussey, a friend and fellow Georgian enthusiast, gave the house an appreciative write-up in *Country Life*.

Then the worst happened. One windy Sunday afternoon in April 1960, while the owner was out working in the woods on the other side of the replanted park, a fire broke out in the library and gutted all the main part of the house, leaving only the office wing, part of the dining-room and the main walls

78

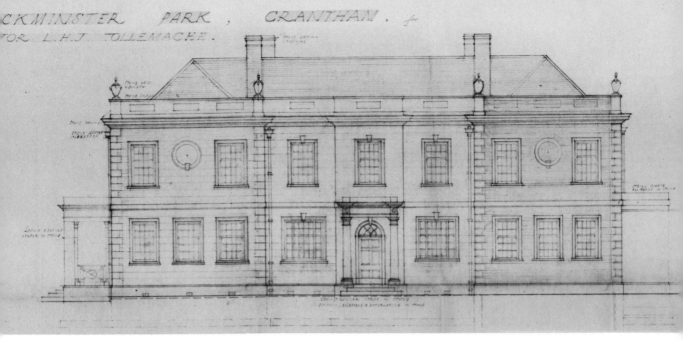

Trenwith Wills's design for the new house at Buckminster Park, Leicestershire.

standing. Most of the contents were destroyed too, including the owner's notable collection of porphyry objects. It never crossed Ralph Dutton's mind not to restore the ruin and he embarked immediately on a programme of rebuilding the house and assembling a new collection to fill the rooms.

The outside largely survived the fire, but as part of the restoration a low attic was substituted for the mansard roof. The interior had to be re-created almost entirely. The opportunity was taken to install a fireproof structure with concrete and hollow pot floors carried on RSJs. Many excellent fittings were bought for the new rooms from demolished buildings elsewhere. The Neo-Classical drawing-room, for instance, has doorcases from Ashburnham Place and two splendid white marble chimneypieces bought in London. In the entrance hall the porphyry chimneypiece from Hamilton Palace survived the fire, but everything else had to be re-created. Four handsome Ionic columns of *Serpentino Antico* scagiola were made by Messrs Fenning at their Putney Bridge works, and they also laid the new marble floor designed by Trenwith Wills; this caused great trouble and had to be taken up and re-laid three times before it was perfect. The new staircase was made of timber with a more graceful Georgian line than its predecessor, and upstairs a clever architectural feature was made of the landing with an urn in a niche. At the same time the first floor was replanned so that the bedrooms are *en suite* with the bathrooms. The library was put back to its pre-war Regency appearance and a new French Empire porphyry chimneypiece found on the Quai Voltaire in Paris replaced that lost in the fire—it is said to have come from the palace of St Cloud. In the dining-room enough of the Adam ceiling survived to enable the remainder to be reproduced

79

The interior of Hinton Ampner House after the fire.

from moulds. The little painted roundels destroyed by heat and water were replaced by new paintings of appropriate character by Elizabeth Biddulph. The opportunity was also taken to colour the ceiling according to Adam's proposals shown on the original drawing in the Soane Museum. Ralph Dutton was helped with the decoration of the new rooms by the London decorator Ronald Fleming, who had started work before the war and together with Mrs Bethell and Lady Colefax was one of the pioneers of the Georgian country house look. He advised on materials for curtains and helped work out colour schemes for each room based on their handsome French Empire carpets. Apart from one or two specialist firms like Fennings, the marble masons, and Jacksons, the plasterers, all the work was done by a local building firm. The original sources for the different rooms range across a period of about seventy years from mid-Georgian in the entrance hall, Adam in the dining- and sitting-rooms, Wyatt-ish in the drawing-room, to Regency in the library and some of the bedrooms. The overall feel, however, is that of an assured and consistent twentieth-century re-interpretation of the past, reflecting an informed and scholarly taste. Of its kind, it is undoubtedly one of the best in the country. It is worth quoting Lord Sherborne's own words on his reasons for rebuilding Hinton Ampner in the Georgian manner:

'No doubt there is much to be said against a restoration of this sort, indeed against the whole conception of rebuilding what was anyhow largely an eighteenth-century replica. Had I been young perhaps a house in con-temporary idiom would have shown more enterprise, but I was not young, and a Georgian fabric was essential as a setting for the furniture and objects which I had every intention of collecting to replace all I had lost. Unquestion-ably, too, rather spacious eighteenth-century style rooms are both pleasant and practical to live in. So, without a qualm of conscience, I encouraged this atavistic work to proceed.'[15]

80

Mural at Castle Howard by Felix Kelly showing 'Ballyshannon Tower, designed by Vanbrugh as eye-catcher. Struck by lightning in great storm, December 1856'.

Hinton Ampner. The staircase

Hinton Ampner. The entrance hall.

81

The drawing-room designed by Trenwith Wills and decorated
by Ronald Fleming at Hinton Ampner House, Hampshire.

NOTES

1 Unsworth, Son and Triggs was started by H. Inigo Triggs. The office records have been dispersed but I was provided with information about the firm by Robin Wyatt, who worked there for a time. Biographical details about individual architects (unless otherwise specified) come from the RIBA files.

2 *Country Life*, 26 March 1959, pp. 662–3.

3 *Country Life*, 9 October 1958, pp. 774–7 and ex info Sir Martyn Beckett. Sir Martyn himself designed some further additions to Pennyholme in the 1960s.

4 RIBAD: A. S. G. Butler albums; *Country Life*, 11 December 1958.

5 Philip Tilden, *True Remembrances* (1954), pp. 168–71.

6 Simon Houfe, *Sir Albert Richardson* (1980).

7 Lanning Roper, *Anglesey Abbey* (1964); James Lees-Milne, *Caves of Ice* (1983) 12, 23 January 1946.

8 Ex info Eric and Simon Houfe; photograph albums at Avenue House, Ampthill; Richardson and Houfe office papers in the Bedfordshire County Record Office.

9 Knight, Frank and Rutley Sale Catalogue, November 1976.

10 *Country Life*, 12 March 1964.

11 RIBAD: RAN 23/G/2

12 Marshall Sisson's design for Okeover was exhibited at the Royal Academy in 1955.

13 *Country Life*, 23 January and 12, 19, March 1964.

14 Trenwith Wills Office Records; I am most grateful to Mrs Dyer for making available to me material relating to her late husband's architectural practice and for her help generally.

15 *Country Life*, 10 June 1965 and 9 September 1965; Ralph Dutton, *A Hampshire Manor* (1968), pp. 80–101.

Top: Hinton Ampner. The library.

Bottom: Hinton Ampner. The drawing-room

V
ARCHITECTS
ERRANT

Standing slightly aside from the mainstream of 'Old Georgians' were the flamboyantly eccentric figures of Sir Clough Williams-Ellis (1883–1978) and Oliver Hill (1887–1968). They were close contemporaries who had begun their architectural careers before the First World War, been highly fashionable between the wars and then carried on designing new houses for a further twenty years in the 1950s and 1960s. Both conducted their lives amidst the trappings of romantic fantasy, had wit, charm and a flair for self-publicity as well as interests wider than the practice of architecture itself. Clough presided over his Italianate holiday village, Portmeirion, in North Wales dressed in knee breeches, yellow socks, a spotted tie and clutching a patent litter-picker, while Oliver Hill affected a high Arts and Crafts manner at Daneway in Gloucestershire, to which he moved in 1948, wearing floppy straw hats and grinding his own flour to bake his own bread in a museum-kitchen where sheets of home-made paper would also be found drying round the Aga preparatory to printing his own poems on his own press.

By the 1950s both architects had perfected their own personal, and immediately identifiable, version of Neo-Georgian, though they had explored other styles earlier in their careers. Clough's very first country house, Llangoed Castle in Breconshire in 1912, had been a handsome exercise in Neo-Jacobean; while Oliver Hill as well as working in Georgian and Jacobean had also gained a reputation in the 1930s as a fashionable Modernist with a series of flat-roofed, white-painted rectangular boxes such as Joldwynds in Surrey. Their executed houses after the Second World War, however, were all Neo-Georgian, though their individual versions of the style were strikingly different. Oliver Hill's owed much to Lutyens, with French inflections, and with their steeply pitched roofs, carefully detailed chimneystacks, many-paned casements and well-chosen traditional materials seem rooted to the ground and have a homely, long-established feel.

Clough's houses on the other hand were a cross between Cape Dutch and the sort of theatrical Italianate usually encountered only in the sets for opera. They have the insubstantial appearance of stage scenery. Their proportions are so attenuated, the swan-necked pediments so improbably curly and the urns so slender-waisted that one feels the first puff of wind could blow them away. A critical Welsh neighbour dismissed his style as 'all pastel shades, grace notes and hydrangeas in pots', and even to his friends this type of architectural treatment was known as 'Cloughing up'.

Both men saw themselves as members of the class for which they worked and their clients as collaborators-in-art rather than employers. This explains the ease with which they attracted country house commissions. Clough was a cross between a Welsh squire and a Hampstead intellectual, who was happy to dash off designs for his neighbours and friends on whatever scrap of paper came to hand. Oliver Hill remained the efficient ex-army officer and friend of the smart, pasting into scrapbooks cuttings about his own career from the gossip columns of *Tatler* and William Hickey, in between making careful drawings for a series of rich clients. Both men at this stage in their careers treated architecture as something of an enjoyable hobby rather than an income-producing profession. Clough possessed inherited money as well as the income from Portmeirion, and Oliver Hill had made enough to live off before the war. Their financial independence made them ideally suited to the sort of private client who likes to potter around building follies in his park, contemplating alternative designs for porticoes and lodge gates, and to elicit an enthusiastic response from his architect without having to face up to too large a bill in fees for abortive schemes at the end of the day.

Both men had (to quote Soane) pursued architecture with the enthusiasm of a passion from their earliest youth. Oliver Hill at school at Uppingham had had as his housemaster the son-in-law of Sir Charles Robinson, Keeper of the South Kensington (Victoria and Albert) Museum. This man was himself interested in the arts, and therefore encouraged his pupil's enthusiasm for architecture, helping him in every way he could. Hill was lucky enough to be let off cricket, and spent his summer afternoons, instead, cycling round Rutland exploring old buildings. He had been brought up in West Surrey in the late Victorian and Edwardian England of the young Edwin Lutyens and Miss Jekyll who had befriended him. As a result he developed a hero-worship for Lutyens and filled a scrapbook with pictures of the great architect's buildings cut out of *Country Life*. On leaving school he determined to become an architect and turned to Lutyens for advice. Lutyens told him to work first in a builders' yard in order to gain first-hand experience of bricklaying and a proper feel for materials—precisely the advice which Ruskin had once given to the young Detmar Blow. Oliver Hill did exactly that and worked as a bricklayer for eighteen months. This gave him his understanding of materials and the basic techniques of construction which is one of the reasons for the greater solidity in appearance of his buildings. He then began a three-year apprenticeship as an articled pupil in the office of William Flockhart, a successful but now largely forgotten Edwardian architect, spending his free time sketching architectural details in the Victoria and Albert, and his evenings studying at the Architectural Association, which was then in its Beaux Arts phase. It was there that he learnt the techniques of architectural draughtsmanship, expressed in a series of beautiful wash and ink drawings throughout his career. He started independent practice at the age of twenty-three in 1910, but in 1914 enlisted in the London-Scottish Regiment, rising to the rank of major. He had a distinguished war and was awarded the MC. He also acquired the slightly gruff military manner which won him the confidence of rich clients in the Twenties and Thirties when he established himself as the purveyor *par excellence* of 'Vogue Regency' and 'Hollywood Moderne'. In this period he aimed at designing not only houses and gardens but 'furniture, décor, upholstery and maids' dresses, summer and winter'.[1]

After the Second World War, his retirement from the brittle world of Chelsea to Daneway, near Cirencester, emphasized his role as heir of the Arts and Crafts, for that magical sixteenth-century house had been occupied previously by Ernest Gimson and the Barnsleys. There he concentrated on a broad range of interests—gardening, photography, writing and landscape painting—in addition to designing country houses. At first his designs for houses tended to be for sites overseas rather than England itself where building licences and strict rationing of materials were still a deterrent to ambitious building projects. His earliest post-war commission was for the Argentine ambassador to Britain, Miguel Angel Carcano—Argentina was then, of course, a strongly anglophile country in which there was a large British financial stake. Oliver Hill's design was for a substantial house to be built on the Carcano estate in the late-Lutyens classical manner of Middleton Park, Oxfordshire, or Gledstone Hall, Yorkshire, with a pedimented centre block, shuttered French windows and flanking pavilions with pyramidal roofs. This ambitious project was exhibited at the Royal Academy in 1946 and illustrated in the architectural press, but not executed because of the Peron revolution.[2]

Another overseas project—for a ranch house in Rhodesia in 1949—was scarcely less grand in scale, though of less sophisticated materials. It was intended as the centrepiece of an estate of 100,000 acres held jointly by four Englishmen, 'members of both Houses of Parliament'. It was a symmetrical design on the model of Holkham, or the Villa Trissino at Meledo, with a rectangular block linked at the corners to four smaller pavilions. The central block had a giant Tuscan portico and contained the principal rooms—dining-room, drawing-room and library—while the four pavilions (described as sleeping rondels) contained separate bedroom accommodation for the four different owners. These pavilions were circular and had steep conical roofs, echoing the form of African huts (or possibly Kentish oast houses) but with tall central chimneystacks inspired by Lutyens. All the roofs were thatched, and the walls were whitewashed brick. The small-paned sash windows had louvred shutters painted green. The portico was rendered, and also whitewashed. Radiating from the centre of each front were vine-covered pergolas and avenues of orange trees stretching out in an extensive cross formation for miles over the estate. The quarters for native staff were segregated and formed a little independently planned model village. The whole set-up was a twentieth-century reinterpretation of eighteenth-century aristocratic 'Improvement' on a scale not possible in immediate post-war Britain or Ireland. Much of the charm of this design came from the deliberate juxtaposition of the sophisticated and the rustic: Lutyens, Palladio and formal avenues; native huts, thatch and whitewash. It was hoped, with what seems extraordinary optimism, that the architecture of this house would 'give a lead to the evolution of a style suitable for the present-day development in Rhodesia and one worthy of the country'.[3]

Back at home, Hill's first post-war house commission of interest was a project for Captain Michael and Lady Victoria Wemyss at Wemyss Castle, in Fife, where they were in the process of stripping Victorian disfigurements and generally remodelling. In 1954 Hill designed a seven-bay arcaded portico with domed and pedimented pavilions to replace the nineteenth-century porch and saloon filling the centre of the house and linking the two end wings. His clients in this case were distinguished connoisseurs who spent more than twenty years after the war making their house into one of the most attractive in Scotland. On their golden wedding their sons commissioned for them a spoof 'Vanbrugh' design from Lawrence Whistler for remodelling the castle in the style of Seaton Delaval. This was engraved on glass in the staircase window and given a tongue-in-cheek historical write-up in *Country Life* as a newly discovered Vanbrugh drawing with the give-away line: 'To have conceived the idea at all, some may think, reveals a certain impudence in the designer.' In the event Oliver Hill's proposal remained, like Whistler's, in the world of architectural fantasy and the treatment of the new entrance front was designed by Captain Wemyss himself with Steward Todd, an Edinburgh architect who acted as the estate clerk of works and carried out the exemplary restoration of the village at West Wemyss. Oliver Hill did get another chance, however, to do a Scottish castle when he reconstructed Inchdrewer in Banff as a romantic tower house with Great Hall, State Room and Oratory in 1965.[4]

In the Fifties and Sixties Oliver Hill produced several variants of a scheme for a Lutyens-esque house with pedimented centre, end wings, steep pitched roof and sturdy chimneystacks. Not all of them were executed, but in 1958 a small-scale version, not really a country house, was carried into effect by Mr and Mrs Arnold Goldetz in the corner of a mature landscaped park at Coombe Hill in Surrey. The site with its good trees called for an eighteenth-century pavilion; the clients wanted a house which was serene, elegant and dignified while at the same time being comfortable and up-to-date in equipment. Oliver Hill responded with what he called a 'modest Bagatelle' which is one of his best post-war works and an excellent piece of nostalgic formal architecture. The exterior was stuccoed and painted shell pink and white to harmonize with the handmade clay tiles of the roof. The segmental-headed French windows to the ground floor repeat the *leitmotif* of all his post-war house architecture.

The interior is ingeniously and unusually planned so as to avoid any upstairs corridors. Access to the four bedrooms at each end of the house is by means of two separate staircases, thereby dividing the accommodation into two suites, for family and guests. The centre of the house is more or less filled by the drawing-room, a surprisingly noble space twelve feet high with coved ceiling supported on Tuscan columns. The illusion of grandeur in this room is helped by the use of wide double doors. For both the drawing- and dining-rooms, Hill designed bolection moulded marble chimneypieces of Lutyens type. The original decoration throughout the house reflected the post-Festival of Britain

Oliver Hill's design for house at Sunningdale.

predilection for bright clear colours, with blue, yellow and white in the drawing-room, and vivid scarlet in the dining-room.[5]

A grander version of the Coombe Hill theme was the house designed in 1962 for Mr and Mrs Andrews at Sunningdale, Berkshire. This too had a three-bay pediment and pantiled roof, but instead of stucco the walls were faced in handmade brick of the highest quality and embellished with a great deal of carved stone detail including the keystones to the ground floor windows and the decoration of the flanking pavilions, the pyramidal roofs of which harked back once more to those at Middleton Park. The deliberate homage to Lutyens is as unmistakable in this design as in the Uppingham School war memorial of 1948 and yet the total impact is different. Christopher Hussey, who knew them both, commented on the comparison between Hill and Lutyens: 'He neither aspired to, nor envied, the architectural qualities that set Lutyens among the great classical architects. Oliver's bent was essentially for visual values, colour and texture in materials and picturesque forms, which he contrived with fastidious though eclectic taste and a romantic gift for fantasies.'[6]

The house which perhaps most successfully expresses these qualities is Long Newnton Priory in Gloucestershire designed for Major and Mrs P. S. Morris-Keating in 1963 to replace an undistinguished early Victorian house which had been destroyed by fire in 1949. Only one three-storeyed fragment remained and this was converted into service accommodation and ingeniously incorporated into the new house. The new main block forms a rectangular pavilion with a five-bay somewhat French façade to the park. It is linked by an arched bridge to the old wing, making the overall plan a T-shape. The front door is placed at the back of the new block under the arch which serves as a *porte-cochère* and introduces a stimulating note of picturesque drama into the harmonies of the design. The main front on the other hand is as serene and

Coombe Hill. The drawing-room.

Long Newnton Priory,
Gloucestershire, *circa* 1865.

Long Newnton Priory,
circa 1965.

Long Newnton Priory. The entrance.

well-bred as could be, with its well-proportioned casement windows, facing of pink-washed stucco and prominent roof of textured grey tiles.

As usual in Oliver Hill's houses the drawing-room is the finest room. It is an exact double cube and the classical distinction of its proportions is matched by a handsome late-eighteenth-century marble chimneypiece (probably designed by James Wyatt) brought from Estcourt Park. The total accommodation comprised the drawing-room, library, dining-room and kitchen in the main block, with five principal bedrooms, a dressing-room and three bathrooms upstairs; and in the wing a garage, store, central heating, playroom and two staff bedrooms. Its architect was satisfied with Long Newnton's air of bucolic elegance and thought that it recalled 'the comfortable Georgian hunting squires that Randolph Caldecott delighted to draw'.[7]

As well as country houses Hill also designed a number of subsidiary estate buildings including gabled Cotswold stone cottages for the Wills family at Batsford Park in Gloucestershire in 1964, and a handsome brick and stone garden pavilion of Palladian derivation at Calstone in Wiltshire in 1965, but his last work was a project for a new family seat for Lord Hereford. This occupied him on and off throughout 1965 and 1966. The owner of an 8000-acre estate in Herefordshire, where he farmed, the thirty-three-year-old viscount had inherited the large, rambling Gothic Hampton Court, near Leominster. He decided to sell this because he found it 'out of keeping with the requirements of the second half of the twentieth century', and to build a new house somewhere else, perhaps in Gloucestershire, though a site was never actually determined. Another reason for moving from Herefordshire may have been boredom with the following dinner-table exchange: 'What's your name?—Hereford. Where do you live?—Hereford. What do you do?—Breed Herefords.'

He could not make up his mind whether he wanted a Georgian-style house or a Modern one. Oliver Hill's first design in 1965 was for a fifteen-bay house with a giant Tuscan portico and formally planned interior with an axial sequence of library, drawing-room and dining-room, as well as all the traditional subsidiary country house accommodation including a gun room. But then Lord Hereford decided that if he was to build a new house it ought to be something for the twenty-first century; after all this *was* the mid-1960s. William Hickey in the *Daily Express* reported in February 1966: 'Viscount Hereford, 33, Britain's premier viscount, is looking to the future—to the 21st century in fact. He plans to live in a house that is built for these times, efficient, electronic, where gadgets replace servants. Somewhere to face the space age. "There is no point," he told me, "in trying to recapture the past by putting up one of those Neo-Georgian places."' So Oliver Hill obliged with an alternative Modern design, L-shaped, two to three storeys high, faced in rough-cast and green Broughton Moor slate, and with a segmental copper roof. In sketches it looks rather like a rustic version of the Royal Festival Hall. The interior was informally planned, but like the Georgian version, ran to a drawing-room, dining-room, library, ample staff accommodation, as well as a large games room (28′ × 30′) complete with stage and cinema screen. The fact that this structure was intended to enshrine an ancient dynasty was indicated by the large amount of wall space provided for the family portraits and the flagstaff on the roof to fly Lord Hereford's personal standard when in residence. In the event this scheme was not executed either. Those people, including most Modern architects, who have moral scruples about building Neo-Georgian houses and yet cannot face living in something looking like the Festival Hall, usually end up doing one thing—they buy a genuine Georgian house. Lord Hereford bought the early-eighteenth-century Haseley Court in Oxfordshire from Mrs Nancy Lancaster.[8]

Clough Williams-Ellis was the son of an academic clergyman from an old Welsh landowning family. Each part of his tripartite name referred to an aspect of his inheritance: brains, land, money. Like Oliver Hill he was educated in the Midlands, but at Oundle not Uppingham. Like Hill he spent his school days cycling round the country in pursuit of old houses and churches, but he had less tolerant masters and was frustrated to find that the most interesting buildings were always just beyond the radius he could attain without infringing school rules and risking punishment. Unlike Hill, however, his formal architectural training was of the shakiest, no more than a couple of months at the Architectural Association before he plunged in and started work for the far-flung network of his, and his wife's, relations and connections. He broke off to fight in the First World War (Welsh Guards), survived, and then embarked on a highly successful career in the 1920s, retaining, it was rumoured, his army batman to make the drawings while he dined out getting commissions, and wrote a number of entertaining polemical books on architecture and what is now called 'conservation'. His fashionable inter-war practice was run from Romney's House in Hampstead, though those years also saw the foundation of Portmeirion, his principal achievement, near the old Williams family home Plas Brondanw in North Wales. Both before and after the Second World War he was almost exclusively employed as the architect of houses—and follies. As he put it himself: 'I never built a block of flats, or offices, or a shop, or a factory, or a cinema anywhere—nor wanted to.'[9]

After the war he was based entirely at Plas Brondanw and, ironically, its reconstruction was to be his first major post-war job. This house had been handed over to Clough on his twenty-fifth birthday in 1908. At that time it was dilapidated and sub-divided into tenements, but over the years he restored it, planted the garden and increased the size of the estate by purchasing two adjoining mountains to protect the landscape. Though, after his marriage to Amabel Strachey, he gradually grafted a considerable dose of theoretical

92

socialism on his basically Tory feudal instincts, his own description of his youthful feelings for the Plas expresses his lifelong atavistic love of the property and the urge to cherish and embellish it, an instinct which he shared with many of his clients and, indeed, many of the patrons described in this book:

'I fully shared my mother's piously dynastic views and regarded everything ancestral with a reverence almost superstitious if not indeed religious. Also I was in the antiquarian phase, and the guardianship of a rambling old Carolean Plas, a "Capital Mansions House" set in a wildly romantic little estate amongst the Welsh mountains that had been held by my family for over four centuries, was well calculated to inflame me.'[10]

On 10 December 1951 it was burnt with all its contents, the flames being fanned by a fierce gale; only the three foot thick outer walls survived. Clough immediately decided to rebuild. The following day his faithful gang of estate builders (responsible for the maintenance of Portmeirion as well as Plas Brondanw) began clearing the debris and propping the shell. Building licences were still in force but, with the support of various amenity societies, one was soon forthcoming for the rebuilding. Even so, materials were extremely scarce, and the whole country had to be scoured for second-hand stuff, in addition to raiding the store of architectural salvage at Portmeirion.

No change was made to the exterior, apart from the insertion of a prominent Venetian window lighting the first floor drawing-room where a fractured lintel made necessary a partial rebuilding of the wall. The new floors were made of reinforced concrete supported on tram rails rescued from a disused quarry. The roof timbers and slates came from the old national school at Llangollen which Clough bought for this purpose and demolished. All the work was carried out by the estate building gang under Clough's direct supervision, apart from the odd specialist job. The reconstruction took two years and in the course of it the opportunity was taken to change the internal planning to make the house easier to manage without staff. The top storey was made into a self-contained holiday flat with its own independent entrance at the rear 'to receive friends for holidays in a way that relieves both hosts and guests of the responsibilities normally attaching to the relationship'. On the ground floor, space was taken off the staircase hall for a new pantry providing a direct link, hitherto lacking, between the kitchen and the dining-room. The architect-owner, looking on the bright side, saw the fire as an opportunity to improve the house and make it more practical to run. Another change was the substitution of a stone staircase for the oak one destroyed in the fire. Most of the architectural fittings were bought from Crowther's, a truckload of eighteenth-century doors and chimneypieces making the journey to Wales. The debris from the fire was used to make a mound at the end of the avenue facing the house. On top of it was erected a stone monument designed by Clough and inscribed:

'This flaming urn raised on the ashes of their home by Clough and Amabel Williams-Ellis celebrates the rebuilding of Plas Brondanw 1953 two years from its burning and the names of those to whom it owes its restoration, viz: Wm. Davies. Tom Davies. Owen Edwardes. Harry Pike. Hugh Owen. Robert Jones and R. O. Williams.'[11]

Having restored and modernized his own house Clough turned a helping hand to those of his Welsh neighbours who found themselves stranded with a huge unmanageable house, such as Lieutenant Colonel J. C. Wynne-Finch at Voelas in Denbighshire. This enormous Venetian Gothic pile, by John Hunger-ford Pollen, was a wreck after wartime occupation and moreover was an example of an architectural style not generally admired at that time. Clough

Voelas, Denbighshire,
by Clough Williams–Ellis.

Voelas. The picture gallery.

Rhiwlas, Merioneth.

had no hesitation in recommending outright demolition and rebuilding. The new house, built in 1958, is a Neo-Georgian rectangular block of nine bays and two storeys faced in painted stucco with a central pediment, sash windows and door with swan-necked pediment on the principal (south) front overlooking the park and River Conwy. The entrance front is informal with a 'Trafalgar' porch off-centre. A special feature of the interior is the gallery, forty-nine feet long and twenty feet wide, which was provided for the owner's collection of family pictures, and also to serve as the principal reception room. The other main rooms are a drawing-room, library and dining-room, the latter with an apsidal recess for the sideboard. There are ten principal bedrooms and five bathrooms. The interior was handsomely fitted out in Neo-Georgian taste with brought-in eighteenth-century chimneypieces, elaborate joinery and plaster-work and a mahogany handrail to the staircase.[12]

Another Welsh house in the Portmeirion orbit, where Clough advised total demolition and a new start, was Rhiwlas in Merioneth, seat of the Lloyd Price family, founders of the Welsh Whisky Distillery, the Rhiwlas Brush Works and other enterprises. Clough tells an amusing story of staying at the house and finding his bags, when he came to leave, plastered with colourful stickers advertising his host's various wares.[13] The old house dated from 1574 and had been remodelled in 1809 in pretty but gimcrack Gothick. The new house was

95

Nantclwyd Hall, Denbighshire. Clough Williams–Ellis's new front.

conceived as a down-to-earth Welsh manor house surprisingly free from the graceful mannerisms which usually bedeck Clough's *oeuvre*. It is informally planned as an L-shape and solidly built in reused local stone with a hipped roof of Welsh slate and sashed windows. Inside, the staircase was given a decorative wrought-iron balustrade, and inscribed sixteenth-century beams from the old house were salvaged and reused in the new one, helping to give it an authentic feel which could deceive those who did not know its true history into believing that it was a genuine old *plas*, modernized in the eighteenth century when the sash windows might have been introduced.[14]

Some of Clough's other clients matched their architect in flamboyance. One house which occupied him on and off in the 1960s was Dunwood in Yorkshire for Mr and Mrs G. Wiles. Here he provided no fewer than five variant schemes for grandifying what was little more than a three-bay villa. Every combination of 'Curzon Street Baroque' pediments, urns, statues and porticoes was suggested for transforming this modest house into a more ambitious affair with a formal setting of avenues, geometrical canals and balustraded forecourts. Suggestions for internal improvements included a library fifty-six feet long with Corinthian pilasters and coved ceiling. The most concrete expression of all this imaginative effort was a cardboard model of Clough's portico scheme, because in the end the owner employed somebody else to do the work.[15]

By far the most important of Clough's post-war jobs was the sweeping reconstruction of Nantclwyd Hall in Denbighshire for Sir Vivyan Naylor-Leyland. The story loses nothing in Clough's own telling: 'An architect should never be surprised by anything, but I did wonder what it might mean when a man of whom I had only heard of but never met, wrote to me suddenly out of

96

the blue to ask if I could arrange to meet him with (mysteriously) ''a view to discussing a project that I have in mind where I think your advice would be helpful''!'[16]

On arrival at his correspondent's large and luxurious house it was to find that he wished to abandon the whole set-up with its 'misguided extensions and muddled clutter' and to start anew in a beautiful setting on another part of the estate. Clough did two alternative drafts for the 'proposed new deal' but could not smother his sympathy for the old one which had a good Charles II front to which 'great lumps of building had been grafted'. The main defect was that the whole giant complex faced north. To the south was an incoherent muddle of miscellaneous outworks, servants' wings, laundries, garages, workshops, kennels and a water tower enjoying the sunshine and views. 'It really all looked just about as welcoming as a railway marshalling yard.' But this jumbled giant of a house had a well-timbered park with tempting opportunities for landscape improvement. Clough was able to convince his client that the best course of action was to retain the seventeenth-century core, demolish the nineteenth-century additions, turn it all back to front, replan the interior, build a new south-facing façade, new entrance drives, lodges, plantations, stables, triumphal arches, follies and much more. The project was carried out. Where the 'marshalling yard' had held the foreground, new terraces and gardens enlivened by four temples, an obelisk, statuary from Scarisbrick, ornamental birds, a folly tower, domed rotunda and a couple of ornamental bridges spanning the specially widened river filled the vistas to the near horizon. A railway line which passed through the park had been made redundant by Beeching and was transformed into the principal drive, entered from the main road through a monumental triple-arched gateway set back thirty feet from the verge and flanked by ornamental pavilions. The 'side' entrances were hardly less grandiose. Other amenities included columns surmounted by eagles, a tall apricot stuccoed arch with a gilded clock turret, giving access to the garage yard 'where guests' dogs can reside in specially provided Palladian kennels'.

Clough enjoyed an architect's dream working with this generous Maecenas of the arts from 1956 into the 1970s. As well as the work which was executed, endless alternative projects were discussed, modified, abandoned or revised. 'Whenever my client visits the place (he mostly lives elsewhere) there will always be a crop of new ideas—not now so readily realized, and anyhow I have now at last told him that at my age I can no longer stand the pace of an exhilarating architectural point to point.' They had their differences like most architects and clients. Sir Vivyan would never agree to the tall fountain jet which Clough wanted in the garden, and he installed *two* heated swimming pools against his architect's advice. The manner in which the work proceeded is indicated in a note by Clough on a whimsical sketch for 'A Duck Tower Boss

Shot' or 'Duck Fort' (a castellated shooting platform): 'Trouble is that if you have anything like a proper stair *inside* the Building (unless a near straight-up ladder) you could scarcely have room to move about or dodge in and out—unless you made the whole edifice over-poweringly large for its site and purpose.' Another difference of opinion was over the best location for the billiard room, which travelled up to the top of the house and down again to the bottom, each time with the necessary strengthening of the floor and the dismantling and reassembling of the table itself. 'My insatiable collaborator and client, a modern variety of eighteenth-century noble builder, ought to have been an architect himself. He will never be content just to sit still and see beauty achieved. He will always itch to improve it.'[17]

The circumstances of Clough's last country house, Dalton Hall in Westmorland in 1968, were hardly less romantic than Nantclwyd. He was just announcing his retirement from architecture because of advanced old age when he was consulted far away from his own habitat in North Wales by a young couple who had inherited 'an extensive and romantically lovely estate' in Westmorland, the Mason-Hornbys. Mrs Mason-Hornby had relations living near Portmeirion which explains why they called in Clough to advise on a problem for which he had gained a reputation, namely what to do with an overgrown, inconvenient and incoherent mansion riddled with dry rot. There was an early-nineteenth-century nucleus at Dalton, but the house had been greatly enlarged in 1859 by the Lancaster architect E. G. Paley so that it resembled one of the larger hotels at Windermere. Clough could not resist the challenge and immediately inspected the property. He found the site perfect, with fine views over a beautifully planted park. At first he thought of ways of reducing and reorganizing the old house to return it to its Georgian character, but the dry rot together with the huge central staircase hall, forever a reservoir of cold air, proved decisive. He reported back to the Mason-Hornbys that demolition and a fresh start on the same site would be the best policy. He came down to breakfast the following morning with plans for a new house on large sheets of paper, remarking, 'You will find the dimensions within 5% of total accuracy.' With his ingrained architect's habits he had paced out the site and the rooms of the old house while visiting it. 'Oh, and you will need to replace the paper linings in the chest of drawers in my bedroom.'

It was unanimously decided to go ahead at once. The new house is of moderate size, symmetrical on all four elevations like a doll's house, with classical centrepieces front and back of applied Tuscan pilasters and pediments. The north (entrance) front has a circular window in the pediment and an elaborate heraldic cartouche over the doorway, while the park front has a small circular window to the pediment and a glazed door. Much of the impact of the house is due to the well-proportioned sash windows and hipped roof of

98

Westmorland slate with a pair of tall chimneystacks. The exterior is stuccoed and painted pink. The new house occupies only part of the site of the old one, and the foundations of the remainder were utilized to make a forecourt with cobbled paving, pleached limes, central grass plot and wrought iron gates, all designed by Clough. One of the great strengths of his work was his interest in the setting of his buildings and the overall landscape effect, often including the design of extensive outworks. At Dalton he also provided a temple as an eye-catcher in the grounds complete with a copper dome and re-using columns from the old porch.

The principal accommodation comprises a grand drawing-room (18' × 21') and a dining-room and kitchen both eighteen feet square, the latter being used as a living-room in the daytime when the family are on their own, though there is also a children's playroom. The drawing-room and dining-room were intended for more formal entertaining as well as a setting for inherited furniture and paintings. There is a lift as well as a staircase and upstairs there are eight bedrooms, a dressing-room, three bathrooms and a small linen room. The house looks well and works well. Architect and clients were equally pleased with it: 'It is not yet decided which of the three of us is most pleased with the final result.' The only criticism is that the scale is somewhat cramped and all the rooms would benefit from being slightly larger, especially the bedrooms. But the house was designed to be as compact, streamlined and easy to run as possible so that if necessary it could operate without any domestic help, even dailies. The nonagenarian Clough recorded, 'It is very warming to have ended my long building career with so satisfactory a last fling.'[18]

NOTES

1 RIBA Library (mezzanine 7.71), Oliver Hill's Cuttings Books 1–13; Jill Lever, Ed., *RIBA Drawings Catalogue, G-K* (1973) pp. 106–29.

2 RA Catalogue, 1946; RIBAD: RAN 16/L/I; *Architects Illustrated* XXV, 1946, p. 89; *Builder*, CLXX, 1946, p. 478.

3 *Building*, June 1949, pp. 189–91; RIBAD: RAN 6/L/9.

4 *Country Life*, 10 June 1971, 6 and 13 January 1966; RA Catalogue 1954; RIBAD: RAN 16/K8.

5 RIBAD: RAN 16/J/10; *Country Life*, 28 December 1961.

6 *Country Life*, 22 September 1969, 750; RIBAD: RAN 16/K/3.

7 *Country Life*, 22 September 1969; RIBAD: RAN 16/K/4, pp. 1–5.

8 William Hickey, *Daily Express*, 17 February 1966; RIBAD: RAN 16/K/10.

9 Clough Williams-Ellis, *Architect Errant* (1971), p. 284.

10 Ibid, p. 92.

11 Ibid, pp. 259–61; *Country Life*, 5 September 1957; RIBA: RAN 33/D/1, pp. 1–39.

12 RIBAD: RAN 33/C/14, pp. 1–4.

13 *Architect Errant*, p. 283.

14 RIBAD: RAN 33/E/17 pp. 1–5.

15 RIBAD: RAN 32/F/22, pp. 1–20. Ex info Mr Richard Haslam

16 Clough Williams-Ellis, *Round the World in Ninety Years* (1978) p. 45.

17 Ibid, pp. 45–7; RIBAD: RAN 33/A/9, pp. 1–40.

18 RIBAD: RAN 32/F/16 1–9; *Round the World in Ninety Years*, pp. 50–3; Ex info Mr Cornish Torbock.

VI
THE MAINSTREAM

Not all the new country houses in the Georgian style built in the last thirty-five years are of architectural interest and in some cases Sub-Georgian might be a better description. One of the more depressing architectural experiences in the United Kingdom is to arrive at the site of a vanished eighteenth-century or nineteenth-century pile and to find in its stead a badly proportioned brick or cement-rendered box with the wrong sort of 'Georgian' windows. One wonders how anybody could have consciously built anything so dreary. An empty site punctuated by the odd romantic fragment would be preferable. But to set against these lost opportunities there is a considerable number of attractive and well-designed houses by a group of architects with similar backgrounds, all of whom trained in the traditional way and none of whom was a product of the big architectural schools. As a result they tend to have a deep love of the architecture of the past, a knowledge of the Classical Orders, and a feel for traditional building materials. On the whole, they have not received much recognition from the architectural establishment. They include Francis Johnson, James Fletcher-Watson, Schomberg Scott, Martyn Beckett and Claud Phillimore, as well as a wider circle of architects who while not specializing in the design of new country houses as such have developed successful practices based on the preservation and repair of a range of historic buildings with perhaps one or two new houses thrown in; Philip Jebb and Donald Insall in England, Robert Hurd and Ian Lindsay in Scotland and Robert McKinstrey in Northern Ireland.

A feature of some of these architects is a strong regional bias, the designers in question having started out working for their relations and neighbours before spreading further afield. This is especially true of Francis Johnson, who is arguably the most distinguished of them, a kind of latter-day Carr of York. Born

Houghton Hall, Yorkshire. The entrance front.

in 1910, he received his formal architectural training in Leeds and started work in the 1930s, but it was only after the Second World War that his large country house practice in Yorkshire developed. For many years a member of the Georgian Group Committee and himself a collector of eighteenth-century paintings, furniture and objects, he is pre-Modern by training and Georgian by inclination. In his own words: 'I have always been an unrepentant Classicist as far as my clients and circumstances would allow.'[1] Fortunately clients and circumstances in Yorkshire from the late 1950s to the 1980s have allowed. Some of his early jobs were creative reconstructions rather than entirely new works and included Houghton, restored by Lady Fitzwilliam for her nephew Captain Rupert Watson (now Lord Manton), and Everingham by the 16th Duke of Norfolk for his eldest daughter, Lady Anne Fitzalan-Howard (now Lady Herries). Both houses were the centres of ancient estates in the East Riding belonging to Catholic recusant families, the Langdales and the Constables, and both had an eighteenth-century nucleus swamped by later additions.

At Houghton the original house, built by Philip Langdale in 1760, had been faced with dreary stucco in the 1820s, when a large Catholic chapel by Joseph Ireland had also been added, and altered again later so detrimentally that the Historic Buildings Council did not deem it worthy of grant aid when the reconstruction was begun in 1957. Francis Johnson's work consisted of stripping away these accretions and replanning the interior. It took three years, being completed in 1960, and produced a house with a Palladian plan of main block and symmetrical wings. Externally the stucco was removed to reveal the brick; glazing bars were restored to the windows; the billiard room, the chapel

102

Houghton Hall. The new dining-room.

(alas) and Victorian porch were demolished. On the garden front dressings of Ancaster stone were added, and so were architraves and cornices to the ground floor windows and a pediment to the central door. On the entrance front a prominent new porch was built with a pediment and massive keystone over the door.

Inside, the rooms were replanned while keeping the best existing features, including the drawing-room with attractive Edwardian plasterwork and the two-storeyed hall with eighteenth-century staircase. The library, opening off the hall through Edwardian arches, was enlarged by throwing in a redundant corridor and embellished with an eighteenth-century-style chimneypiece. The old dining-room was converted into a smoking-room, and a new one made nearer the kitchen out of space formerly occupied by the lowest flight of the back stairs and a ground-floor bedroom. The retention of the upper flights of the back stairs posed a problem as the underside of the steps jutted into the room; but the architect got round this by giving the room a Soanic ceiling with a segmental arch over half the space. The poor lighting was overcome by inserting a large Venetian window in the west wall. Both the wings were replanned: the west to contain rationalized domestic offices, a servery (off the dining-room), pantry, kitchen, scullery and staff rooms; the east to contain the

owner's bedroom suite.[2]

At Everingham an even bigger problem presented itself. The house had been let since the Duke of Norfolk's mother (Lady Herries in her own right) had died in 1945. When the lease fell in the Duke considered selling but changed his mind and in 1960–2 restored the house and gave it, together with the 3000-acre estate, to his eldest daughter, who was destined to inherit the Herries barony when the entailed dukedom passed to a second cousin. The house, built in 1760 to the design of Carr of York, had been greatly altered and extended in the nineteenth century by the 10th Lord Herries. He had turned it back to front, making a new entrance, added a large dining-room wing, and tacked on to one end a Catholic parish church on the scale of a Roman basilica. Again, it was decided to reduce and replan the house but to retain the church as a detached structure on the lawn alongside. The dining-room, domestic offices, large bay window, porch and clock tower were all demolished, leaving the Carr block in pristine isolation. This was restored externally to its original form and a Doric porch added. Internally, with the exception of the drawing-room, considerable portions of Carr's interior had disappeared in the Victorian remodelling. The entrance hall, dining-room and staircase all had to be re-created. For the

Everingham Hall, Yorkshire. Before.

Everingham Hall. After.

Everingham. The new staircase with mahogany handrail.

Everingham. The entrance hall designed by Francis Johnson.

reconstituted hall an appropriate eighteenth-century chimneypiece was found in one of the bedrooms and brought downstairs, while the rest of the decoration (including plaster wall panels, pedimented doorcases and a modillion cornice) was designed to match. The staircase hall in the centre of the park front posed a similar problem. Nothing survived of the original treatment except some carved decoration on the former landing. Here again Francis Johnson devised an appropriate wall treatment and inserted a magnificent cantilevered staircase in wood with gentle risers and elegant turned mahogany balusters. This was made by Anelay's of York, who did all the building contract. The work at Everingham is a triumph of sensitive re-creation. Anybody who did not know that much of what is seen today dates from the 1960s would find it completely convincing, even down to details like the little ivory disc inlaid into the swirl at the bottom of the staircase handrail.[3]

Another Francis Johnson job which involved the imaginative reconstruction of an eighteenth-century house to create something new, but with a convincing feel, is Settrington House in the North Riding for Lord Buckton (Sir Samuel Storey, Bt, created a life peer). The old house had been gutted by fire and Francis Johnson was asked to reinstate it without the top storey of redundant servants' rooms. He suggested a more radical treatment, cutting away parts of the first floor as well, keeping the central three bays and adding a pediment to create a stepped-up Burlingtonian-Palladian effect. Lord Buckton was that comparatively rare client, an Englishman who can understand architectural drawings, and he immediately grasped the point and approved the scheme. The interior was also rebuilt to Francis Johnson's design. It is as theatrical and dramatic as the exterior, with a spinal corridor carrying Soanic arches and plaster vaults and dramatically lit from semicircular clerestory windows. The effect of the main rooms was heightened with more elaborate plasterwork than had existed in the old house. The result was to transform a run-of-the-mill Georgian mansion into something rather special, a modern Palladian villa.

Country house fires are often disasters, but they can also provide opportunities, as at Settrington and also Sunderlandwick in the East Riding. This latter estate belonged to Sir Thomas (Rob) Ferens of the Hull business family whose wife was a cousin of Francis Johnson's. The Hall, heavily remodelled in the 1840s, had been burnt to the ground on VJ Day in 1945 while the RAF were in occupation. Only the detached stable block in a late Classical style reminiscent of St Petersburg survived. Francis Johnson was asked in 1963 to design a new house for the old site which would sit quietly beside the stable block when seen from the approach drive, but would hold its own from across the park. The answer to this problem was an L-shaped plan with the main rooms—study, drawing-room and dining-room—facing the park, and the kitchen and other domestic offices forming the other arm. The main front looking west over the

Settrington House,
Yorkshire. After the fire.

Settrington House,
reconstructed by
Francis Johnson.

park has an elliptical bow in the centre flanked by Wyatt windows under blank arches, a feature of which Francis Johnson is fond. The ends are strengthened by applied pilasters and to the north is an asymmetrical loggia with columns, screening the gentlemen's lavatory and gun room behind. The outside is faced in pale pink brick made by Wray's of York. The entrance is on the east from the forecourt, between the stables and office wing, and is through a semicircular bow. The hall has an easy-rising mahogany staircase with a yew handrail, and gives access to a transverse gallery the full width of the house with a plaster-vaulted ceiling. As at Settrington this, together with the arcaded landing at the top of the stairs, gives the interior a sense of architectural grandeur often lacking in Neo-Georgian houses. Throughout, the finishes are of high quality and the Classical detail impeccable. The drawing-room, for instance, has good decorative plasterwork, fitted mahogany china cabinets with traceried patterns, and an excellent brought-in marble chimneypiece.

The overall quality of the design is partly due to the care with which the architect made full-size drawings to guide the craftsmen. This would probably not have been necessary in the eighteenth century, but with the narrowing of

107

Sunderlandwick Hall.

the scope for building work of quality, it is necessary to give craftsmen detailed guidance which they would not have required when there was a more widespread and consistent demand for well-designed architectural decoration.

As well as the main house at Sunderlandwick Francis Johnson and his partner also designed a smaller Regency-style house on the estate for the Ferens's daughter (though this was somewhat modified in execution) and he has designed several other Regency-style houses of moderate size such as Whitwell in the North Riding for David Brotherton, an industrialist, on a new site, taking advantage of the dramatic view over the plain of York. The old house at Whitwell, by Pritchett, was sold and is now a country club. The new house is of brick with two segmental bows flanking a Doric porch *in antis*, of Ancaster stone, which gives access to an oval entrance hall.

New houses have several times materialized when a property has changed hands and the purchaser has wanted a 'new deal'. The most notable example in Francis Johnson's work is the Warter Priory Estate in the East Riding. Following the purchase of this large property by a family trust of the Marquess of Normanby in 1976, the main house, a not very distinguished (and unlisted) mainly Victorian '*château*' was demolished. Lord Normanby already had his principal seat in Yorkshire at Mulgrave Castle, near Whitby, and merely wanted a subsidiary shooting lodge or retreat on the Warter Estate. Francis Johnson had done some alterations at Mulgrave, so it was not surprising that he was asked to design the new house at Warter. They were lucky in that one of the farmhouses, though altered later and in poor condition, had a Jacobean wing with shaped Flemish gables. This was developed to form the nucleus of a symmetrical U-shaped house. The Jacobean part was made into the centre block, the paint cleaned from the stonework, a pedimental doorcase added and the interior rebuilt apart from a good seventeenth-century timber staircase

108

made partly from old bits, perhaps from nearby Londesborough. A plain early-nineteenth-century wing to one side was remodelled in a more architectural style with Wyatt tripartite windows and a wing duplicating it altered on the other side. The forecourt thereby created was paved in patterns with Portuguese granite setts inspired by the attractive pavements in Lisbon. The result has been to transform a derelict farmhouse into a small country house of distinction which looks like a Jacobean lodge extended in the Regency period and serves as an ideal *pied-à-terre* for the owners.

As well as new houses and substantial reconstructions, Francis Johnson has on many occasions been employed to add a room or carry out internal alterations to existing houses, and these have often been of considerable interest. They have included several rooms for Mrs Sheffield at Sutton Park, Yorkshire, the library in the Gothick taste for Mrs Sheila Sutcliffe at the Mansion House, Tetford, Lincolnshire, the Jacobean long gallery at Burton Agnes, Yorkshire, for Marcus Wickham-Boynton, interior remodelling and a Gothick pavilion at Halecat, Westmorland, for Michael Stanley and the central hall for Lord Shuttleworth at Leck Hall, Lancashire, as well as the sumptuous dining-room in a new wing for Charles Mills at Hillborough, Norfolk, with mahogany doors, Adam-style plaster ceiling and marble chimneypiece—a room which cost £30,000 fifteen years ago. The remodelling of a single room has in some instances led to something more ambitious. At Garrowby, in the East Riding, the remodelling of the old wing to form a handsome classical library *circa* 1973 for the late Lord Halifax (contractors: Anelay's of York) was the overture to the almost complete rebuilding of the house by his son, the present Earl. Garrowby is Francis Johnson's and his partner Malcolm McKie's most ambitious country house and is one of the finest built in England since the Second World War. The recent work there completes

Garrowby. The retained tower contains the chapel.

the process whereby a small shooting box on the edge of the Yorkshire Wolds has developed into the principal seat of one of the more interesting twentieth-century aristocratic families: Charles Lindley Wood, the 2nd Viscount (who died in 1934) being the learned champion of Anglo-Catholicism, while his son, the 1st Earl, was Viceroy of India and Foreign Secretary. The present Lord Halifax has the distinction of two Prime Ministers among his great grand-fathers: the Liberal Lord Rosebery and the Conservative Lord Derby.

The Woods were a Whig family from the West Riding who rose to prominence in the early nineteenth century. Their main seat was at Hickleton in the West Riding. Garrowby, a small hunting lodge surrounded by farmland, had been bought by the second baronet in 1827 and it was used mainly for holidays in the late nineteenth century. The second baronet's grandson, the 2nd Viscount, enlarged this house in romantic semblance of an old manor round two courtyards (one the stables) and made the park by removing hedges and planting avenues and clumps of trees. From the late nineteenth century Hickleton was increasingly affected by coal mining and so more time was spent at Garrowby. In the Viceroy Lord Halifax's words: 'Gradually we began going more to Garrowby, which we always loved. Originally a small rambling self-contained house along two sides of a cobbled courtyard with a cottage and stabling attached, my great grandfather had acquired it in the first stages of the nineteenth century as a good shooting property . . . It was and is wonderful riding country . . . As the family visits to Garrowby became more regular and longer, my father began to think about building on to it . . . 1892 saw the start . . . The alterations gave the house a south aspect with a gabled roof, adding a large sitting-room on the ground floor, a small entrance hall and the chapel, with two or three bedrooms above.'[4]

During the Second World War Hickleton was requisitioned by the army immediately after Dunkirk and for some time it was used as General Alexander's HQ. When it was derequisitioned at the end of the war, the proximity of heavy industry, together with the size of the house, made it seem no longer feasible to maintain it. It was let as a school, and Garrowby became the Halifaxes' main base. The Hickleton estate, however, was retained, part of the stables converted into a cottage for occasional visits and the old brewhouse kept going. Visitors to Garrowby are still served Hickleton beer.

Garrowby, though an attractive house in pleasant country, was not entirely ideal. The piecemeal way in which it had developed created a far from convenient plan, with long narrow corridors and ill-connected small rooms. It was not in sound condition, the bricks in particular were beginning to spall, and though designed by C. E. Tower (a pupil of the great Victorian church architect G. F. Bodley), it was not an especially important piece of Victorian architecture and it was not listed. When the present Lord Halifax inherited he at first intended to keep and repair the Victorian house, and Francis Johnson and Malcolm McKie did a project showing how this could be done. But it would have cost the earth and still been unsatisfactory, so a more radical scheme for demolition of the main block and reconstruction was adopted instead. Though daunted by the cost, Lord Halifax decided that this would be the best long-term solution as it would give the chance to devise a flexible plan adaptable to differing circumstances. Work began in 1980 with William Birches as the contractors, and the last touches are still being added at the time of writing.

The new Garrowby forms three sides of a quadrangle. The rear (north) wing is the original 1803 house and contains Francis Johnson's library of 1973 with guest bedrooms over. The 2nd Viscount's little castellated tower at the west end has been converted into a chapel by removing the first floor and opening the interior to the full height. This has created space for the large Victorian Gothic altarpiece with woodcarvings made in Oberamergau to Tower's design and the Jacobean-style gallery and pews from the previous chapel. The new chapel also contains many of the family's religious relics and mementoes and reflects their strong High Church tradition. Regular services are held here, a local clergyman serving as chaplain.

The long east wing is also old, but remodelled inside to contain the family's own accommodation opening off a long corridor partly with plaster vaulting. It includes a private entrance at the side of the house with a hall where wellingtons and dog leads can be left lying around, the nursery and a large cheerful kitchen with an eating area for informal meals. Upstairs in this wing are the family bedrooms. The main block, facing south over the freshly re-landscaped park, is entirely new and contains the drawing-room, summer sitting-room, dining-room, front hall, main staircase and principal bedrooms. The house is cleverly planned so that it can be expanded or contracted as required and each section has its own independent electric circuit. This makes it economical and easy to manage. When on their own the family can retreat to the east wing and shut up the remainder. In winter the library, which overlooks the courtyard and therefore has no view, is used as a sitting-room, while in the summer the south-facing rooms in the main block come into their own. There are twelve bedrooms, both the library and drawing-room are large and the dining-room can sit twenty with ease, so the house is as well-adapted for large-scale entertaining as for comfortable family life.

The interior is beautifully finished throughout and is a tribute to the great care taken by the architects and Lord Halifax himself. It demonstrates that a high standard of craftsmanship is still possible in England if both the client and the architect care enough. The library has architectural bookcases designed round inset paintings and at one end is a screen of Ionic columns with capitals copied from the temple at Bassae. The main rooms have decorative plasterwork

111

designed by Francis Johnson and handsome chimneypieces: that in the sitting-room is designed by Francis Johnson and made by R. Reid of York, but the others are eighteenth-century ones reused. The mahogany panelled doors downstairs are all new but the painted ones upstairs are from the old house. The dining-room has an apsidal serving recess with built-in electric hot plates flanking an equestrian bronze of Louis XIV, a nice combination of modern convenience and eighteenth-century grandeur. The entrance hall is divided from the staircase by Doric columns painted to resemble Siena marble and the wrought iron balustrade was made by Hammond's of Kirkby Moorside from Francis Johnson's full-scale drawings.

The exterior is sturdily Georgian in the manner of Carr of York. The two old wings have remodelled fenestration, that in the library comprising Wyatt windows under segmental arches. The front door in the main block, facing the library, is set in a full-height canted bay, and has a simplified Doric porch of Ancaster stone. The main façade of seven bays faces south and is strongly modelled, so as to read from across the park, with big simple mouldings, a sprocketed hipped roof and pedimented dormers. The central three bays have a pediment, and so has the garden door on the ground floor. The proportions are carefully worked out; the lower windows are longer by one row of panes than those on the upper floor and the ends are defined by simplified pilasters supporting the bold moulded cornice. The facing material is honey-coloured Stamford brick. In addition to the main house, the improvements at Garrowby have extended to the park and include a lake, stone ha-ha, new tree planting, a pedimented temple made from columns removed from the Victorian house (shortened to improve their proportions), an inner entrance lodge, and new formal garden to the west with yew hedges. It will be many years before they reach maturity, but Lord Halifax's children will enjoy the same experience as Osbert Sitwell in growing up year by year with a garden created by their father.

A contemporary of Francis Johnson's who paralleled the regional character of his work in another part of the country is James Fletcher-Watson in East Anglia. He too trained in the 1930s, first as an articled pupil to his uncle Cecil Upcher in Norwich and then in London in the office of Aston Webb & Son (by that time headed by Maurice Webb), where he found himself surrounded by Edwardian grandeur—drawings for Buckingham Palace, the Mall, Admiralty Arch, the Victoria and Albert Museum. He also attended the Royal Academy Schools and the architectural lectures given there by Lutyens had a great influence on him.

This Edwardian approach to architecture was enhanced by his interest in watercolour painting. He was always interested in painting as much as in architecture, and since he retired from practice in 1980 has devoted himself entirely to watercolour in the Cotman tradition, recalling those nineteenth- and early-twentieth-century architects who were talented watercolour artists in

Right: The temple at Sheringham by James Fletcher-Watson.

Far right: The Wicken House.

their own right. He qualified in 1939 but did not start work till after the war when he entered his uncle's office in the Cathedral Close at Norwich, eventually inheriting the practice. He remained in Norwich till the end of the 1950s when he moved to London, but through his family connection maintained strong links with Norfolk. One of his smaller works in the county was a domed hexagonal temple, on a site suggested by Repton, in the park of his cousin Tom Upcher at Sheringham Hall near Cromer. This earned a back-handed compliment from an aunt who glancing out of a window remarked, 'How nice that old stone temple looks, I'd never noticed it before.'

Fletcher-Watson found that his training as a proper draughtsman under his uncle, at the Royal Academy and in a great Edwardian's office, as well as his talent for watercolour, enabled him to design in the round and to explain to clients exactly what they were getting. Like his hero Lutyens he had a feeling for vernacular materials, and this is demonstrated in his early works such as the new Bishop's House in Norwich, with its panels of Norfolk cobble, and the Wicken House near Castle Acre for Sir Kenneth Keith, with colour-washed brick and a roof of black-glazed Norfolk pantiles (now in fact only obtainable from Scandinavia as they are no longer made in East Anglia). The Wicken involved the conversion of a plain but substantial farmhouse built by Coke of Norfolk into a proper country house following Sir Kenneth's purchase of 3000 acres from the Earl of Leicester in 1955. Fletcher-Watson reroofed it, added a pediment, columned doorway and louvred shutters to the ground-floor windows. The work included a small stable block with cupola and a staff cottage. Further alterations have since been carried out by other designers, including enlargements at either end of the house which have somewhat spoilt its proportions. An enclosed swimming pool has also been built and decorated by David Hicks, while the interior of the house was done with the advice of Francis Egerton of Malletts.

Another Coke of Norfolk farmhouse—contemporaries remarked that he had provided 'gentlemen's houses for his tenants'—remodelled to make a fully-fledged country house was Warham House near Holkham for Lady Mary Harvey, sister of the Earl of Leicester, and her husband in 1957. The façade of

Norwich. The Bishop's House. Garden front.

the old three-bay farmhouse with windows in blank arches was retained, but enlarged by pyramidal-roofed wings at either side. A small pediment was added to the centre, and a new doorcase. Seen across the paddock from the village it forms a picture not unlike a Portuguese *quinta* with its pink-washed walls and warm red tiles. The whole of the interior is Fletcher-Watson's and comprises eight bedrooms with large walk-in cupboards on the American model and bathrooms with fitments designed by the architect, who was responsible for the Georgian-style built-in china cabinets in the drawing-room.

Fletcher-Watson often designed fittings and items of furniture for his houses, including chandeliers. When he remodelled Kimberley for Lord Kimberley he designed a set of dining chairs each with different game birds carved on their backs. On the whole he was working for people with strong taste who themselves played a large part in arranging the interiors of their houses. These are comfortable and elegantly decorated but do not have the architectural originality or the spatial excitement to be found in some of Francis Johnson's houses, though a feature is often made of the staircases which tend to be semicircular in the late-Georgian manner. On the whole the architectural impact of his houses is external and owes much to visual refinements learnt from Lutyens.

Fletcher-Watson's largest Norfolk house, Watlington Hall, built for the Popes in 1965, demonstrates this, as does its smaller precursor Wichwood House, Hethersett, near Norwich designed for Michael Watt in 1956. Watlington is a seven-bay house of red brick with a hipped roof and a three-bay centre with pilasters and a pediment. It is a formula which could be merely Chelsea-

114

ish Neo-Georgian, but in fact works partly because of good proportions and partly because of subtle visual adjustments. Thus the ground floor windows are a few inches wider than those on the upper floor and the tall square chimneystacks have a slight batter, of one inch in ten, which has the same effect as entasis in a column. Watlington was built on an old site (formerly occupied by one of Donthorn's gaunt Tudor-Gothic piles burnt down in 1943) and so it was possible to make use of the existing foundations and approach drives, but even so it was remarkably economical. It represented quite an achievement in the mid-1960s to build a large house of traditional quality within a budget of £50,000.

The contractors were Carter's, then the best building firm in Norfolk. They were responsible for executing most of Fletcher-Watson's houses (and his remarkable New England-style church at Bawdeswell near Norwich) just as Anelay's of York have done most of Francis Johnson's. Reliable building firms with a range of traditional skills are as essential as a competent architect and sympathetic client in creating a decent Neo-Georgian house. An interesting aspect of the architect-builder relationship at Watlington was that the contractor was able to produce an estimate for the cost of the work from the plans

Warham House, Norfolk. Before.

Warham House. After.

without any detailed specification because he knew Fletcher-Watson's methods so well, and this guestimate proved entirely accurate.

Another of Fletcher-Watson's Norfolk houses is East Carleton Manor, done for Colin Chapman in 1964. It is slightly smaller than Watlington but is an interesting variation on the same theme; it also has a seven-bay front and hipped roof but is given an entirely different character by a two-storeyed portico of elongated Tuscan columns with a first-floor balcony. The materials are red brick with white-painted trim including the modillion cornice of projecting brick ends, a nice visual joke. The proportions are well managed, although Fletcher-Watson would have preferred smaller dormer windows. The columns of the portico may seem excessively attenuated, but that was deliberate as the portico was inspired by East Coast America and was intended to give the house a flavour of New England. Colin Chapman had spent a lot of time in the United States, greatly admired the old Colonial houses there and wished to commission something similar himself with these largely satisfactory results.

In Scotland naturally there was a strong regional bias and the most active traditional architects in the country house field in the 1960s were natives: Ian Lindsay, Leslie Grahame MacDougall and W. Schomberg Scott. Ian Lindsay was employed chiefly for scholarly restorations of historic houses, reducing them to their pre-Victorian condition and enhancing their integral architectural character. His work is a model of excellence, Aldie, Mertoun, Bemersyde, the Hirsel, Druminnor all being exemplary self-effacing restorations. But Schomberg Scott, in addition to restorations of this type, was also responsible for a number of new houses and substantial reconstructions. They are of particular interest because of their distinctive Scottish flavour, with harling, gables and carved heraldic decoration, drawing inspiration from sturdy pre-Adam northern Classicism and Scottish vernacular.

Schomberg Scott owed his initial interest in the Scottish domestic tradition to a period in the office of Reginald Fairlie (Lorimer's chief pupil and therefore representing the 'Apostolic tradition' in Scottish architecture). He then spent some time in London in Sir Edward Maufe's office in the years leading up to the 1939–45 war. On demobilization he returned to Scotland, joining Ian Lindsay and becoming his partner, before setting up his own office. The background to

his career was therefore strongly traditional and this was reinforced when he became consultant architect to the National Trust for Scotland. This post gave him wide opportunities for steeping himself thoroughly in the traditional techniques and character of Scottish domestic building and this found expression in his house jobs, both new and restorations. His three most interesting country houses are Monteviot in Roxburghshire for the Marquess of Lothian; Dupplin, Perthshire, for Lord Forteviot; and Gannochy Lodge, Angus, for the Fosters.

Monteviot, carried out in 1962–3, involved the replanning and partial reconstruction of an existing house which had grown in stages into a monster. The original small fishing lodge was a charming three-bay eighteenth-century house on a superb site overlooking the River Teviot. To this had been added in the late eighteenth century two projecting wings on the south with canted ends and Venetian windows. In the early nineteenth century Blore was commissioned to replace the house with his usual brand of Tudor-Gothic. Work began on the east side with a large L-shaped wing of domestic offices and a new dining-room, but then ceased, leaving a gap between it and the eighteenth-century house. Succeeding generations tried to link the two disparate parts by adding a congeries of passages, a chapel and a billiard room to the north side. When the present Lord Lothian inherited in 1961 he asked Schomberg Scott (who had already restored Crailing for him) to remodel Monteviot and to clear away the impossible muddle. The Georgian south front was retained, as was the Blore wing, though replanned inside; but all the northern extensions and the chapel were demolished and replaced by a new front of simple Scots Georgian character: white-harled with tall sash windows, carved heraldic panels and the front door surrounded by a moulded architrave and surmounted by a coat of arms. Behind the new front a large transverse hall or saloon with a segmental ceiling was built for showing the bigger family portraits from Newbattle Abbey (the former Lothian seat, now a training college), as well as two new staircases. The former servants' hall in the Blore wing was made into a private Catholic chapel with carved wooden fittings inspired by the chapel at Falkland Palace and redolent of modern Scottish craftsmanship. The rest of the Blore wing was converted into self-contained staff flats and at the west end independent quarters were made, following his marriage, for the eldest son Lord Ancram, with their own access, nurseries and so forth. At the same time the interior was redecorated by Mrs Hourigan, who had kept Colefax and Fowler ticking over during the war and had worked with John Fowler since 1936, and the garden redesigned by Percy Cane.

Dupplin was designed *circa* 1970 for Lord Forteviot to replace a William Burn house which had been mutilated after a fire in the 1930s and was in poor condition. It was a larger job than Monteviot and not without difficulty. The site

Far left: East Carleton Manor, Norfolk.
Left: Portico at East Carleton.

Dupplin Castle, Perthshire.

Dupplin. The entrance front.

Dupplin. The staircase.

posed problems as it was on the brink of a steep hill. This was overcome by retaining the extensive substructure of the previous house and covering it with a reinforced concrete raft to make the foundations for the new one, a factor which controlled the outline of the new house even though it was built entirely from scratch. It is austerely Scots Classical, harled, with an unhistorical columned porch on the north front, and a large semicircular bow in the centre of the south front. The hipped roof is partly concealed by a parapet. At the west end is the office court with garages and staff accommodation. The interior is planned round the large central drawing-room behind the bow window (the main bedroom over is circular), with the library and dining-room to the west and Lady Forteviot's sitting-room to the east.

More strikingly planned is Gannochy Lodge for the Fosters in Angus where there was no constraint provided by retaining portions or foundations of a previous house. It is based on the Palladian model of a centre and flanking pavilions with quadrant links. The gabled centre block comprises the main accommodation while the south pavilion contains a garden room and the north a utility room and garage. This makes an attractive composition, less austere to Sassenach eyes than Monteviot or Dupplin.[5]

Far more prolific than any of the architects discussed so far is Sir Martyn Beckett. He has designed about twenty completely new country houses as well as restoring or altering about seventy old buildings, none of which are remotely alike because in each case the site, character and wishes of the client have been respected. He was born in 1918 and educated at Eton and Trinity College, Cambridge, succeeding to his father's baronetcy in 1937. During the war he served in the Welsh Guards, winning the MC, and it was only on demobilization in 1946 that he started to look around for something to do. He was already interested in buildings and drawing and so was naturally drawn to architecture. His brother-in-law Lionel Brett (now the 3rd Viscount Esher) was an architect, which helped to settle his mind in that direction though he had no illusions about the solid hard labour involved in getting qualified. A. S. G. Butler's work at Pennyholme for Lord Feversham, Sir Martyn's half-brother, provided an opening and Sir Martyn entered his office as an articled pupil, spending three years there. Butler was working on his massive three-volume study of the architecture of Sir Edwin Lutyens and his enthusiasm for the master rubbed off on his new pupil. Sir Martyn became steeped in Lutyens and came to know all his work in detail. He passed his intermediate exam from Butler's office, but knowledge of the Classical Orders and traditional country house work was not considered enough to pass architectural finals so he spent a further year at the Hammersmith School in 1951 before setting up on his own in 1952. It was a risk for a newly trained architect to embark immediately on independent practice, but it paid off and jobs soon began to come in, some of

119

Gannochy. The entrance front.

them being houses to which he would return again and again over the years.

One of these was Bruern Abbey in Oxfordshire which belonged to Michael Astor. There he was responsible for three phases of alteration and improvement. His first job *circa* 1955 was the formation of the library and dividing the large hall into a dining-room and new staircase beneath a central dome; further work in the 1960s included internal alterations and staff cottages; the final phase in 1972–3 involved substantial external reconstruction. A later block at the back was demolished and a new north front designed with a central pediment and segment-headed windows picking up the rhythm of the 1720s south front. The latter is now the only original feature to survive at Bruern; the rest is almost entirely a post-Second World War creation. The interior had been burnt in the 1880s, and plainly reconstructed. Parallel to Sir Martyn's alterations, elaborate schemes of decoration were carried out in the 1950s and early 1970s by John Fowler, and these successfully disguised the Victorian gawkiness of the rooms. Following Michael Astor's death Bruern was let for a time to 'Taki', the *Spectator*'s 'High Life' columnist, but has recently been sold.

Another house where Sir Martyn made a number of alterations over the years is the Manor House at Hambleden near Henley for Viscount Hambleden of the W. H. Smith family. These have included a billiard room treated as a Moorish tent, a domed octagonal conservatory intended for shooting lunches (the South Seas atmosphere and sub-tropical vegetation forming an amusing contrast to the winter cold outside), and a symmetrical bathing pavilion decorated with

120

trellis. The latter was the reworking of an unexecuted early scheme for an aviary for Sir Alfred Beit at Russborough in Ireland. It had been hoped that the drawings for the Hambleden bathing pavilion might be exhibited at the Royal Academy Summer Exhibition but Hugh Casson turned it down on the grounds that it was scenery not architecture.

Sir Marytn Beckett's most unusual country house, and one of the most curious built since the Second World War, is Callernich on North Uist, designed in 1962 for Earl Granville, who had bought the island and wished to live there. Lord Granville invited Martyn Beckett to North Uist and taking him to the northernmost point, a barren rock jutting into the Atlantic, in a gale so strong it was impossible to stand upright, said, 'I would like to build a house here.' There was no shelter of any kind, the island's nearest shop was fourteen miles away; it would have been hard to think of a less auspicious spot for a new country house. Nor was it to be a small house. Lord Granville wanted fourteen bedrooms and eight bathrooms, all on one floor. Martyn Beckett hit on the idea of a circular house on one level round an inner court rather like a bull ring, but in fact inspired by the 'Round Square' at Gordonstoun, where he had been responsible for some work for the school. This solution cut down the building's vulnerability to the Atlantic gales. The battered walls two feet thick were built of concrete, harled and whitewashed in the traditional Scottish manner, and the double-glazed windows had damp-resistant teak frames. There were no builders on the island capable of doing the job, so a task force had to be sent

specially from Glasgow. Despite the remoteness of the place they enjoyed the job and worked well. Lord Granville gave them free shooting and fishing and the job was finished in record time. The remoteness of the site was possibly an advantage as it was too far away for the client to visit while work was in progress and that prevented any of those mid-flight changes of mind which can slow down a job considerably. The exterior of the house pays tribute to Scottish vernacular with crow-stepped gables. The interior is planned with the entrance archway on the landward side giving access to the central court round which runs a continuous corridor. All the main rooms face outwards and the principal drawing-room is on the side opposite the entrance, looking straight out over the Atlantic fifty yards away and to the distant outlines of Lewis and Harris.

Most of Sir Martyn's houses are more conventional and there are a number of formal Georgian ones as well as some informal ones of mixed materials showing the influence of Frank Lloyd Wright. This is partly the fruit of a trip to America in 1960 paid for by Denis Berry in connection with a design for a new house at Brockenhurst in the New Forest. This project was abandoned at contract stage, but Sir Martyn enjoyed the visit to the United States and was able to see many famous American buildings, including Wright's Falling Water, and to develop new ideas. His more conventional Georgian houses include the new house at Sudbury in Derbyshire built for Lord Vernon in 1965 to replace the old house when it was given to the National Trust. It is a five-bay brick pavilion, the sprocketed hipped roof being covered in cedar shingles which gives it a slightly Chinese air. It is carefully sited so as to enjoy a good view over the lake without being visible from the old house. Another Georgian-style house is Hunter's Hill in Kent built for Lord Byers, formerly the Liberal leader in the House of Lords. It is red brick of five bays, but the design was spoilt in execution by the omission of the intended pilasters to support the pediment which as a result is left looking top-heavy and disjointed. It is not clear whether Lord Byers's objection to pilasters was due to economy or because he thought they were inconsistent with Liberal politics and would create the wrong image, like Sir Gilbert Scott, the Victorian architect, who denounced Classical porticoes as synonymous with cold, arrogant feudalism.

Perhaps Sir Martyn's most successful Georgian house is Neasham Hall in County Durham, built in 1971 for Sir John Wrightson, Bt, to replace a nineteenth-century Jacobean-style remodelling by Dobson of an older house. The new one is on the old site and takes its cue from the pre-Dobson house, bits of which survived and were salvaged at the time of demolition, notably a pair of semicircular bow windows with stone Tuscan columns as mullions. The new house is built of brick made at Darlington from the same clay as the original house, though the moulded cornice is fibreglass. Neasham is a compact square house with the two bows on the garden front, a square porch on the entrance

Neasham Hall, Durham.

front opposite, and a crowning parapet with urns. The interior is arranged around a central top-lit staircase, the garden front having the large drawing-room and sitting-room, while the transverse entrance hall also serves as the formal dining-room; in winter the family eat in the kitchen when on their own and in summer in the glazed loggia at the side of the house.

Sir Martyn's most recent work (1981–3) is the enlargement of Beamsley Hall on the Bolton Abbey estate in Yorkshire for the Marquess of Hartington, eldest son and heir of the Duke of Devonshire. This has included remodelling the drawing-room, the addition of a large billiard room and garages as well as a total renewal of the internal services and decorations. Lord Hartington will now live here on the Cavendishes' secondary English estate while his father continues at Chatsworth in Derbyshire.

The creation of subsidiary houses for heirs-in-waiting or dower houses for widows has been a feature of late-twentieth-century country house building. David and Lady Caroline Somerset (now Duke and Duchess of Beaufort), for

123

instance, have made a very attractive house and garden at Badminton by enlarging and remodelling a cottage in the village. Philip Jebb, an architect like Ian Lindsay whose work has mainly involved the splendid restoration and adaptation of existing houses, has also designed a handsome late-Georgian-style dower house, influenced by Nash, at North Port near Lennoxlove in Scotland for the dowager Duchess of Hamilton; and Claud Phillimore has designed several, including the dower house of Lavinia, Duchess of Norfolk at Arundel.

Claud Phillimore has the distinction of being the most prolific designer of country houses in England since the Second World War, having been responsible for forty 'new' ones as well as a large number of restorations and adaptations. He became the leading country house architect by a mixture of personal inclination and luck. He was lucky in having the means to enable him to specialize in this not very lucrative branch of the architectural profession, and he was lucky to be around in the 1950s and 1960s when many landowners were in need of an architect to design a new Georgian-style house for them. In a sense he became the architectural equivalent of John Fowler, the obvious choice that a traditional landowner would make. It has to be admitted, however, that his houses are slightly disappointing. His initial drawings sometimes show elaborate and unusual geometrical layouts, but these never made it to the final stages, and invariably as executed his houses are conventional Neo-Regency with plain exteriors, though the interiors are more stimulating. He was especially interested in this aspect of design and went to great pains to provide detail drawings of fittings such as radiator cases or the pavement patterns of hall floors, and in several instances collaborated with John Fowler. Clients who might have insisted on cutting costs outside were more prepared to spend money on the rooms in which they were to live.

Phillimore belonged to the generation which was brought up on Georgian architecture as rediscovered and made fashionable in the 1920s and 1930s, and became one of the committee members of the Georgian Group in the 1950s. Born in 1911, he was the second son of the 2nd Lord Phillimore and educated at Winchester and Trinity College, Cambridge, where he read architecture, graduating in 1933. He received no further architectural education, but travelled a lot looking at buildings—while cycling round the Palladian villas in north Italy, he called at the Villa Malcontenta and was later left it by Bertie Landsberg. Phillimore formed a good architectural library of his own with all the standard eighteenth-century tomes. He set up practice in London in 1937 but only did one or two small jobs before enlisting in the Royal Artillery as a territorial in 1938. He served in the Middle East during the war and was promoted to major. He started work again in 1947 and the following year took into partnership his school and university contemporary, Aubrey Jenkins.

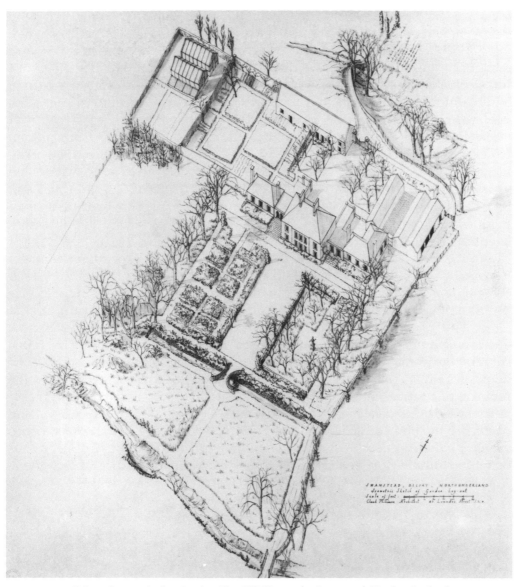

Belsay. Isometric drawing by Claud Phillimore for Swanstead, Northumberland.

They embarked immediately on a long series of new houses, many of them for old-established landowners wanting new houses to replace 'white elephants'. The first was for Sir Stephen Middleton at Belsay in Northumberland, where, as we have already seen, there was trouble with building licences, and others were Lockinge in Berkshire which came to nothing as Christopher Loyd chose

125

to enlarge Betterton Farmhouse to Claud Phillimore's design, rather than build a new house on the old unsatisfactory site; Clovelly Court in Devon where it was found impossible at the time to do more than patch up the fire-damaged remains of the old house; Abbotsworthy in Hampshire, an ingenious Regency transformation of an ugly red-brick gabled Victorian house for Esmond Baring; and Fosbury Manor in Wiltshire, a similar Neo-Georgian remodelling for C. W. Garnett.

His first really large-scale project was the reconstruction of Knowsley in Lancashire for the 16th Earl of Derby in 1953, a grandiose project sparked off by Lord Derby's appointment as Lord Lieutenant, the Queen's projected state visit to Lancashire in 1954 and the relaxation of building licences. Knowsley as it had developed from the seventeenth century was a huge inchoate L-shaped mass with bits of different dates and in different styles, Classical and castellated. A start on transforming this into a Neo-Georgian house had been made before the First World War for the 15th Earl by the smart Edwardian architect Romaine Walker—so smart he would not have a telephone in his office. Claud Phillimore's work was to all intents and purposes the completion of this project. In the process a quarter of an acre of redundant Victorian buildings at either end of the house was demolished, including the libraries, service quarters and the old estate office. The more compact house resulting from this surgery was replanned with a new front porch, elaborate forecourt and new domestic offices at basement level, which were opened to the light of day by the removal of a terrace in front of the house. The state rooms on the *piano nobile* with elaborate Edwardian features in different 'Period' styles were retained and decorated by John Fowler, the gallery being converted into a library for which Claud Phillimore designed new Classical bookcases to house the famous Stanley natural history collection. The most astonishing feature of this whole

project, completed in 1956, was the scale of the staff accommodation, with rooms for a secretary, valet, housekeeper, comptroller, butler, estate agent, footmen, housemaids, and a servants' hall for in-staff, a club for estate staff and a canteen for dailies. It was the last time in England that provision was to be made for servants on this scale, and that it was an error of judgment is proved by the fact that only ten years later Lord Derby decided to part-let Knowsley to the police (keeping only the estate offices, library, and the Queen's Rooms in case of a royal visit) and to build an entirely new house for himself in the park.

Claud Phillimore produced a striking cross-shaped plan with bowed ends and a circular entrance hall, an interesting demonstration of his largely frustrated penchant for geometrical planning. In this case Lord Derby said that he had never seen anything he disliked more and the new house as built in 1963 is a large plain rectangle of brick with only a bowed porch on the entrance front to recall the originality of the first design. The new house was big enough for all the best pictures and furniture and comprised an entrance hall, garden hall, study, dining-room and a drawing-room thirty-eight feet long arranged around a huge central staircase hall rising the full height of the house with an imperial-plan staircase. Marble chimneypieces were removed from the old house and inserted in the new one and the decoration of the main rooms once again was done by John Fowler. Though reduced in scale the staff accommodation was still generous by late-twentieth-century standards and included four maids' bedrooms, two lady's maids' bedrooms, four menservants' bedrooms, a brushing room, utility room, china room, pantry, larder, three stores and a deep freezer, scullery, staff sitting-room, staff dining-room, two staff WCs and a back staircase. This was to service a house with two bedrooms for Lord and Lady Derby and a maximum of eight guest bedrooms.[6]

From the late 1950s onwards Claud Phillimore and his partner were fully employed, with two or three new houses turning up every year, often leading from one to another along a chain of relations or neighbours. Thus Aughentaire in County Tyrone for John Hamilton-Stubber, Lord-Lieutenant of that county, was followed by Bartlow in Cambridgeshire for his brother-in-law Captain (later Brigadier) Breitmayer; and a whole group of houses popped up around Ascot in Berkshire, including a remodelling for Peter Palumbo the property developer. Most of these houses are in a similar Neo-Regency style, usually brick or stucco, with casement rather than sash windows, low-pitched roofs and bracketed eaves and somewhat attenuated Tuscan columns.

The style crystalised in the plan for a new house for the Duke and Duchess of Norfolk at Arundel. This was the brainchild of the Duchess who found that large-scale opening to the public after the war had drastically reduced the family's privacy in the castle. She conceived the idea of building a new house in the park which would in the long term serve as her dower house, there hitherto

127

The new house at Knowsley as built.

Top: Arundel Park, Sussex, painted by Felix Kelly.
Bottom: Arundel Park, Sussex. The garden front.

Dalton Hall, showing the forecourt
also designed by Clough Williams-Ellis.

being none on the Arundel estate. A site was chosen at the south end of the park facing Hiorne's Tower, a Gothick folly. A site at the north end looking down over the Arun valley might have provided better views but would not have been so convenient; the town end was chosen specifically to make it easy to get dailies. In applying for planning permission it was not at first admitted that the new house was intended for the Duke; it was pretended that it was for the manager of the racing stables and gallops established in the park during the war; and only after permission was forthcoming did the truth out.

The tripartite layout of the house with a central block and two little pavilions was the Duchess's idea, inspired from a stay before the war with the Trees at Ditchley in Oxfordshire, so that the pavilions could be self-contained with the staff in one, and her four unmarried daughters in the other. It was only after deciding on the site and form of the new house that the Duchess discovered the architect, when in the course of her work for Sussex charities she visited the Edward VII Hospital for Officers at Horsham and met Claud Phillimore, who was recovering from TB. He in turn had spent his convalescence dreaming up schemes for an 'ideal house' of Palladian derivation with a main block and wings. This coincided with the Duchess's project, and he was appointed to the job. It was intended that the new house should be compact and comfortable but would have an air of grandeur, otherwise the Duke might have thought it too like a farmhouse and have retreated to the castle. The grandeur was supplied by the full-height staircase hall with a Soanic vaulted ceiling and top-lighting. The main rooms are the drawing- and dining-rooms end to end on the garden front. They can be opened up for parties, with drinks tables in the bow windows at either end, to accommodate as many as 150 guests. A less formal sitting-room next to the hall is treated as a library. Claud Phillimore took great trouble over the details of the interior. The double doors are copied from those in the Double Cube Room at Wilton and the ormolu door handles were made specially in Paris. Old marble chimneypieces were bought for the main rooms and the front door is that from Norfolk House, St James's Square, London, demolished in 1938. The interior was decorated by John Fowler drawing on the smaller pieces of eighteenth-century French and English furniture in the castle, where they looked incongruous against the Victorian Gothic setting. The colour of the staircase hall in particular caused John Fowler great trouble; he was determined it should be neither too dark nor too light and kept mixing different colours till he finally hit on a subtle shade which gave satisfaction —'Thames Mud'. The exterior is pink-washed and has one or two nautical touches, recalling the proximity of the sea, including porthole windows in the links and an admiral's walk on the roof for viewing the racehorses. After twenty-two years the Duchess is still pleased with the design and 'would not change a thing'. Claud Phillimore himself says that if he were to do it again he

129

Top: Dalton Hall, Westmorland,
Clough Williams-Ellis's last house.

Bottom: The conservatory designed by Sir Martyn Beckett
at The Manor House, Hambleden, Oxfordshire.

would add a foot to all the dimensions. This touches on the central problem of modern Georgian houses: the difficulty of achieving a compact or economical design without making the proportions too cramped. The new house at Arundel was never intended for house parties but was used in conjunction with the castle, where the Duke had his study and chapel, and which was always opened up properly for Goodwood Week, the high spot of the Sussex social year. It now serves the purpose for which it was intended, as a dower house, while the present Duke, when he is at Arundel—he has other houses—uses the castle.[7]

A larger version of the Arundel centre block, with segmental bows, is Tusmore in Oxfordshire built on the site of a demolished Robert Mylne house for Lord Bicester in 1960. Its proportions are more satisfactory than Arundel and it is faced in Oxfordshire stone with a stone-flagged roof, which immediately gives it an advantage over stucco or roughcast. The interior is beautifully finished in every respect. The entrance hall has a stone and marble floor relaid from the old house, the marble eighteenth-century chimneypieces were also re-

Tusmore, Oxfordshire. Claud Phillimore's new house from the air.

Top: Arundel Park. The staircase.
Bottom: Arundel Park. The library.

used, while Claud Phillimore designed the Regency-style joinery, including reeded door architraves and the radiator cases.[8] Many detail drawings were made and this was altogether his favourite new house, with Aske Hall, in Yorkshire, a substantial reconstruction rather than an entirely new job, the runner-up. At Aske, for the Marquess of Zetland, parts of the eighteenth- and nineteenth-century house were demolished and a new front of stone designed by Claud Phillimore with a large porch and projecting ends with high-shouldered Victorian windows. For this and his other reconstructions, he employed a demolition contractor who was prepared to pay to remove redundant bits for their salvage value. This gave his client a few thousand pounds towards the cost of the new work before it started.

Claud Phillimore largely retired from architecture in the early 1970s, handing over his remaining jobs to a former pupil, Donald Insall, who has designed a couple of new country houses including Broad Oak, Carmarthen, in 1960 for Viscount Emlyn (now Earl Cawdor). This is a rectangular brick house in the Phillimore manner with a semicircular portico of slim Tuscan columns. Otherwise he has developed a successful practice as a professional conservation architect, working on all types of historic buildings rather than specializing in country houses.[9]

NOTES

1 Letter to the author, 6 April 1983.
2 *Country Life*, 23 and 30 December 1965.
3 *Country Life*, 15 and 22 February 1968.
4 Earl of Halifax, *Fullness of Days* (1957), pp. 40–3.
5 W. Schomberg-Scott's architectural drawings are at the Scottish Monuments Record in Edinburgh.
6 RIBAD: RAN 47/D/1/1 J/5/1–19.
7 RIBAD: RAN 47/H/1/1–22; *Times*, 11 November 1984; *Connoisseur*, June 1963, pp. 72–83.
8 RIBAD: RAN 47/I/2, 3, 4, 5, 6.
9 Information used in this chapter for which no documentary source is given comes directly from conversation with the architects and owners.

VII
MODERNS

Though most large new country houses in recent years have been Neo-Georgian, there are nevertheless a number of substantial houses in the Modern style. In some ways these are more interesting than the purely traditional houses (if not necessarily as satisfactory in visual terms) because of their brave effort to reinterpret in an entirely different architectural vocabulary 'the low spreading country house, spaciously planned, which has long been an English speciality'. The design of a country house which could hold its own externally in a majestic setting and inside had the quality 'not to say grandeur which the term country house implies', posed an insoluble conundrum for the Modern architect. The *Architectural Review* pointed out in 1977, 'The idiom in which he [the Modern architect] worked had not been devised with the country house in mind: it was rather like making a shrine from parts manufactured for a motor bicycle.'[1] Historically the Modern Movement had produced two alternative approaches to the problem. One, derived from Frank Lloyd Wright, conceived the house as an extension of the surrounding landscape; the other, derived from Le Corbusier, conceived it as a classical statement, fresh, white, new, owing nothing to anything and 'dropped down like an egg on the grass'. In this chapter houses of both types are discussed, stark white self-contained creations like Eaton Hall, or more 'natural' houses designed round the view, like Exbury, where the scale of the house is deliberately played down and the building is continued into the landscape by the walls of the garden.

It is tempting to generalize about the type of client who would commission a Modern, rather than a Georgian-style house, and to claim that he is altogether a more efficient, versatile, progressive sort of fellow. But this is not by any means the case, though it is true of some. Lord Walston, for instance, the Socialist life peer who has advanced views and is a highly mechanized farmer, in 1970 moved out of a large Edwardian Neo-Georgian house to a smaller Modern house, designed by Sir Leslie Martin, as a deliberate gesture. But many of the more efficiently managed and progressively farmed estates boast a Neo-Georgian house, while certain Modern houses rise in pristine contrast to an estate littered with thistles, dead elm trees and broken fences. In several instances the choice of a Modern-style house has been dictated as much by the nature of the site as by the personal taste of the owner. The new Eaton Hall is an example. It was felt there that a Neo-Georgian house would have been impossible cheek by jowl with the remains of Waterhouse's Victorian Gothic palace. Though many of the Cheshire neighbours were greatly disappointed that the Westminsters did not opt for a full-scale replica of the seventeenth-century Eaton Hall, it was decided, rightly, that only a house in the Modern style would make a sufficiently bold statement to stand alongside the dominating Victorian chapel and stables, which it was always intended to retain.

Nor are the patrons of Modern houses narrowly utilitarian in outlook, aesthetic Roundheads versus the Georgian Cavaliers. Many of them are men of wide culture who undertook their houses as considered acts of patronage and filled them with specially commissioned furniture and contemporary works of art, as did Lord Sainsbury at Ashden, Leo Rothschild at Exbury or Gerald Bentall at Witley Park. One of the big problems with country houses in the Modern style is that of evolving a sympathetic setting for inherited possessions. Glass walls, for instance, do not leave much room for hanging family portraits; and it has to be admitted that high-quality eighteenth-century furniture tends to look incongruous in non-Classical settings, whether Victorian Gothic like Arundel Castle or Modern as at Eaton Hall. Perhaps for this reason the Modern style has more often been chosen for subsidiary houses by people who already have one large country house, and wanted a more relaxed and informal place to get away to, rather than a substitute for their principal seat. Thus Mr and Mrs Hugh Cavendish have built a Modern house in Wigtonshire as a place to retire to for a few days every month as a respite from their more formal life at Holker. This allows both themselves and the staff at Holker to recover from the strain of large-scale entertaining. Similarly Lord Montagu of Beaulieu has built a cedar-boarded cottage called Warren House to the design of Casson and Conder on a remote part of his estate at Beaulieu as an informal bolthole from the Abbey. Lord Crawford has Pitcorthie, designed by Trevor Dannatt, adjoining Balcarres; Lord Esher has built Tower House to his own design on the Watlington estate; and Lord Sainsbury, though he originally built Ashden as his main house, has since bought a more traditional house and keeps Ashden as a subsidiary 'holiday home' for friends and relations. This is perhaps the ideal solution for those people who want, and can afford, the best of both worlds. For the owner of a Baroque palace stuffed with Rubenses,

134

Top: Warren House. A small beach house on Lord Montagu's estate with built-in hi-fi.

Bottom: Modern. Warren House, Beaulieu, Hampshire, designed by Casson and Conder.

Eaton Hall, Cheshire. The most ambitious Modern house in England.

Reynoldses and Roman sculpture it makes a pleasant change to have a stark little Modern house elsewhere to escape to from time to time.

By far the grandest of Modern-style houses is the Duke of Westminster's new Eaton Hall in Cheshire. Indeed, it is one of the most ambitious houses built since 1945, and for this reason helps to throw light on the problem of trying to express a traditional idea in radically new clothes. The previous house at Eaton, a Victorian masterpiece by Alfred Waterhouse, was unfortunately demolished by the Grosvenor Estates trustees following the surrender of a lease by the War Office when National Service came to an end. With what proved unnecessary pessimism, the trustees decided that the Duke of Westminster would never live properly at Eaton again and the old house was progressively demolished between 1961 and 1963, leaving just the chapel and stable block. When the 5th Duke inherited in 1967, it was to find a mess of nissen huts and other traces of army occupation adjoining a hole in the sky where formerly the Wagnerian bulk of the house had filled the central axis of the estate. The Duke nevertheless decided that the family should carry on living at Eaton and should build a new house to replace the old one, a decision which was greeted with general approbation on the estate at the time and which can be generally saluted as

136

Eaton Hall and the Victorian clock tower.

entirely right. A first move was the restoration and replanting of the gardens where architectural features were repaired and the bedding-out replaced by modern planting of shrub roses and ground cover. The architect chosen for the new house itself was John Dennys, whose wife, Laura Littleton, was the sister of the Duchess of Westminster. He had already remodelled the interior of Saighton Grange, a subsidiary house on the Grosvenors' Cheshire estate, in a grand Neo-Georgian manner, incorporating genuine eighteenth-century features brought in from elsewhere. The choice of the Duke's brother-in-law is perfectly understandable but it is perhaps regrettable that such an important commission did not go to an architectural practice like, say, Arhends, Burton and Koralek, a firm at that time in the process of making spirited additions to Keble College, Oxford—a not dissimilar Victorian Gothic challenge—or even to Powell and Moya, whose Cripps Building at St John's, Cambridge, was then generally considered to be the perfectly planned and sensitively detailed 'Modern statement' in a historic setting. The sad fact is that, while from a distance the new Eaton has some of the classic Modern impact of the Corbusier dream with its rectangular symmetry, white cladding and sleek bronzed window frames, close up it is rather disappointing, the centre of the garden front, with an awkward staircase, and the *porte-cochère* on the entrance front both being unsatisfactory features. The basic problem is that, however hard it tries, the new house is not able to hold its own on a central axis of such splendour. On one side it faces the most spectacular gilded wrought-iron gates in England, a large obelisk and an avenue two miles long, while on the other side formal gardens with terraces, statuary, canals and temples, all to rival the scale of Vaux-le-Vicomte, stretch far into the distance.

Rather than risking a brave failure it might have been wiser to have set the new house to one side of the main axis, facing the south garden. There it would have counterbalanced the Waterhouse chapel opposite and allowed the grand central vista to have swept uninterrupted in between, rather like Le Nôtre's layout at Chantilly which is centred on the open space between the Grand and Petit Châteaux and not on any of the buildings themselves. It was also a mistake to clad the building in Travertine mosaic rather than beautiful pink Cheshire sandstone from the Storeton Quarry, which at that time was still functioning to supply Liverpool Cathedral and would have been easy to obtain. To have sited the house off-axis, however, would have been too radical a break. The point, and the interest, of the new house was that it was a strict attempt to repeat the attributes of its predecessors in different architectural dress. It had to stand on exactly the same site as Samwell's, Porden's and Waterhouse's Eaton (facing east-west) and like the latter two had to have a *porte-cochère*. When John Dennys's design was unveiled in 1970 some of the Westminsters' fellow dukes were shocked. The Duke of Bedford wrote, 'I was interested to see . . . a sketch

138

model of Eaton Hall. It seems to me one of the virtues of the Grosvenor family is that they frequently demolish their stately home. I trust future generations will continue this tradition if this present edifice, that would make a fine office block for a factory on a by-pass, is constructed.'[2]

An attempt to give the building a height and scale appropriate to the setting was made by raising the main rooms over a sub-storey, containing a games room and heated swimming pool; this makes the house three storeys high. Ingenious use was made of the fall in ground levels to contrive a split level entrance from the *porte-cochère* with a wide flight of steps leading up to the entrance lobby on the *piano nobile*. The centre of the house is filled by the large hall which serves as a general sitting area on the Edwardian model. It forms the main internal feature and is spatially interesting as it rises through two storeys, has views through glazed doors and windows to the gardens, and is spanned by a bridge at second-floor level linking the principal bedroom suites in the north and south corners of the house.

The principal rooms are the dining-room, library and drawing-room which face the garden and have large windows with marvellous views eastwards across the terraces to the Cheshire Plain and Peckforton Hills. There is also plenty of wall space for the paintings, a specific requirement of the client, for though 'Bendor', the 2nd Duke, sold all the Old Masters of religious subjects on the grounds that he did not like religious paintings, the Westminster collection is still one of the finest in England and contains notable works by Rembrandt, Velasquez, Zurbaran, Van Dyck, Claude and Stubbs, which are frequently lent to exhibitions. The main rooms have wood-block floors, the drawing-room is hung with silk, and the library has fitted bookcases. These, like all the internal joinery, are of teak and cedar supplied by Venables of Stafford. The standard of workmanship throughout is of an impressively high standard, closer to the norm in American architecture than English. The remainder of the main floor is occupied by a study, separate gentlemen's and ladies' lavatories, and at the north end adjoining the dining-room, the kitchen, larder, staff sitting-room and staff lavatory. The rest of the service accommodation is beneath the kitchen, on the lower floor, and the service entrance is by sunken access, concealed from the forecourt by a parapet wall. The floors at that level are tiled or of re-constituted marble, and the swimming pool at the south end is surrounded by Cosmati-work columns and marble statues salvaged from the Victorian house.

The top floor contains twelve bedrooms, two dressing-rooms, two private sitting-rooms, seven bathrooms, a laundry, servery, linen rooms, and valet's room. The family bedrooms face the garden; the rather small guest bedrooms overlook the forecourt, Belgrave Avenue and the distant Welsh hills. Additional bedroom accommodation for larger house parties has been made in

141

Capel Manor, Kent.

Waterhouse's stable block, which also contains a picture gallery for the overspill from the collection. The magnificent Victorian chapel and clock tower have been carefully restored, too. The latter contains a carillon of bells which is still capable of playing 'Home Sweet Home' whenever the Duke arrives.[3]

Several Modern country houses derive much of their architectural impact, like Eaton, from the romantic counterpoint between retained fragments of a previous building resourcefully incorporated into a new one. Michael Manser's house at Capel Manor, Kent, designed for John Howard MP, is a good example, with the retained terrace supporting a new glass box in startling contrast to a half-ruined Tuscan colonnade romantically enclosing the swimming pool at one side. Perhaps the best-known example of this type of approach is Stratton Park in Hampshire where John Baring retained the noble Doric portico when he demolished the rest of George Dance Junior's important Neo-Classical house. The portico was incorporated as a piece of dramatic scenery into the new house built on the site in 1963–5 to the design of Stephen Gardiner and Christopher Knight. It is L-shaped, the short stroke of the L facing the portico and being linked to it by a formal rectangular pond, with the other wing running parallel along one side. Most of the rooms, including the dining-room, the kitchen, nursery and family bedrooms, are in this long wing which was intended to form a self-contained unit for the family when on their own. The other part of the house was intended for entertaining and comprises a glazed full-height conservatory on axis with the pond and portico; the pond is continued into the conservatory itself and is crossed by a bridge to the main staircase. This provided an irresistible temptation for rowdy young men to push each other

142

into the water when drunk at parties. The large drawing-room, at the top of the staircase, fills the first floor and is open to the conservatory, enjoying jungly vistas over its tropical plants as well as the Repton park beyond the portico. The guest bedrooms and bathrooms are situated beneath the drawing-room on the ground floor so as not to waste the best outlook on them.[4]

The construction of Stratton is part steel-framed and glass and partly dark brown brick with African mahogany panels and window frames, making a sombre contrast to the pale stone of the portico. The architect had wanted the whole house to be steel and glass, but the client had vetoed this on practical grounds. Both were right. There is no doubt that the conservatory wing is the more effective visually, while the solidly clad wing is the more practically habitable part of the house. Though Stratton is cleverly planned, and detailed in a style reminiscent of Arne Jacobsen at St Catherine's College, Oxford, it has to be admitted that it was an impractical house. The electrically operated blinds soon broke down so that the solar gain from the conservatory in summer made half the house uninhabitable. This, combined with the excessive humidity from the pond and plants, must have had a deleterious effect on the Quattrocento Italian paintings on wooden panels in the adjoining drawing-room. It is not entirely because the M3 motorway is being built through the park (destroying Repton's planting and threatening George Dance's London Lodge) that John Baring has sold Stratton and bought back the adjoining Grange estate, which Lord Ashburton had been forced to sell in the late nineteenth century when Baring's Bank came within an inch of failing. His intention was never to restore William Wilkins's Greek Revival house at the Grange, which after being a conservation *cause célèbre* in the 1970s has been taken into guardianship by the Department of the Environment and restored as an Ancient Monument, but to build a new house, called Lake House, on the site of the kitchen garden and incorporating part of its wall. This faces south over the lake but cannot see Wilkins's improbable Hampshire Parthenon. The new house has been

Stratton Park. The entrance with mini and catalpa tree, symbols of the Sixties.

Stratton. The drawing-room.

Stratton. The conservatory.

Top: Eaton Hall, Cheshire, from the garden.

Bottom: Arundel Park, Sussex, designed by Claud Phillimore. The entrance front.

designed by Francis Pollen, a Baring cousin for a time in partnership with Lionel Brett and perhaps best known for his sensitive Catholic church architecture. Though Modern, it is a much more straightforward building than Stratton, built with vernacular materials, brick and flint, and in its own way paying homage to Lutyens though plainly detailed and informally planned.[5]

Perhaps the most successful Modern house to incorporate part of an old one is Glen Tanar in Aberdeenshire, designed by the Edinburgh architect Professor James Dunbar-Nasmith (Law and Dunbar-Nasmith) circa 1970 for the Honourable Jean Bruce, daughter of the last Lord Glentanar and heiress of the Coats cotton-thread fortune. This replaced a large baronial edifice designed by George Trufitt for the 1st Lord Glentanar, which had been 'murdered beyond recall' in the 1930s. It was decided to demolish all except the large ballroom of 1910 and to incorporate that into a modern version of the Highland shooting lodge. The ballroom, which is single-storeyed and built of local granite with a steep slated roof, was linked to the two-storeyed new house by a glazed conservatory; but, as both parts are the same height, the result balances well. The walls are harled with granite quoins and full-height bay windows, carrying little pyramidal slated caps. They help to give the house a Scottish baronial air though the architectural detail is all Modern.

Glen Tanar was designed for all the year living as well as large-scale seasonal entertaining. The old ballroom is furnished as a large drawing-room and is well suited to big parties. It has an amazing interior with an open timber roof lined with tier upon tier of stags' antlers like a *schloss* in Germany or Austria. The new drawing-room and dining-room are both spaciously proportioned and rise the full height of the two-storeyed new wing, so that they do not seem too paltry after the grandeur of the old drawing-room. The entrance hall is also large, and is furnished as a sitting-room so that it too can be used as a living-room in the manner of many Victorian and Edwardian houses. All the joinery in the new house, including the boarded ceilings of the main rooms, is of Douglas fir grown on the estate, and old stone chimneypieces are reused from the previous house as well as various other decorative features, including a large Victorian stone carving of the Glentanar arms in the front hall.[6]

Law and Dunbar-Nasmith have done quite a bit of country house work in Scotland, including Leuchie for the Hamilton-Dalrymples in East Lothian, and an unexecuted scheme for Mrs Findhorn in Nairn, but their other major country house is in England. This is Leopold de Rothschild's house on the Exbury estate in Hampshire. It was built in 1964–5 on the site of the kitchen garden—always a good place for a new house because walled gardens were usually sited to catch the sun—and enjoys splendid views across the Solent to the Isle of Wight. As a bachelor, Mr de Rothschild did not have to accommodate a large family, but as a keen musician he wanted his new house big enough for

Top: Kings Walden Bury, Hertfordshire, designed by Raymond Erith and Quinlan Terry. The entrance front.
Bottom: Waverton House, Gloucestershire, designed by Quinlan Terry.

chamber music concerts for up to fifty people. The design therefore was evolved around a large music room capable of holding two grand pianos, a harpsichord (specially made for the house by Tom Gough) as well as guests and a chamber group. The other main stipulation of the client was that all the living-rooms and the main bedrooms should face south towards the sea and the sun. The architects evolved a complicated open-plan layout with the music room as the nucleus of the house and rising through five different levels, making a room too high for its width but providing a concert platform and a gallery for the music library and stereo. The different levels are connected by an open staircase spiralling round a free-standing chimneystack. In addition to this unusual space, the house also contains a more conventional drawing-room and dining-room, four main bedrooms, two dressing-rooms and two staff bedrooms. The ground floor—sunk below garden level and partly concealed—has a car underpass giving direct access to the entrance hall and a lift to the different levels, a gun room, wine cellar and so forth. The house is L-shaped and two- to three-storeyed, with the garage and service rooms in the smaller back wing. The external treatment plays down the scale by sinking the house into the ground and affecting a cottagey tiled roof with secret windows to the second floor. Most of the decorative fittings were specially commissioned as works of art in themselves and include a large tapestry by Sax Shaw, cast aluminium balustrade supports for the gallery and staircase by Ann Henderson and sculpted crystal doorknobs by Helen Weir.[7]

Built-in work by modern artists is a feature of another large Modern house, Witley Park in Surrey. The estate of 1400 acres was bought by Mr Gerald Bentall in 1954. The Edwardian house of the shady financier Whitaker Wright, complete with such amenities as a glass-domed billiard room under the lake, had been gutted by fire in 1952. The Bentalls decided to build anew on a virgin

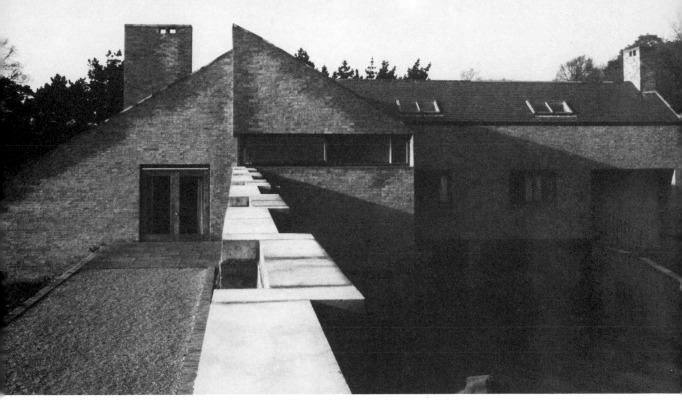

Exbury, showing how the scale of the house is partly concealed.

site in the park, so there was no question in this case of having to pay respect to the remnants of the previous layout. Mr Bentall chose as his architect Patrick Gwynne, perhaps best known for his restaurants at the Theatre Royal, York, and overlooking the Serpentine in Hyde Park; but also responsible for some interesting domestic work. He is one of that small pioneer group of English architects capable of designing distinguished Modern-style buildings before the war, and who carried on developing his own bent after 1945, never prolific but turning out a number of small buildings, including two houses at Coombe Hill, Surrey, all of which show careful thought, attention to detail, and considerable flair. Witley Park is his only full-scale country house design.

The new site was chosen for its extensive outlook and the house was designed to take advantage of the sun round the clock. The architect rightly rejected the idea of having fully glazed walls. Glass houses are only really suitable in woodland settings where the trees can provide pattern and shadow. This is successfully demonstrated by Peter Walmesley's houses at Loch Aire and elsewhere in Scotland. At Witley it was decided to have corner windows to frame the outward views, and this led to the development of a hexagonal plan. The house is formed of two hexagonal wings meeting at the obtuse angle. The

147

Exbury, Hampshire, from the garden.

hexagon theme is developed to run through the whole design, including the section of the concrete columns supporting the main floor, and even the shapes of the flower beds in the rose and iris gardens—a nice visual joke. The other deciding factor in the design was that the house should be easy to run with just one live-in couple (cook and butler) and one daily for cleaning; and otherwise with as many labour-saving devices as possible. Indeed, Witley Court marks the high water mark in England of lavish 1960s electrical gadgetry, before the 1973 oil crisis led to more frugal and energy-conscious architectural attitudes. The ground-floor service room is fitted with a burglar-proof parcels receiver, intercom, water pressure warning lights, and an electric goods lift. The kitchen has three sinks with mixer and spray taps and automatic waste disposal unit, an Aerovap humidifier, high level ovens and rack grill, as well as conventional electric cooking ranges, extractor fans, retractable cook book supports etc. Between the dining-room and the drawing-room is a revolving section of wall with drinks cupboard, built-in refrigerator and 'wine chambering compartment'. There are also built-in gramophones and televisions and a projector room. The dining-room fireplace has an integral fireguard and an automatic flue with draught control and an ash chute to the ground floor. The garage doors, opening windows and retractable blinds were all electrically controlled. One could spend all day happily pressing buttons.

Witley is built of concrete, faced on the ground floor with brown Hornton stone, and the upper part with panels of pre-cast Derbyshire spar suspended from the fascia beam. The main rooms are either panelled with Austrian elm, or hung with silk. The two hexagonal wings dictated an interesting plan with unconventional room shapes. The ground floor is occupied by the estate office, garage and service areas, including a laundry and wine cellar. All the main rooms are on the first floor, with the drawing-room, dining-room and kitchen round an inner hall twenty-nine feet long filling the big hexagon, and the bedrooms in the other, smaller, hexagon. The position of the individual rooms was dictated by the outlook and the sun: the drawing-room faces south and west to get the best views, the dining-room west to enjoy summer sunsets, the kitchen north and the staff flat west to get the advantage of the evening light when 'the couple' were off-duty, and the bedrooms face east for the early-morning sun. Much of the furniture was specially designed for the house by Patrick Gwynne. Paintings by Stefan Knapp and a Finnish tapestry were commissioned for the upper hall; while the dining-room had sliding aluminium doors with etched Chinese patterns by Peter Thompson, and the dining-room servery hatch is embellished with enamels by Stefan Knapp.[8]

On the whole, despite this type of discriminating artistic patronage, few of those who built Modern houses employed the most famous names in the architectural profession: there are no country houses by Stirling, or the

149

Smithsons, or Powell and Moya, or Norman Foster, or Richard Rogers. Sir Basil Spence did one post-war country house, the new drawing-room block at Rossie Priory in Perthshire for Lord Kinnaird in a not unattractive Tudorish *Moderne*. In 1967 Lord Esher (Lionel Brett) designed a subsidiary house for himself, Tower House, Christmas Common, near Watlington, in the form of a four-storeyed gabled brick tower with a turret for the lift. Sir Denys Lasdun was commissioned by Timothy Sainsbury to do a very large concrete house, a sort of far-spreading version of the National Theatre, Thames House near Newbury in Berkshire. Sir Hugh Casson's firm has also done a certain amount of country house work, including internal redecoration and new bedroom suites at Windsor and Sandringham, the stud farm and guest house for the Aga Khan at Sheshoon, County Kildare, in 1982 (whence Shergar was kidnapped), and a large house at Ashden, Kent, for Timothy Sainsbury's brother John, now Lord Sainsbury, and his wife Anya, the former ballerina. This was built in 1964, though much added to later, and is a long low single-storeyed building crisply and neatly detailed with white weatherboarding affixed to six-inch thermalite blockwork walls, a black-painted eaves fascia and a monopitch roof. The choice of materials was intended to pay respect to the Kentish vernacular, a point also made by the circular brick oast house bathroom at one end.

The house occupies the site of another, which had been destroyed by fire,

Ashden. Bedroom. The furniture was designed by the architects.

just below the summit of a ridge overlooking Romney Marsh so that the four main rooms of the open-plan interior, a 'gay and colourful' kitchen, dining-room, living-room and 'ballet practice area' can all enjoy the glorious view towards 'one of the most extraordinary landscapes in Europe' and the distant Channel. 'The landscape seems an integral part of each room, and enormous sliding windows frame the views. On especially warm days they can be rolled back, unifying house and garden, and a giant orange canopy can be lowered for shade.' As well as the main living-rooms, Ashden had on the same floor bedrooms for family and guests, the main bedroom suite being ingeniously arranged as three parts with fitted cupboards as room dividers to make a bedroom, dressing-room and bathroom. Much of the bedroom furniture was specially designed by the architects for the house and complemented the 'successful blend of antiques' chosen by Anya Sainsbury as well as the Sainsbury collection of modern art by Fry, Hubbard, Irwin, Key, Soto, Kitaj, Richier and Rodin. The interior finishes were deliberately kept simple as an understated backdrop, with plain white walls and ceilings, floors of parana pine boards or hexagonal industrial tiles. 'The white walls are an important factor in emphasizing the unusual sense of spaciousness . . . they also form the best of all backgrounds for the Sainsburys' modern pictures and sculpture.'[9] In photographs, frozen into a still life, Ashden has a similar impact to a painting by Mondrian. It was greatly admired at the time of its completion and received

151

the ultimate 1960s accolade: a write-up in the *Sunday Times* colour supplement with photographs by Lord Snowdon.

One of the best features of the design was its flexibility, and over the years it has been enlarged and altered; an extra guest suite erected, the central open terrace covered over to make a glazed conservatory, a nursery and playroom made for the children, and a cedar-boarded bathing pavilion, complete with sauna and its own living-room, erected by the swimming pool. Ashden demonstrates how very much more flexible a Modern house can be than a formally planned Neo-Georgian one. It was intended from the beginning to grow and expand with the family, and from that point of view proved highly successful. Though various partners in the firm were involved in the design at different stages, Lord Sainsbury was very anxious that Sir Hugh Casson should personally supervise the design, and consciously commissioned the house as a deliberate piece of patronage. This was another reason for the house's success: 'Few houses in England have so felicitous an atmosphere, created perhaps by the mutual respect and friendship with which patron and architect began and completed this project.'[10]

Another knighted Modern architect who has designed several houses on different scales is Professor Sir Leslie Martin, head of the architectural school at Cambridge and best known for his new buildings at that university and at Oxford. His fully-fledged country house is Town's End Springs at Thriplow, Cambridgeshire, designed in 1970 for Lord Walston to replace an Edwardian Neo-Georgian house sold at that time. It is of brick with a flat roof and rectangular outline, and acts as the centre for an agricultural estate of 3000 acres, most of which is farmed in hand and demonstrates Lord Walston's progressive views on the future of the landed estate in England.

Arguably the most successful English country house in the Modern style, however, is Freechase at Warninglid in Sussex, designed for Sir Gawaine Baillie, by Tom Hancock and Tony Swannell in 1975. It is flat-roofed, freely planned and with squat proportions redolent of the 1930s Modern Movement, but combines this successfully with a strong feeling of formality and an American standard of finish. Seen from outside, it 'paraphrases the confident eighteenth-century porticoed house, monarch of all it surveys'. The walls are clad in lightweight, heavily insulated panels of rough grainy aluminium but these are relieved by asymmetrical 'porticoes' of square structural piers faced in stone and supporting the flat projecting roof; these give the house its considerable presence, not to say grandeur. Inside, the architects have paraphrased the eighteenth-century house's 'graceful interior, with its fine plaster skin—of a quality rarely seen nowadays—and its recessed mouldings'. The overall plan is L-shaped with a triangular centre. One leg of the L contains the kitchen connected to the octagonal dining-room by a butler's pantry on the ground

Freechase, Warninglid, Sussex.
Section of the exterior.

floor, and the main bedrooms upstairs. The other part of the L contains guest rooms on the ground floor, and a large studio, sauna, and photographer's darkroom upstairs, while the whole of the centre is filled with a double-height drawing-room and gallery reached by a spectacular elliptical stair. All these rooms are 'consistently pleasant; but without doubt, what makes the house memorable is the circulation which joins them up: ample, leisurely, with splayed walls to give a sense of complexity and puzzlement and to provide long and unexpected vistas as you move through the house'.[11]

So far there has been no significant Post-Modern country house built in England, largely because the reaction away from the Modern Movement has been catered for in the country house market by the 'New Palladians'. But one Post-Modern design was made in 1981, though, alas, not executed, for Girsby Manor in Lincolnshire for the Varley family. The architects were Rick Mather and Associates, and the site was that of a demolished house, of which one or two bits survived. The client was open-minded about style and merely specified that he wanted the chief rooms (dining- and drawing-rooms, main bedroom and conservatory) all on one floor and facing south in a line overlooking the existing terrace, the park and the village in the valley below. The hall, TV room, office, kitchen, breakfast-room and services were to be on the north side, together with three guest rooms for visiting members of the family. This chain of spaces was to have been expressed in the external elevation by variations in plane and height, and the playful Post-Modern detailing would have complemented the Edwardian 'Free Style' of the surviving bits of the old house, including a game larder, water tower and Neo-Baroque gateway of 1910. To these the new house was to have been linked by walls and yew hedges. Sadly, this house was not built because the owner's son, who was going to take over the farming of the estate, was killed in a motorcycle accident in Spain on his summer holiday and the scheme was abandoned.[12]

NOTES

1 *Architectural Review*, May 1977, p. 314.
2 AA Notes, December 1970, no 19: letter from Duke of Bedford to the editor.
3 *Architectural Review*, May 1975, pp. 293–8.
4 June Park, *Houses for Today* (1971).
5 Ex info Mr Francis Pollen.
6 *House and Garden*, April 1972, p. 66.
7 *Architectural Review*, April 1966, pp. 295–8.
8 *Country Life*, 19 December 1963; *Architectural Review*, March 1963, pp. 169–73. The hexagonal plan can be enjoyed from the air by anybody flying into Heathrow from the Continent on a clear day.
9 *House and Garden*, December 1966, p. 47; Ex info Mrs Pamela Robinson of Casson and Conder Partnership.
10 Ibid.
11 *Architectural Review*, May 1977, p. 314.
12 *Architectural Review*, September 1981, pp. 101–2; Ex info M. Green of Rick Mather and Associates. Ian Ritchie's amazing Hi-Tec house near Crowborough, in Sussex, is not a country house.

VIII
THE NEW
PALLADIANS

Perhaps the best-known new country house in England is Kings Walden Bury in Hertfordshire, designed by Raymond Erith and Quinlan Terry for Sir Thomas Pilkington and completed in 1971. It is a large and highly original Neo-Palladian house with proportions worked out in Venetian feet, and was intended to be a full-blooded demonstration of its authors' commitment to the cause of genuine Classical architecture, both Raymond Erith and Quinlan Terry seeing themselves as preachers in bricks and mortar. For that reason their work is different from the Neo-Georgian houses so far discussed in this book which, on the whole, are easy-going and undogmatic. The architecture of Raymond Erith and Quinlan Terry by contrast is more vigorous and intellectual and has made them the self-declared vanguard of a crusade for the survival of Classicism. Their houses exude a single-minded conviction and sense of purpose which is lacking from the work of more accommodating and worldly architects, especially as their dedication to Palladian principles is matched by their vehement dislike of Modern architecture.

Raymond Erith at the end of his life (he died suddenly in 1973) had become the best known of modern Classicists and something of a cult figure, but this success was late in coming and the first half of his architectural career had been singularly unproductive. Born in 1904, the son of an engineer, he had received little formal education due to a childhood illness and as a result developed a habit of independent thought and a tendency to question received ideas, which he retained for life. He entered the Architectural Association at the age of seventeen, winning several prizes, and then completed his training in Morley Horder's office. He set up in private practice in 1928 but had little success before the war and almost gave up architecture for farming in the 1930s. In 1946 he began again, opened a new office in Ipswich and built up an architectural practice dedicated to propagating the Classical architecture he loved. He embarked on a series of careful drawings for the annual Royal Academy Summer Exhibition and travelled in Italy to study the work of Palladio. In 1958 he moved his office to the Old Exchange at Dedham in Essex and from there he concentrated on designing a series of remarkable Classical buildings which put into practice the accumulated ideas of a lifetime and, as well as houses, included work at Oxford, Gray's Inn and the exemplary reconstruction of Numbers 10 to 12 Downing Street for Harold Macmillan when he was Prime Minister.

Erith hated what he regarded as the shoddiness and brutality of most Modern architecture. He did his best to ignore it and concentrated his mind on continuing and developing the Classical tradition. 'My aim has always been,' he wrote in 1959, 'to recapture the essential quality of architecture, by which I mean the quality which began to disappear some time during the eighteenth century and which had practically vanished before 1850 . . . I do not pretend to know the whole answer but by studying old buildings I have managed to get a fairly clear view of the thing itself and I think I have found the method, or a method by which it was produced.'[1] His Italian-derived Classicism was grafted on to the English vernacular and it was this which gave his buildings their sense of originality combined with a comfortable feeling that they had always been there. He was convinced that the Classical tradition could be expanded to meet new needs, and quoted Soane to the effect that the architect's job is 'to make Classical architecture progress and absorb in itself the new needs of a new age'. To an extent he saw himself filling a doleful gap between Soane and our own time.

To Erith his architectural work, and especially the design of country houses, was a vehicle for knocking the idea 'that for a big building there is no *alternative* to the established (Modern) style of architecture'. All his buildings testify to a passionate belief in Classicism as a living tradition and his determination to keep the lamp of that tradition if not alight then at least smouldering. In a letter in 1971, two years before his death, he put into words his enduring faith: 'All my life I have been waiting for the revival of architecture. I do not think it *will* happen but if the right idea could be put out at the right time I think it could happen. How wonderful it would be. The world could be beautiful again. And nothing, really, but a blind spot stops it.'[2]

His houses are imaginative and full of idiosyncratic enlivening touches, though soundly based on Classical precedent. He made intelligent use of standard source books, especially Palladio's *Quattro Libri*, the 1825 Paris edition of *Palladio's Works*, the 1832 Venice edition of *San Michaeli's Works*, Letarouilly's *Five Books* and the standard treatises on the Orders, and the buildings of Ancient Rome, Renaissance Italy and eighteenth-century England. When

Gatley Folly, Herefordshire. Designed as a
dower house by Raymond Erith.

tackling a job he would search through his sources to see how Palladio or Inigo
Jones or an eighteenth-century master builder might have faced the same
problem. Often the answer was progressively adapted to the situation in hand
so that it became distinctively his own. In this way, as a design was developed
at the drawing board, it took on a life of its own.

All this is expressed in a series of houses from the 1950s onwards, some of
them alterations to existing buildings and some of them entirely new; including
the reconstruction of Hunton Manor in Hampshire, a thorough remodelling at
Blackheath in Suffolk, additions and a new front at Morley Hall in Hertfordshire for John Buxton, 1955–7, a swimming pool at Culham Court in Oxfordshire for Michael Behrens in 1957, additions to Wellingham House in Sussex for
Ian Askew, 1955–71, and to Sternfield House in Sussex for Lieutenant Colonel
Eric Penn, 1967, and a francophile new house called The Pavilion at Little
Horkesley in Essex in 1969 for Richard Duthy. These all show a lively wit and a
flair for eye-catching detail such as the two little square cupolas with large lead
hipknobs added to the wings at Hunton, or the octagonal Chinese Room with
eighteenth-century wallpaper from demolished Panshanger at Wellingham.
The most striking demonstration of Erith's quirky individualism is the Folly at
Gatley Park in Herefordshire built by Captain Thomas Dunne in 1960 as a
dower house for his mother. It is elliptical, of stone quarried on the estate, with
a concave-roofed verandah on the ground floor and basket-shaped dome on
top, looking for all the world like an old lady's straw hat; it gives to a
geometrical Neo-Classical concept a comfortable vernacular feel. The interior of
Gatley was sympathetically decorated by John Fowler with an understated
scheme of beige, cream and brown, natural linen, rush matting and wardrobes
in the main bedroom designed as little Saracenic tents.[3]

Larger than any of these houses is Wivenhoe New Park in Essex, a Palladian villa reinterpreted in modern terms. It was commissioned by Charles Gooch to replace his inconvenient old house, Wivenhoe Park (famous as the subject of a painting by Constable), when that was sold to the new University of Essex, the proceeds of the sale paying for the replacement house. The new Wivenhoe was intended as a home for the family and a centre for the estate. Mr Gooch specifically asked for a Classical house as he was used to spacious Georgian rooms and he did not want a house in the Modern style. He was lucky to have an Essex neighbour and architect in Raymond Erith, eager to design a sizeable country house as a demonstration of his Classical beliefs. The result is a free rendering of the Palladian villa theme which is in many ways the ideal model for a modern country house, combining utility and a sense of grandeur. The Palladian style is so acclimatized in England that it does not look foreign, though Erith drew his inspiration directly from the sixteenth-century Veneto rather than English eighteenth-century Palladianism. The plan comprises a central block and flanking wings making a front 174 feet wide. Among other things, this plan is a relatively economical way of achieving presence and bulk—as demonstrated by so many Irish eighteenth-century houses. Wivenhoe cost five guineas per square foot, which is very good value for money considering the height of the rooms. Those in the main block are twelve feet four inches high.

The exterior is simply but immaculately detailed and makes an impact through carefully worked out proportions. The main block is given sufficient height in relation to the length of the house by raising the central three bays to form an attic storey with a pediment. Wivenhoe is entirely astylar but on the garden front there is a dramatic two-tier arcaded loggia introducing a strong

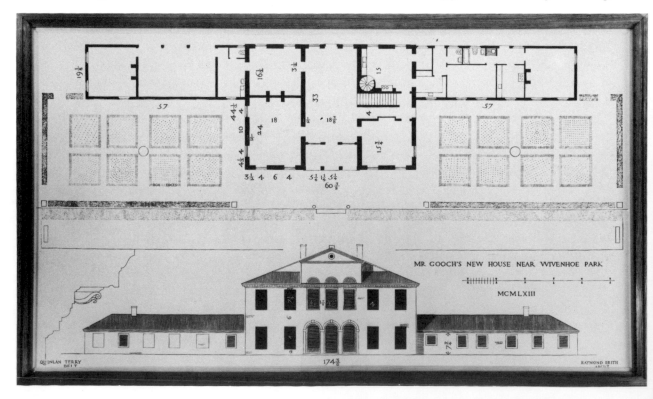

Wivenhoe. The park front.

whiff of the Veneto to the mild Essex landscape and perhaps expressing a yearning for long hot summers. The building materials are local pink brick for the walls with red pantiles for the roof and a restrained use of Portland stone for trimmings including the handsome modillion cornice round the building and the architraves of the ground floor loggia arches. The windows in the central block are casements; those in the wings are sashes. The entrance front is less successful as it lacks the interest given to the garden front by the dark recesses of the loggias, and as a result seems somewhat flat. It was intended originally to have a carved stone coat of arms between the first-floor windows over the front door but this was never executed. It was also intended to flank the forecourt with ranges of farm buildings on strict Palladian lines, but this idea, too, was abandoned.

The internal layout is as Italianate as the exterior. The wings contain the estate office and garage in one and a staff flat and larders in the other. The main rooms, including the kitchen, are in the central block and open off a large transverse hall (33′ × 18′).

This, as well as serving as the entrance hall, is used for shooting lunches, parties and committee meetings, emphasizing the role of the house as a focus for the estate and local affairs generally. The polished timber floor is of oak grown on the estate and there is a plain bold cornice, stone doorcases and chimneypiece. The austere monumental character of the hall is continued through a double archway to the main staircase which has a rising barrel-vaulted ceiling like the staircase of an Italian palace. The library, drawing-room and dining-room are relatively plain, comfortable rooms, the two former with

159

Wivenhoe Park, Essex. Raymond Erith's
design drawn by Quinlan Terry.

old marble chimneypieces. Much of the charm of the interior comes from the use of strong bright colours, Egyptian yellow in the hall, Pompeian red in the dining-room and blue in the drawing-room. These colours form a good background to the family pictures and furniture from the old house.[4]

Kings Walden Bury, begun in 1968, like Wivenhoe draws its basic inspiration from the sixteenth-century Veneto, but uses a more elaborate architectural vocabulary. It was commissioned by Sir Thomas Milburne-Swinnerton-Pilkington to replace a hideous 1890s Neo-Elizabethan house which he had inherited from his maternal grandfather, Major J. F. Harrison, and had decided to make his family home to replace the old Pilkington seat, Chevet Park in an industrialized part of Yorkshire. It is one of the few new houses to have been widely published in the architectural press and in John Cornforth's view is 'arguably the most handsome country house built since the war'.[5] It has an originality and vitality that makes much Neo-Georgian architecture seem tame and stultified by comparison. It is moreover entirely satisfying in its scale and proportions. The client wanted a house on an ample scale and the main rooms are sixteen feet four inches high, a dimension partly dictated by two large glass chandeliers in the drawing-room. Unlike many new houses it has no feeling of being cramped or stinted. The site, close to the parish church and model estate village, is that of the previous house and overlooks mature Victorian parkland. The overall plan is H-shaped with a service court to one side containing the garages in a handsome little building reminiscent of P. F. Robinson's evocations of North Italian and Swiss farm buildings. The facing material is hand-

Kings Walden Bury, Hertfordshire.

161

Top: Wivenhoe. The loggia.
Bottom: Wivenhoe. The hall.

Kings Walden Bury. Detail of entrance front.

made red brick from Mr Minter's brickworks at Bulmer Tye in Suffolk. The actual building work was carried out by Kerridge of Cambridge. The roof is covered in second-hand pantiles. This use of well-chosen materials gives the exterior a nice variety of tone, and already it has a mellow feel. The architectural detail is partly of stone and partly of painted plaster, the masons being Collins and Curtis of Ipswich and the plasterer George Cook of Cambridge. The system of 3:2 proportions that runs throughout the house gives it harmony and ease, as does the consistent use of the fourteen-inch Venetian foot (a fad of Raymond Erith's) for all the measurements rather than the English foot. The wings are plain with six-pane double hung sashes, while the centre has nine-pane sashes and an elaborate two-tier frontispiece of Doric and Ionic columns, the details of these Orders having a deliberate bucolic simplicity.

The interior has a cool formality and, like Wivenhoe, is planned round a large austere central hall with a stone floor and a barrel-vaulted staircase opening off

162

Kings Walden Bury. Dining-room.

one side. The four main rooms are in the projecting wings: kitchen, dining-room, sitting-room, drawing-room. All the mouldings of cornices and architraves are taken directly from Palladio, while the slightly idiosyncratic marble chimneypieces made by J. Whitehead and Sons of Kensington were derived from the same source. That in the principal bedroom is a fantasy on a theme inspired by Palladio's design for the Tuscan Order.

The house works extremely well and admirably solves the modern problem of living on a spacious scale with a modicum of domestic help. In this context it is difficult to refrain from quoting 'Jennifer's Diary' in *Harpers and Queen* for September 1983, as it gives a good picture of a new house in full fig:

'After a delicious dinner, produced by Nicky and Lucy's splendid young chef, we all drove on to Kings Walden Bury where Sir Thomas and Lady Pilkington gave a truly super dance, to celebrate the twenty-first birthday

164

of their elder daughter Miss Sarah Pilkington, and for their eighteen-year-old son and heir Mr Richard Pilkington, who had just come back from working on a farm in South Africa . . . A spacious marquee, lined with pretty soft green and white material, had been built out from one side of the house . . . A profusion of exquisite white flowers were superbly arranged throughout . . . It was a joy to stroll out on to the lawns, and to see some of the beautiful floodlit trees, including a spectacular copper beech. Lord Colwyn's Three B band played for dancing, also Ruffle's Discotheque run by Mr John Benson, who went on playing until 6 a.m.'

At Kings Walden Bury Raymond Erith had been assisted in the design by Quinlan Terry, who had come to work for him in 1962 and become his partner in 1969. Since Erith's death in 1973 Terry has continued the practice, working from the same office in Dedham, the walls papered with old copies of *The Times*, and has been responsible for a series of houses inspired by Kings Walden Bury though smaller in scale. In this he has been able to take advantage of the profound swing in architectural taste in the 1970s away from doctrinaire Modernism towards stylistic pluralism. Kings Walden Bury had been thought of by its client, and perhaps by its architect, as the last in a tradition. In the event it has turned out to be the father of an increasing progeny. It was completed just in time to benefit from the widespread loss of faith in the Modern Movement and the renewal of interest in architectural decoration and traditional building materials. To a younger generation who did not think it morally necessary to try to twist a factory aesthetic to suit an antipathetic purpose, the Kings Walden Bury formula seemed the perfect answer to the problem of designing a gentleman's house in the late twentieth century. In the last ten years New Palladianism has become the norm for country houses, fulfilling the role provided in the public and commercial field by Post Modernism and Hi-Tec.

Quinlan Terry aims to continue Raymond Erith's brand of Anglo-Palladianism but draws on the more Baroque and Mannerist Palladian detail to be found, for example, in the Palazzo Thiene at Vicenza, or the Villa Foscari. He mixes classical details and proportions to create his own brew, which he is still perfecting. Within the broad discipline of the canon of Classical architecture he has been able to devise new permutations, and the variety of detail in his houses and the thought that goes into them are very impressive. He has an almost religious faith in the rightness of the Classical Orders which he believes were divinely revealed to Moses on Mount Sinai with the Ten Commandments, and used by Solomon in the Temple at Jerusalem from where they spread throughout ancient civilization, to be transmitted to us in the Italian Renaissance. He likes to express the character of his clients through the use of a particular Order for their houses: Corinthian for the flamboyant, like Michael Heseltine in the pavilion at Thenford, or Doric and Tuscan for the more diffident and understated.[6]

Waverton House in Gloucestershire, designed for Jocelyn Hambro in 1977 and built in 1978–80, is Ionic. It combines Classicism with Cotswold vernacular, having Renaissance Ideal Proportions of 2:1 (the height of the house is equal to half the elevation, and the windows are all double cubes) while the materials are sturdily rustic and the details boldly simplified. The windows are surrounded by flat stone bands, not moulded architraves, and the modillions are omitted from the sloping cornices of the pediments. The high-pitched roof is covered in Cotswold stone flags and the walls are faced in stone salvaged from three demolished barns. This use of local materials was insisted on by the planning authority to the immeasurable benefit of the design. The main cornice and the entrance doorcase are Ionic, the latter with the unusual feature of the volutes in the capital projecting beyond the abacus. A precedent for this is not to be found in Palladio but in San Michaeli.

The layout comprises a central block and long single-storeyed wings like Wivenhoe. The house stands well on a balustraded terrace though it may be felt that the central flight of steps to the garden, based on Palladio's detail of the Villa Godi, is too steep and narrow for its situation. A wider flight, or even a double flight, would have been more satisfactory visually. Waverton is smaller than Kings Walden Bury, as befits its function as the centre of a stud rather than the focus of a large landed estate and dependent village. It was the stud which drew the Hambros from Hampshire to Gloucestershire in the first place. The Waverton Stud had been started twenty-five years earlier by William Hill and proved excellent for horses. But it had no house on it and Quinlan Terry was called in. The Hambros wanted a house with a specific number of principal bedrooms, and a large imperial plan staircase reminiscent of their previous house in Hampshire. Within a week he had sent a sketch plan showing the layout of central block and subsidiary wings for staff, a gunroom and garages. He then spent some time looking at Cotswold buildings in order to get more of a feel for the *genius loci*. The plan stayed the same, but the elevations were developed as the design progressed.

The principal internal feature is the staircase with treads of reconstituted Portland stone and a wrought iron balustrade incorporating a pattern of Hs (for Hambro) made by Rathbone of Kingham, the local blacksmith. There are seven principal bedrooms and two dressing-rooms. The ground-floor rooms are a dining-room, study, drawing-room and kitchen. The interior decoration was done by Imogen Taylor of Colefax and Fowler, and incorporates pictures and furniture from the Hambros' old house. The staircase hall has a large patterned William Kent wallpaper in shades of off-white and the drawing-room has a Doric bookcase designed by Quinlan Terry.[7]

Waverton perfectly demonstrates Quinlan Terry's own definition of a

166

Waverton House, Gloucestershire.

Waverton.
Front door.

'genuine Classical' building. The plan is symmetrical; the front door is in the middle; the windows are the right size and shape and come in the right place; the roof is pitched and simple in outline; the materials are traditional; the walls solid and loadbearing; the proportions of the house are expressed by one of the Classical Orders and the proportions of the ground floor by a smaller Order round the front door. In other words it is a variation on the theme developed by Palladio, anglicized by Inigo Jones and adapted by the Georgians. He compares his houses to the labels on wine bottles. 'If you look at the label you will often find a building of this kind and it is significant that the good things in this life are expressed in terms of material objects like vineyards and Classical buildings. I have never yet seen a Modern building on a wine label and the reason is obvious: people do not associate the Modern Movement with comforting, reassuring and genuine things.' He pays due tribute to his clients 'whose courage in commissioning and financing these schemes has kept the lamp of Classical architecture flickering. Patronage is not a fashionable concept today, but without it there would not be much art for us to see and there could be no architecture for which a large capital is needed.'[8]

A typical client is Michael Abrahams, chairman of Weaverscroft Carpets in Bradford, who wished to build a new Georgian house on his estate at Newfield near Ripon. He first designed the house himself and got a local surveyor to draw out the plans but was not happy with the result and called in Quinlan Terry to redesign it. He had strong views about what he wanted. He felt that a true country house should not be an isolated building in a landscape but the centre of a self-sufficient and well organized farm. He had studied Palladio and

Newfield. Garden front.

Newfield. Entrance front.

Newfield. Front door.

Newfield. Garden door.

Two chimneypieces from Newfield. *Left*: from the hall; *right*: from the drawing-room

had been struck by the Palladian idea of 'a city being as it were a great house or on the contrary a country house being a little city'. A by-product of this was that Quinlan Terry won £5,000 in prizes from the Philip Rothier Foundation European Award Scheme for the Reconstruction of the City by submitting the design for Newfield as a work of architecture that contributes 'to the reconstruction of the world that is common to all, permanent, solid and beautiful'.

Newfield has a symmetrical plan with a large forecourt flanked by timber barns for hay, animals and farm machinery. The house itself comprises a main block, with a tripartite layout of central hall, drawing-room and dining-room-kitchen, and small projecting wings containing a staff flat and service rooms. The whole is approached by a straight axial avenue of newly planted lime trees. The house has an Ionic Order and is built of local stone. The windows are smaller than Waverton as befits its more exposed position on a hilltop in Yorkshire. Many features of the design were directly specified by the client who intended it to be an expression of his own personality. As he put it: 'When you see a building across a field, in a split second it tells you a lot about the chap who commissioned it. That he has done well, has been civilized, is fond of the land, likes hunting, is either moderate or extravagant.' In a sense a new country house is a form of immortality. It should still be there in two hundred years' time saying *Si Monumentum Requiris* . . . Newfield is Quinlan Terry's most successful house so far.

Other examples of munificent architectural patronage in Terry's career are the small but sumptuous garden pavilion of 1982 at Thenford in Oxfordshire for Michael Heseltine, and an unexecuted Baroque scheme in 1983 for enlarging the old rectory at Hampton Lucy in Warwickshire for Keith Hunt, a

170

Top: Thenford summer house.

Bottom: Thenford summer house, interior. The painted decoration on all the walls is by Marcus May.

Birmingham businessman. The latter involved adding a new stone front with a two-storeyed picture galley, saloon and dining-room to an existing brick-built house. It was essentially an excuse for a palatial formula with giant ringed Doric columns in the centre and flanking wings with large Venetian windows. The client commissioned it out of love of architecture rather than any practical need and, unfortunately, financial difficulties have, for the moment, prevented its execution. The pavilion for Michael Heseltine is also an exercise in Baroque detail, with contrasting fluted pilasters without entasis against the smooth central columns with entasis. The leafwork of the Corinthian capitals to the pilasters is a further variation in contrast to the column capitals. The keystones are all different and express the relative importance of the arches. It is also an exercise in using two different kinds of stone: smooth pale Clipsham for the columns, cornices and architraves, and rough brown Hornton for the walling. This reinforces the architectural detail with variations in the colour and texture of the materials. Inside is a handsome echoing room which serves as a summerhouse and changing room for the nearby swimming pool and has an Italianate fireplace of Portland stone, a geometrical pavement of Portland and blue Westmorland slate and *trompe l'oeil* wall paintings by Marcus May.[9]

Quinlan Terry has recently completed a house on the Berkshire Downs near Hungerford the theme of which is pure geometry. The client wanted a simple house, with no frills and no valley gutters, just a good solid design which would last for two hundred years without any maintenance problems. The key to this is a large plain tiled roof with a pitch of 48°, big enough to contain attic bedrooms. A superimposed Order with pediment round the front door forms the centrepiece and demonstrates the size of the main cornice.

Quinlan Terry is not as isolated a phenomenon as was Raymond Erith. There are now several other architects of about the same age, between forty and fifty, who practise a similar Palladian philosophy. One is Harry Graham who

NORTH ELEVATION

Harry Graham, design for a house in Nigeria, 1982.

172

The stable block at Sevenhampton rebuilt as guest rooms
by Nicholas Johnston for Ann Fleming, 1975.

submitted the only literate Classical entry to the National Gallery Hampton site competition and has recently designed a large Palladian house for a tribal chieftain, Mr Hyde Onoagulachi, in Nigeria. It was exhibited at the Royal Academy Exhibition in 1983 and a nice punning touch is that in the frieze the triglyphs and metopes read as the client's initials HO, HO, HO. The client unfortunately is unwilling to pay the English scale of architect's fees, it being the custom in many African countries for architects to accept very low fees and to make their living in the form of payments from the building contractor. It therefore seems unlikely that this house will now be built.

Another country house specialist is Nicholas Johnston, who is responsible for several new jobs including houses at Llangoed (succeeding Clough Williams-Ellis's castle) and Llanstephan in Wales. He was also responsible in 1971 for the immaculate replica 'stable block', with shaped gables and a cupola, containing guest bedrooms for Ann Fleming at Sevenhampton Place in Wiltshire, so the *Quattro Libri* continues as the fountainhead of at least one strand in the English country house tradition.

NOTES

1 Lucy Archer, Ed., *Raymond Erith RA (1904–1973)* (Royal Academy Exhibition Catalogue, 1976).
2 Ibid; *House and Garden*, February 1966, pp. 32–5.
3 Ibid.
4 *Country Life*, 22 July 1965, pp. 218–20.
5 *Country Life*, 27 September and 4 October 1973.
6 Frank Russell, Ed., 'Quinlan Terry', *Architectural Design* (1981); Clive Aslet 'To the Manor Reborn', *The Times*, August 1983.
7 *Architectural Review*, September 1981, pp. 157–60; *Country Life*, 6 August 1981.
8 Quinlan Terry, lecture at the RIBA. 16 November 1982.
9 Ex info Quinlan Terry.

IX
GENTLEMEN
AMATEURS

One thread in the English country house tradition over the last three hundred years has been the work of the talented or eccentric amateur—designing his own house or that of his friends, and sprinkling his estate with follies. Many eighteenth-century examples are well known, notably Horace Walpole's piecemeal embellishment of Strawberry Hill or John Chute's theatrical staircase at The Vyne or Lord Strafford's Gothick farm buildings, or the 11th Duke of Norfolk's remodelling of Arundel and Greystoke castles. In some cases the owner was assisted by a surveyor or architect but the overall effect nevertheless was largely his own creation. Perhaps as the result of the development of strict professionalism in the nineteenth century, the amateur architectural tradition became somewhat attenuated, but since 1945 there has been a remarkable flowering of amateur activity. Indeed, some of the finest houses built or remodelled in the period are the work not of professional architects but of private owners or people with a general interest in eighteenth-century architecture, including antique dealers, painters or goldsmiths. One reason for this strong amateur showing has been the indifference to country house work of a large section of the architectural profession and this has thrown the landowner back on his own devices. The loss has been the profession's rather than the landowner's. It is difficult, for example, to think of many architects in the 1960s who could have done as good a job as Roger Hesketh's additions to his family house, Meols Hall in Lancashire. All the houses designed by amateurs pay homage to Georgian architecture and often incorporate materials and features from demolished buildings. They are the architectural equivalent of musical variations on themes by eighteenth-century composers, and there seems no reason why these houses should not be treated as equivalent works of art.

174

The earliest case of an owner reconstructing his house to his own design after the war (in fact partly during the war) is Basil Ionides at Buxted Park, Sussex. Buxted, an early-eighteenth-century house, had been gutted by fire in February 1940 leaving only the outer walls standing. Fortunately the house and its contents were fully insured so it was possible to face the catastrophe with a degree of cheerful resilience; it was decided at once to rebuild without the top storey, and to re-create the interior, drawing on fragments and fittings of demolished houses which Mr Ionides had been collecting for a number of years and salting away in a warehouse in London. Work started immediately after the fire and was completed in 1947. Embarking on the reconstruction of a large country house in the darkest year of the war may seem a rather improbable project but at that stage building licences were less difficult to obtain than later, and it was ascertained from Sir George Chrystal, the minister responsible, that there was in fact considerable unemployment among builders in Sussex. The project received official sanction provided that no timber was used. This condition was met by making the floors and new roof of concrete. The shell was repaired and the new flat roof erected first, and then the interior was slowly reinstated and decked out with borrowed plumage over several years. The removal of the second floor reduced the house to two storeys and made it more manageable, though it gave the exterior an uncomfortable truncated look. It was hoped to add a balustrade round the new roof, but this never materialized. It would have improved the external appearance and its omission is to be regretted.

Perhaps it is slightly stretching things to call Basil Ionides an amateur, for he had trained as an architect, but, having married a rich wife, did not need to practise on a commercial scale and was enabled to spend his time advising friends on the decoration of their drawing-rooms, collecting eighteenth-century furniture and embellishing his own house at Buxted which he and his wife had bought in 1930. There is a good description of him, and the house, in James Lees-Milne's diary: 'Was met by Basil Ionides, who motored me out to Buxted Park. He is a pleasant, jolly *bon viveur*, large and well-fed. He told me in confidence that on his wife's death her estate would be worth £2 million. We went all round the house, which was burnt out in 1940. Immediately afterwards they began reconstruction and are still continuing. They took off the top storey altogether so that from the outside the house looks grotesque. Nothing of the inside is left at all except two plaster overmantels of coats of arms and mantling. Everything else is new or imported.'[1]

The principal change in the planning of the house was to move the entrance to the west end and to create a new front door and forecourt there. The balustrade of the forecourt was salvaged from Chesterfield House in London and the new front door, with a pediment and stalactite rustication, came from

Buxted Park. The porch with doorway brought from
West Harling, Norfolk, by Basil Ionides.

West Harling Hall in Norfolk. The new entrance hall is a plain Georgian-style room skilfully put together out of old fragments. The skirting boards come from Norfolk House in St James's Square; the mahogany doors from an Adam house in Portland Place; the chimneypiece from 19 Arlington Street. It could be an obituary to the terrible demolitions of London houses in the 1930s. In the adjoining staircase hall, the splendid timber staircase in purest Palladian taste came lock, stock and barrel from 30 Old Burlington Street. The former two-storeyed hall in the centre of the house was subdivided by the insertion of a new floor. The lower part was converted to a garden hall and embellished with a chimneypiece from Queensberry House, Richmond, doorcases from Kingston House, Kensington Gore, Ionic columns from 19 Arlington Street and marble urns from Wanstead. The drawing-room has a chimneypiece from Clumber and a plaster frieze copied from a house in Richmond. The Neo-Classical saloon has mahogany doors from 38 Berkeley Square, Adam plaques from the Adelphi and two chimneypieces of *rose brèche* marble from Kingston House, Kensington, while the window architraves were rescued from Chesterfield House. In the library the chimneypiece came from Felix Hall, Essex, and

176

Top: Waverton, the drawing-room. The Doric bookcase was designed by
Quinlan Terry and the decoration is by Imogen Taylor of Colefax and Fowler.

Bottom: The library at Meols. The paintings of Sir Peter Hesketh-Fleetwood's
Arab stallion by James Ward dictated the height of the room.

the overmantel from the State Dressing-room at Stowe. The same story is repeated in all the other rooms, even the bedrooms—which tend to be Regency in contrast to the mid-to-late-Georgian character of the main rooms. The result is curiously similar to the sequence of 'period rooms' formed in the Victoria and Albert Museum after the war to display eighteenth-century furniture and fittings. It is not, however, a dead creation; it has a strong personality of its own, though it is synthetic. Mr and Mrs Ionides were hybridizers of genius and their house is fascinating as an informed and sensitive response to the decorative arts of the eighteenth century before the advent of professional architectural history took some of the fun out of the subject.

The Ionides' taste parallels the views on the eighteenth-century interior propounded by Margaret Jourdain and Christopher Hussey in the 1940s and early 1950s. Christopher Hussey himself wrote in *Country Life* in 1950: 'Buxted with its contents and setting illustrates the arts of the eighteenth century more vividly and comprehensively than perhaps any original building of the epoch. . . The house is so arranged that, along the vistas and through planned connections, the results of some remarkable alliances are perceived. Under its new flat roof we find, combined into a fresh unit, authentic traits of, it may be, William Kent and Robert Adam, with distinct Rococo characteristics yet a complexion rather Chinese. . . yet transformed by a cross with Greville grandeur from Stowe or a touch of Lord Burlington's pedantry.'[2] In some ways it represents an artist's view of the eighteenth century, with evocative assemblages of old details in compact and convenient twentieth-century rooms. However convincing, or indeed genuine, the detail in this type of interior, it could never be mistaken for a real eighteenth-century house because the plan and the purposes of the rooms are entirely different. These rooms were intended for relaxed and comfortable living, or for drinks parties, not for parade and formality. In a genuine eighteenth-century house, however altered and rearranged over the years, the bones of the original apartments and axes are still discernible through the later accretions, and the effect is very different from a twentieth-century Georgian house.

Another amateur purveyor of romantic, eclectic eighteenth-century-style interiors, younger than Basil Ionides, was Felix Harbord who died in 1982, though most of his work dates from the 1950s and 1960s. He was a painter by training, having studied at the Slade in the 1920s. In a sense he was an interior decorator, though he never had a smart shop in London. His work is really that of an amateur architect and involved the complete remodelling of rooms, and even whole houses, as romantic, elegiac variations on an eighteenth-century theme. He had started out before the war with work at Chichely in the 1930s and a total revamping of the interior of Kingston Russell in Dorset for the Vesteys, complete with plaster palm-trees, tent rooms, Dufours wallpaper and

177

Luttrellstown Castle, County Dublin. The
Grisaille Room designed by Felix Harbord in 1950.

some fairly extreme *chinoiserie*. After the war his major interior jobs were the reconstruction of Oving, Buckinghamshire for Lord and Lady Hartwell, proprietors of the *Daily Telegraph*, The Park House at Wilton for the Honourable David Herbert (younger brother of the 16th Earl of Pembroke) and Luttrellstown Castle near Dublin for the Honourable Mrs Brinsley Plunkett. Luttrellstown, a typical early-nineteenth-century Irish stucco castle, had been given to her by her father, Ernest Guinness, as a wedding present in 1927. Beginning in 1950 the interior was thoroughly remodelled in Georgian taste. The Victorian Banqueting Hall was demolished and replaced by a large new dining-room in a very grand mid-eighteenth-century style with plaster swags, carved marble chimneypiece, white and gold side tables from Wilton and an oval painting in the centre of the ceiling. Another new room, the Grisaille Room, was decked out in Adamesque taste to form the setting for nine *grisaille* paintings by Peter de Gree representing Irish trade and commerce. Latterly the staircase hall was remodelled and a ceiling painting attributed to Thornhill from a demolished house in Suffolk inserted in 1963. Other rooms were embellished with brought-in chimneypieces, doorcases, new plasterwork and marble floors to create an ensemble which for thirty years was among the most admired in Ireland.[3]

Felix Harbord's most interesting post-war country house is Ockham Park in Surrey created in the 1960s for Felix Fenston, a property developer who had bought the estate. Ockham was originally a Jacobean H-plan house remodelled, it is thought, by Hawksmoor between 1725 and 1729, and again in stucco Italianate taste in the mid-nineteenth century. The main block was destroyed by fire in 1948 leaving only the shell of the large kitchen wing, an unprepossessing stuccoed block with a Victorian tower. Beneath the stucco, however, the early-eighteenth-century brick walls survived and it was decided to use them to form a new house in the Hawksmoor manner. The stucco was stripped, revealing the brickwork; thick barred sashes were installed in the windows; the Victorian tower was demolished and replaced with a copy of the idiosyncratic early-eighteenth-century clock cupola combined with a chimneystack shown on a sketch of 1726 by Hawksmoor formerly in the possession of the late Rupert Gunnis. The interior was completely rebuilt and fitted out with eighteenth-century panelling from demolished buildings in London. The kitchen block had been so mutilated in the nineteenth-century alterations that it is not known whether it was by Hawksmoor or not, but future generations could well be deceived into believing that Felix Harbord's reconstruction was Hawksmoor's work with its curiously proportioned little Venetian windows and central chimney turret. The fact that the brickwork is largely eighteenth-century will add verisimilitude to the deception.[4]

One of the most successful houses created since the war to the design, and under the direct supervision, of its owner is Meols Hall, Southport, Lancashire,

Ockham Park, Surrey, in 1947.

Ockham Park in 1966.

extended and remodelled by Roger Hesketh between 1960 and 1964. It is a remarkable and romantic story. A house has stood on the site since the reign of King John and has passed down by descent (sometimes through the female line) to the present owner. In the early eighteenth century, following the marriage of Roger Hesketh of Meols to Margaret Fleetwood, the heiress of Rossall, the family moved to Rossall Hall and Meols was reduced in size and became the agent's house. The development of the town of Fleetwood in the 1830s by Sir Peter Hesketh-Fleetwood led to financial difficulties and the sale of most of the Lancashire estates in the 1840s. About half of the North Meols estate, including Meols Hall itself, was saved, with assistance from other members of the family, by Sir Peter's younger brother the Reverend Charles Hesketh, then rector of the parish. On the latter's death in 1876 his widow, not wishing to move out of the old rectory, an attractive early-nineteenth-century house, built another for the new incumbent, retaining the old one for herself and her successors. In 1898 their grandson, father of the present owner,

180

Meols Hall. Gazebo.

succeeded to the estate. A few years later he bought Stocken Hall in Rutland with its surrounding estate, which then became his principal home, Lancashire being visited for only a few weeks in each year. Immediately after the First World War he decided to make Meols Hall his base in Lancashire, the old rectory, now rechristened The Rookery, being sold and subsequently demolished. In 1938, under a family arrangement Meols Hall passed to its present owner.

From early in his life Mr Roger Hesketh had dwelt on the possibility of restoring Meols as a proper house, and it was this ambition which helped to form the impetus for his, and his brother Peter's, interest in eighteenth-century architecture. From the start, they accepted that the only appropriate style for such a project was that of Palladio, as translated into English by Gibbs and Leoni, and the way in which the resulting Anglo-Palladian manner had been used in Lancashire in the eighteenth century. Both brothers studied architecture at the Architectural Association, Peter having previously done so under Professor Richardson at London University. During the inter-war years both had travelled in Europe, England and America, looking at buildings with friends like John Summerson and Christopher Hussey. As a result, they both gained a detailed practical knowledge of Classical architecture. With the Hall now at his disposal, Roger Hesketh and his brother, both unmarried, moved in and a start was made.

In the same year, 1938, a cousin, Thomas Knowlys Parr, died and left back the contents of his house in Hampshire, 'the wreck of Rossall', which comprised the nucleus of the Fleetwood-Hesketh family collection, inherited from Sir Peter's widow. These chattels arrived back in Lancashire after an absence of

181

ninety-four years barely a week before the outbreak of the Second World War. This gave new meaning to the project for reconstructing the house at Meols.

The war brought everything to a halt. When it ended progress was again delayed because at that time it was not yet possible to get the necessary building licence. It was, however, found that a licence could be granted for purely agricultural purposes, so by 1952 Mr Hesketh was able to complete a symmetrical Palladian shippon which he designed for a herd of Jersey cattle. Meanwhile, in the same year, he had been elected Member of Parliament for Southport. This imposed a further delay, since, with most of his time being now spent in London, adequate supervision of the work would not have been possible. The 1950s, however, had not been inactive architecturally, for it was then that the plans for the house had gradually evolved. Certain minor amendments were called for by the fact that Mr Hesketh was now married with a young family for whom nursery accommodation had to be provided. It was not until after Mr Hesketh's retirement from the House of Commons in 1959 that work could be started in earnest.

To a large extent the replanned house was designed from the inside out and the different parts were evolved, down to the hanging of the pictures, before the elevations were finally approved. The latter were dictated by the priorities of the internal disposition, and the need to retain the two remaining seventeenth-century parts of the old house, namely the centre of the entrance front and the gable wing enclosing the south end of the house. The principal external alteration was the new east façade of three storeys facing the park. It is in the style of the 1730s. 'A devotee of Colvin and Pevsner would immediately wonder about the identity of the follower of Gibbs who practised in what was then a remote and desolate spot . . . Almost inevitably the Smiths of Warwick come to mind . . . But that would be quite the wrong track.'[5] Various models and drawings were made for this front, with and without pilasters. In the end, an astylar version was chosen with quoins at the corners and a handsome rusticated and pedimented doorcase. The latter is in fact by Giacomo Leoni and, like most of the excellent dressed stonework at Meols, was rescued as it was about to be dumped into a disused dock at Liverpool following the demolition of Leoni's east wing at Lathom in 1960. The red bricks are also eighteenth-century and were acquired when Tulketh Hall, Preston, a former family property, was demolished in the same year.

The use of old materials gives the house an authentic, established feel; the retention of the seventeenth-century parts also adds to the sense of the house's historical development and gives it a nice sense of chronological growth absent from an entirely new house. All the Classical detail is impeccable and is the result of a great deal of careful thought. The main cornice of pre-cast stone is derived from Alberti and the convincingly Lancastrian coping to the parapet is

Top: Meols. The drawing-room.
Bottom: Meols. The dining-room.

copied from the eighteenth-century church tower in the village, while the prominent windowsills in the south wing are another local feature which can be seen, for instance, in the Georgian houses in Preston. It is this balance of mainstream Renaissance and Lancastrian variation which makes Meols so convincing a design. The illusion of organic growth is further emphasized by the treatment of the flanking kitchen wing at the south end and library at the north, as 'later' additions in the style of circa 1800. To complete the eighteenth-century character of the east front, a garden wall was demolished and replaced by a ha-ha, opening up the view into the replanted park and to the distant Pennines. This view is framed by a pair of embattled brick gazebos modelled on an eighteenth-century original at Rossall and embellished with Lathom door-cases and carvings of the Hesketh and Fleetwood arms.

Peter married during the war and now lived at Hale, near Liverpool, only some thirty miles away. Having been so closely involved in the project since its inception, he was thus still readily available, both during the planning stage of the 1950s and while the work was actually in progress, to discuss problems as they arose and offer alternative solutions. It was, for example, at his suggestion that Alberti's design was finally selected for the cornice of the south front.

All the alterations at Meols were carried out under Mr Hesketh's own supervision. No clerk of works or contractor was employed. All the work was done by local craftsmen and builders on a time and materials basis. This cut down the cost for, as Mr Hesketh explains, 'A contractor is bound to add something to his tender to cover contingencies that may never arise. Similarly if one changes one's mind when building is already in progress, and things do not always look quite the same in reality as they do on paper, the additional cost can be accurately gauged from the time sheets, while there is no means of precisely assessing the "extras" on a contractor's account which in conse-quence tends to increase disproportionately.' During the four years the alter-ations were in progress, the Heskeths remained in the house and moved from room to room as the work advanced. In this way it was possible to supervise the building very closely.

The interior of Meols is as successful as the exterior and there is a nice sense of variety between the smaller, low-ceilinged rooms in the old house and the larger scale of the new rooms such as the library, which is used as a sitting-room in summer. In the winter the smaller and warmer Yellow Room in the old house takes its place. The proportions of the library were dictated by the fittings and pictures, the width by a fitted Regency bookcase from Bold Hall and the height between the dado and the cornice by the large picture of Sir Peter Hesketh-Fleetwood's Arab stallion painted by James Ward in 1828. The cornice is copied from that over the main staircase at Tulketh and the door architraves and dado mouldings from Carr of York's work at Lytham Hall, across the Ribble estuary

184

to the north. The three rooms behind the new east front are treated as a formal enfilade of drawing-room, stone-floored garden hall and dining-room. These three rooms are given a unified look by having identical cornices and coved ceilings (copied from the Hermitage at Bayreuth), and marble chimneypieces of similar colour and pattern, two of which are eighteenth-century while that in the drawing-room is a copy made by Stubbs of Liverpool in 1962. Much of the formal character of these rooms comes from the eighteenth-century pattern of picture hanging with the portraits and landscapes hung in tiers filling the space between dado and cornice. The details of the picture hanging were worked out on paper before a brick was laid and it is one of the factors which conditioned the proportions of the house. A feature of the new rooms at Meols is the clever provision of thoughtful conveniences such as the 'shutter space' in the window recesses of the dining-room, which forms cupboards to store the salts and peppers and other articles from the table when not in use. It was considered replacing the rather cramped old staircase with another in the new part of the house, but in the event the old stairs were kept and improved, the upper flight being given a late-seventeenth-century balustrade from Harrock Hall.

Other owners who have played a part in the design of their own houses have had at least some assistance in making the plans and supervising the building work. At Shane's Castle in Northern Ireland, Lord O'Neill built a new house in 1958 with the help of Arthur Drury, a Belfast architect. Like many of the best post-war Georgian houses, it has a strong local character, in this instance drawing inspiration from eighteenth-century Anglo-Irish architecture. It is the

Shane's Castle, County Antrim.

third house to be called Shane's Castle. The estate, on the north-east corner of Lough Neagh, is one of the oldest in Ireland because the O'Neills, descended from the ancient Irish royal house, were allowed to keep their lands after the Plantation of Ulster. The earlier house was built in the seventeenth century and remodelled by Nash in 1815, but was said to have been burnt by the family banshee the following year. The ruins survive on the estate in a romantic situation overlooking Antrim Bay, and in their present state have the character of a decorative folly. A new house was built in the nineteenth century on a different site near the Georgian stables (to avoid the banshee?), but this was burnt in the Troubles in 1922. Over thirty years were to elapse before the present house was built on the other side of the stables. It is a good and convincing Neo-Regency design in the Classical manner. The well-proportioned principal elevations are each of seven bays. The entrance side has a deeply recessed centre. There is a low-pitched roof behind a parapet, tall sash windows and handsome fanlights over the doorways. Many of the details were chosen by Lord O'Neill from other Irish houses of appropriate date and style. The interior has a fine drawing-room and elegant semicircular staircase divided from the entrance hall by fluted Ionic columns.[6]

Torry Hill near Maidstone in Kent is another house designed by the owner with some assistance. In this case the style chosen is 'William and Mary' of *circa* 1700. It is built of hand-made red brick with a steep-pitched hipped roof, segmental-topped dormers and prominent panelled chimneystacks in the Kentish manner. Torry Hill is the work of Robin Leigh-Pemberton, since June 1983 Governor of the Bank of England, and occupies the site in a beautiful park with very good beech trees of an ugly Victorian house which had been

186

Top: Shane's Castle. The staircase.
Bottom: Shane's Castle. Dining-room.

Left: Torry Hill, Kent, in 1865. *Right*: Torry Hill, present day.

inherited. The new house was built between 1956 and 1958, the Leigh-Pembertons moving in in January 1958 by which time work was almost completed. The builders were a local firm, H. Butcher and Son of Sittingbourne, and they were responsible for the excellent brickwork which contributes so much to the handsome appearance of the house. The design was largely Robin Leigh-Pemberton's own with help over the details and in drawing up the plans from the late H. G. Freemantle of Hindhead. Mr Freemantle was not a professional architect either, but was knowledgeable about traditional building methods and was recommended to the Leigh-Pembertons by a neighbour as a freelance adviser. He had ideas which did not always appeal to Mr Leigh-Pemberton, but equally were often good. Together they evolved a solid and convincing design. The house is square in plan, of seven bays by five, and has doorcases of a different character on each front. It is only one of the latter, with an unhistorical form of broken pediment, which gives the game away. Even *The Buildings of England* was forced to admit: 'It aims to deceive and it nearly does,' and added, 'the date incredibly *circa* 1960'. It is to be hoped that the date will seem less incredible to readers of this book![7]

There has in recent years been a considerable vogue for the erection of follies in the grounds of country houses. At Garmelow Manor, Eccleshall, Staffordshire, for instance, Arnold Machin, the sculptor (best-known perhaps for the profile of the Queen on British postage stamps), has constructed in the garden a Gothick tower, boathouse and an ambitious subterranean top-lit grotto approached by a spiral staircase. He was assisted in the design by his son, Francis, who has subsequently developed a successful line in the sale of prefabricated Gothick conservatories and garden temples. These have had something of the effect in popularizing follies that Laura Ashley has had with Colefax and Fowler-type interior decoration. The number of follies, gazebos and other subsidiary estate buildings designed by the owners themselves since 1945 are too many to mention in detail. The Palladian shippon and castellated gazebos by Roger Hesketh at Meols have already been described. There has

188

Right: Gothick temple at Hill Court.
Far right: Chinese temple at Hill Court.

been considerable enthusiasm for *chinoiserie* or Gothick pavilions often of light timber or trellis construction. At Hill Court in Herefordshire in the 1960s the late Mr J. L. Trafford was responsible for one of each—a Gothick octagon with a tiny onion dome on top and an open Chinese pavilion enshrining a wickerwork elephant.

Some of the 'amateur' houses have been designed by people well known in other fields. At Ranston, near Iwerne Minster in Dorset, the house was rebuilt in 1961–3 for the Gibson-Fleming family with four reset façades on a new structural brick core and a rearranged interior reusing eighteenth-century decorative features. The architect was Louis Osman, also artist, medalist and goldsmith, the maker of the crown used by Prince Charles at his Investiture as Prince of Wales at Caernarvon.

It is not of course accurate to call Louis Osman an 'amateur' in this context for he was trained, and has practised, as an architect since 1936. He studied at the Slade and under both Sir Albert Richardson and Henry Corfiato. They drew like eighteenth-century architects and artists, and he himself has always drawn and regarded the ability to draw as essential to any architect's creative ability. He was once told by Graham Sutherland, while working with him on the cross of Ely, 'You are the only architect I know who can draw.'

Osman has been responsible for a number of distinguished buildings including the reconstruction of the two eighteenth-century blocks gutted during the war on the north side of Cavendish Square, London, and the new bridge linking them, with the Epstein Madonna and Child. His country house work includes a circular, Cotswold stone, beehive-domed, stone-roofed library in Gloucestershire and the reconstruction and extension of Valley Farm, Edgeworth, for Anne, Lady Hollenden. A free-standing, circular, cantilevered, green-oak staircase five feet wide is under construction there by Roger Capps at the time of writing.

Osman says he does not design in the eighteenth-century or medieval or Modern manner but creates for the life style of the client. 'Nowadays,' he says, 'this is usually a Jekyll and Hyde affair.' Ranston, when inherited by the present owner, comprised a central cube of 1753 flanked by later accretions, all

riddled with dry rot. Osman was commissioned to demolish the old and build a Modern house in the eighteenth-century park with its lake and Palladian bridge. He was sure that this would not suit his clients and that what they would really like was the revived Palladian central block.

A steel scaffolding structure was built right through the house supporting the original roof, the four external walls were demolished and the original stonework carefully numbered. The original sash windows with their crown glass and doors were also preserved for reuse and the magnificent rococo plasterwork of the interior was coated in clay, boxed and taken down. The back of the plasterwork thus exposed with its blanket of dry rot fronds was removed from the site and steam-fumigated. The sale of the Casali painted panels already removed was stopped, the polished mahogany joinery of the interior with its mercury-gilded fittings, original locks and hinges, and the stone staircase with wrought iron balustrade and cross-barred mahogany handrail was removed. So were the Corinthian columns from the hall and the original panelling and carving. All was fumigated. Every bit of structural timber was removed and replaced with concrete. Rebuilding then started on a reorientated plan so that the main rooms in their original form would face south and the entrance and staircase be on the north. New kitchens were made on the west side, giving straight into the dining-room.

The basements were remodelled with concrete vaults and a ramp down so that cars could drop their passengers under the centre of the house, the drive passing right underneath and out again on the other side.

A new structural brick shell was built on each of the four sides exactly to the original dimensions. On the east front a new centrepiece was formed with a stone doorway and Venetian window over. On the south front the opportunity was taken to build the twin balustraded steps with wrought iron balustrades intended in 1753 but never hitherto executed.

All the original rococo plaster work and all the original joinery finishes were refixed and the series of painted panels, in their rich stucco frames, representing the Liberal Arts and Grecian gods and goddesses, were reset in the drawing-room and library ceilings, and the entrance hall where there is a large panel on each wall—Juno and architecture; Apollo and music; Mercury and sculpture; Minerva and painting, and on the ceiling Bacchus and Ariadne. All are by Andrea Casali, and were commissioned for the house by Thomas Ryves.

The contractors for this extremely complicated and involved work were Messrs Dove Brothers of Islington for overall management and the foreman in each trade, with the local builder cooperating and supplying the labour force, a duality which worked well and economically. It is interesting that the final cost was about half that of a completely new building of equivalent space and

Felix Kelly, The Dower House, Tillmouth Park.

quality. Ranston is among the most distinguished and stylish houses created since the last war.

Felix Kelly, the painter of romantic landscapes and views of buildings, has likewise designed one or two country houses for friends. At Tillmouth Park in Northumberland he was responsible for the Gothick 'Dower House' evolved out of a plain three-bay farmhouse for Sir Michael Blake. This is the fourth seat on the estate and succeeds the mad Twizell Castle and even more mad Tillmouth Park, both built by Sir Francis Blake in the 1770s and demolished in 1888, and the Victorian Jacobethan Tillmouth Park, now let as a hotel. When Sir Michael inherited the estate and baronetcy he lived at first in a plain farmhouse with two bay windows. But after his marriage he found it necessary to extend the accommodation. Felix Kelly had been a friend for years and Sir Michael asked him for his advice on how to give the little house more room and more character, preferably in a style which would perpetuate the Gothick tradition of Sir Francis Blake's eighteenth-century follies, but smaller and more light-hearted. 'Instead of racking his memory box for the name of a twentieth-century architect specializing in the design of Gothick houses, he offered to have a go himself.' Sir Michael was enthusiastic. Such commissions had been the order of the day in the eighteenth century. If a dramatist could design a palace like Castle Howard, why should not a painter design a Gothick country house in twentieth-century Northumberland? So Felix Kelly went ahead and after preparing the plans and elevations was lucky to find a local builder, Peter Young of Coldstream, who 'was an enthusiast, a craftsman of the highest order

191

and ready to go'.

Then a snag occurred—planning permission. The local council turned out to be strongly prejudiced against Gothick and resisted the plan at every stage. To them, Gothick was a mausolean style more suitable for 'the dark nether world' than a house in an 'area of outstanding natural beauty'. The battle raged on, and it was only after a change in membership that a cautious permission was given for one façade to be 'gothicked' in order to see what the result would be like. So Sir Michael, Felix Kelly and Peter Young went ahead in 1976 and added battlements, quatrefoils, Gothick glazing bars, a third bay window and two trellis porches and flanking conservatory. On seeing the result the council finally gave permission for the rest to go ahead. A large castellated porch with four pointed windows and a front door with a Gothick fanlight was added to the entrance front. Overall the house was doubled in size. Sir Michael's own chief contribution to the design was the retention and duplication of the bow windows, which he considered were very important for catching the sun in a northern landscape. The planning and fitting of the kitchen were Lady Blake's contribution to the effort.[9]

The work at Tillmouth Park has encouraged other owners to employ Felix Kelly to create Gothick houses or pavilions on their estates. At Henbury Hall in Cheshire, for instance, Sebastian de Ferranti has employed him to remodel a former keeper's cottage as a Gothick *trianon* called 'The Cave', which is a smaller version of Tillmouth. The Henbury estate is in pretty, undulating country near the foothills of the Peak District and was bought by Sebastian de Ferranti's father in the 1950s. The Victorianized house, formerly the seat of the Liverpool shipowners, the Brocklehursts, was demolished in 1957, except for the foundations and cellars. It has long been Sebastian de Ferranti's intention to replace it with a new house on the same site, a prominent, elevated position clearly visible from all sides in the park. The nature of the site suggested a free-standing house with four show-fronts which would look equally good from all sides and would also have a strong silhouette. This line of thought led directly to Palladio's Villa Capra (or Rotonda) near Vicenza, several versions of which had been built in England in the eighteenth century, most notably Chiswick, Mereworth, Nuthall, and Foots Cray. Why not erect another at Henbury? A twentieth-century version of the Rotonda became Mr de Ferranti's dream, and he asked Felix Kelly to paint a design showing it, looking 'as if Palladio had been reinterpreted by Vanbrugh'.

A sophisticated Classical composition such as Henbury, however, will depend heavily on its detailed design, unlike the more light-hearted Gothick, part of the charm of which is its very lack of accuracy. For a couple of years Mr de Ferranti and Felix Kelly have been looking for an architect capable of interpreting the Henbury Rotonda as a full-blooded Classical design. That

192

Felix Kelly, Henbury Hall, Cheshire.

takes the story beyond the realms of the amateur and for the result the reader must now turn to the postscript.

NOTES

1 James Lees-Milne, *Caves of Ice* (1983), p. 43, 29 April 1946.
2 *Country Life*, 4 and 11 August 1950.
3 Desmond Guinness and William Ryan, *Irish Houses and Castles* (1971); Christie's Sale Catalogue, September 1983, pp. 139–43.
4 *Country Life*, 29 December 1950, p. 2218, illustrates Hawksmoor's designs for Ockham. The reconstruction of Ockham was halted by Mr Fenston's death. His widow lives in the restored stables and hopes one day to finish the house.
5 *Country Life*, 25 January and 1 and 8 February 1973; ex info Mr Roger Hesketh.
6 Ex info the Lord O'Neill; Mark Bence Jones, *Burke's Guide to Country Houses*, Volume I, Ireland (1978) p. 257.
7 John Newman, *The Buildings of England: North-East and East Kent* (1969) p. 317; Ex info Mr Robin Leigh-Pemberton.
8 Edward Croft-Murray, *Decorative Painting in England 1537–1837*, II (1970) pp. 182–3; Ex info Mr Louis Osman.
9 *House and Garden*, February 1979, p. 59.

Top: Newfield, Yorkshire, the entrance front.

Bottom: Shane's Castle, County Antrim. Built in 1958 to the design of Lord O'Neill and Arthur Drury.

POSTSCRIPT

Work on the new Henbury Hall started on site in the spring of 1984 and it is likely that the house, when completed, will be among the most distinguished built since the war. The detailed working drawings and scale model have taken a year to prepare. Julian Bicknell was appointed as architect in April 1983 to implement the idea for a new Palladian Rotonda conceived in the first place by Sebastian de Ferranti and Felix Kelly. It is to be an ideal house, four-square and perfect, on an eminence in the centre of the eighteenth-century park at Henbury. The design was evolved as a response to the landscape, and the park is to be improved as part of the overall concept; new vistas will be created, the lake dredged and extra planting added to enhance the general effect. The main approach will be from the north and through the park, sweeping round to the west, south and east of the building before debouching in front of the north portico, so as to give the visitor distant and close-up views of all four sides of the new house before he arrives.

Julian Bicknell was appointed on the strength of the three rooms which he has designed at Castle Howard for George Howard (now Lord Howard of Henderskelfe). He studied under Sir Leslie Martin at Cambridge, and until he received the commission at Castle Howard, had not worked with Classical detail. It was while preparing the designs for the new library, picture cabinet and garden hall (with paintings by Felix Kelly) for George Howard that he first studied the Classical vocabulary; this involved two things, learning the language and learning how to use it. At Castle Howard, the key to the design was the extension of the rigorous proportional system established in the original interiors by Vanbrugh and Hawksmoor. The new Order in the garden hall has a module two thirds that of the Order in the Great Hall and that in the library one third of the major scale. Working with Vanbrugh was the ideal introduction to the Henbury rotonda, for the intention there is to produce a version of the Palladian villa, such as Vanbrugh himself might have designed in the decade of the Temple of the Four Winds at Castle Howard.

While working on Henbury, both the architect and the client have made a careful study of the various eighteenth-century English versions of the Villa Rotonda: Chiswick, Mereworth and Foots Cray. Henbury will be smaller than its predecessors, the central domed hall being the same size as the interior of the temple at Castle Howard. The house will be a cube of fifty feet measured to the drum of the dome, the eaves of the roof being forty feet above ground.

194

These proportions and the scale of the cube were decided by the client's requirements. The house will have a rusticated plinth with four Ionic porticoes, one on each front; that on the south only will have a flight of steps down from the *piano nobile*, the others being simply belvederes.

The structure will be of load-bearing brick faced with stone, partly French limestone and partly reconstituted stone. Stucco is not a practical proposition in the wet windy climate of north-west England. An obelisk is being built in the park to display three different samples of stone before a final choice is made. The roof will be covered with traditional stone Macclesfield flags, the only touch of local vernacular in the design. The dome will be clad in lead over a steel structure. The chimneys will be concealed round the base of the drum of the dome. The lantern on top of the dome is to have a miniature Corinthian Order, a light-hearted reference to the traditional hierarchy of the Orders through the house with Ionic on the *piano nobile* and Doric in the ground-floor hall. The section of the dome is inspired by ovoid domes of Baroque Rome rather than Palladio's perfect hemispheres, and this will give it a more dramatic silhouette, while the pattern of the leadwork is copied from the dome at Mereworth.

The main entrance will be in the plinth of the north portico through a heavily quoined and pedimented doorway. The ground-floor hall will have the kitchen on the east, a games room on the west and a staff flat at the south end. The main staircase in the north-west angle will be oval and cantilevered, the plotting of the oval being based on the system best known through the work of Borromini. The centre of the house on the *piano nobile* is a tripartite hall running from north to south, the ends having oval groin vaults and the centre rising fifty feet into the dome. This hall is flanked to the north by the drawing-room and dining-room, both eighteen feet high, with a serving room (reached from the ground floor by separate food and passenger lifts), and the library and the morning-room to the south. The top floor comprises two principal apartments each made up of a bedroom, dressing-room and bathroom for Mr and Mrs de Ferranti. There will also be four guest bedrooms and bathrooms. The central hall on the main floor, the interior of the dome and the openings to the main staircase will all contribute to an exciting spatial progression through the house. When completed the interior should be as impressive as the exterior silhouette when first glimpsed through the woods and across the lake of the park.

In many ways the design of Henbury marks the culmination of the architectural trends studied in this book, combining as it does the romantic vision of the amateurs, inspired by the English eighteenth century, and the recent scholarly revival of Palladianism as the style best suited to the design of a 'gentleman's house' in the late twentieth century. The owner had originally considered building in the Modern style and in the 1960s had approached Yamasaki and other modern architects in the United States with an eye to commissioning a

Modern house. He also looked over most of the world for a Modern house that would provide a suitable model for Henbury, but found nothing which gave him the particular excitement he derived from the villas of Palladio. This, combined with the visual demands of the English park setting, more or less dictated a Classical house and has led to Felix Kelly and Julian Bicknell. Most builders of country houses since the war have reached a similar conclusion for similar reasons. A country house is a traditional architectural form intended to embody a traditional way of life, and it is not surprising therefore that many people have been happiest expressing it in traditional architectural language. This has helped to perpetuate the Romantic Classical aesthetic evolved between the wars by Neo-Georgian architects, Romantic painters like Rex Whistler and the pioneer interior decorators.

Post-war country houses demonstrate that independent private patronage can still play a stimulating role in architectural development. This is partly a matter of attitude, and only partly of money. Some of the houses in this book have been built by rich men. Many, however, have been built by people who, by American or Middle Eastern standards, are not especially rich but who nevertheless wished to perpetuate a tradition and to create something permanent. As the architect Quinlan Terry has put it, 'If you build a house it is a monument to this age, to what you think. And it goes on for your son and grandson.' If it had not been for the encouragement of George Howard and Sebastian de Ferranti, for instance, Julian Bicknell might never have extended his architectural vocabulary to embrace Classicism, and the new rooms at Castle Howard or the Henbury rotonda would not even have reached the drawing board. As this book shows, new country houses have been instrumental since the Second World War in supporting a number of interesting specialist architectural practices in England, Scotland and Ireland. Thanks to such commitment and enterprise the country house has been kept going as a living tradition despite an unsympathetic political and architectural climate, and has been prevented from degenerating entirely into a dead museum world.

I hope it will be agreed that there have been enough houses built since 1945 to be taken seriously as a social and architectural phenomenon. All the pointers indicate that the building of country houses will continue. Indeed, the current ethos in Britain would seem to be far more conducive to this type of architectural enterprise than it has been in recent years. It is also likely that the Classical style will remain the most appropriate and popular one for such houses. In the hands of a stylish architect and confident client, it can still produce admirable buildings as has been so triumphantly demonstrated by the designs for Henbury.

GAZETTEER

Abbey House, Audley End, Essex
For the Honourable Robin Neville
Large additions 1967–8
By Philip Jebb; interior decoration by Dudley
  Poplack

Though Audley End House itself passed to
the nation after the war and is now kept by
the Department of the Environment, the
estate still belongs to the Neville family, and
Abbey House was done up for them so that
they could continue to live there.

Abbots Ripton Hall, Huntingdonshire
For the 3rd Lord De Ramsey
Alterations to house, garden pavilions and
  swimming pool 1960s/70s
By Peter Foster, architect; Humphrey
  Waterfield, gardener

Replaces Ramsey Abbey as the family seat.
Lord De Ramsey has made very large and
ambitious new gardens with several temples
and follies, a Gothick rondel, enclosed
swimming pool, thatched tennis pavilion,
several trelliswork features, and a five-and-
a-half-acre lake.
(*Country Life*, 21 March 1974)

Abbotsworthy House, Hampshire
For Esmond Baring
Reconstruction 1950
By Claud Phillimore

The old house was a gabled, red-brick,
Victorian-Tudor affair. Claud Phillimore
demolished the billiard-room wing and
Georgianized the rest, adding segmental
bows, stucco and trelliswork. Inside he
formed an oval library.
(RIBAD: RAN 47/B/5)

Abercairney, Crieff, Perthshire
For Major J. Drummond-Moray
New house *circa* 1960
By Claud Phillimore

A large Neo-Georgian house with segmental
bow windows and single-storeyed recessed

porticoes. It replaced Richard Dickson's
superb Gothic abbey but is more or less the
same size as its predecessor. The old house
was demolished as much because it was
Gothic as because it was too big. If the
Victorian tower by Thornton Shiells had
been removed it would have been perfectly
manageable.
(RIBAD: RAN 47)

Abergeldie, Aberdeenshire
For John Gordon
Restoration of tower house 1963
By John Lamb (of Barnett, Mitchell and
  Sons)

Mr Gordon, a descendant of the original
owners, inherited Abergeldie from a cousin
in 1963 and decided to live there. He
removed an eighteenth/nineteenth-century
wing and reinstated the original tower with
great care. The restored external harling is
painted a mellow terracotta colour.
(*Country Life*, 21 February 1974)

Aboyne Castle, Aberdeenshire
For the Earl of Aboyne
Restoration of tower house 1982
By Robert Hurd and Partners

Lord Aboyne is the eldest son of the 12th
Marquess of Huntly and has restored
Aboyne so that he can live on the family
estate. Massive Victorian extensions were
demolished, leaving the sixteenth/
seventeenth-century tower. Its interior was
virtually rebuilt and the exterior harled in
the traditional manner. Much of the work
was done by 'direct estate labour' and it
received an RIBA award in 1983 as an
example of 'rehabilitation work'. The jury
remarked, 'It has conjured a phoenix out of
a white elephant with the aplomb of a Celtic
William Burgess.' The interior decoration is
by Michael Player 'the most talented pupil of
John Fowler'. *See page 22.*

Moorish garden feature by Peter Foster at
Abbots Ripton Hall, Huntingdonshire

House of Aldie, Kinross-shire
For the Hope-Dickson family
Tower house restored from ruins 1950s
By Ian G. Lindsay

Really an exemplary restoration rather than
a new or reconstructed house, but important
in the history of the post-war Scottish
country house as the earliest example of the
reinstatement of an old tower as a family
house. Mr. Hope-Dickson bought the
property in 1948 and the work proceeded by
stages over a number of years. The exterior
harling was restored and painted white and
a new entrance formed by roofing over a
small court. The interior was simply
reinstated with plain timbered ceilings
except where original decorative plasterwork
had survived.
(Sheila Forman, *Scottish Houses and Castles*
(1967) pp. 44–6)

Anglesey Abbey, Cambridgeshire
For the 1st Lord Fairhaven
Picture gallery wing 1955–6
By Sir Albert Richardson, PRA

The two-storeyed picture galleries are
reached by a bridge over the back drive. The
style is vaguely Tudor to blend with the rest
of the Abbey. The builder was Percy
Golding. *See page 65.*
(Robin Fedden, *Anglesey Abbey*—National
Trust Guidebook 1968)

Angmering Park, Sussex
For the 14th Baroness Herries
New house 1982
By William Bertram of Bath

Large house of flint with Gothick touches, a
prominent hipped roof and a central
semicircular bow window. Lady Herries sold
Everingham in Yorkshire (qv), bought a
3000-acre portion of the Arundel estate from
the family trustees and built a new house on
it because she wished to live in the south
near her childhood home at Arundel Castle.

Arderne Hall, Cheshire
New house *circa* 1975
By David Brock of Liverpool

Arderne Hall was Victorian Gothic and the
capital seat of the Utkinton estates held by
the Ardernes since time immemorial. It was
demolished in 1958 and the land sold. The
present house was built for a new owner on
the old site and sold again in 1983. It is
Modern, comprising two interlocked
cyclinders with flat roofs. The facing
material is black and red Jacobean brick.
Most of the rooms are circular with exposed
brick walls and timber ceilings. The living-
room has a diameter of 29'4", the drawing-
room 28' and the dining-room 22'5".

Ardwell, Wigtownshire
Restored and refronted *circa* 1955.
By Anthony Wheeler

The Victorian house, by Maitland Wardrop,
was demolished and the older house (which
had become the kitchen wing) was
remodelled and refronted to form a new
house.

Arundel Park, Sussex
For the 16th Duke of Norfolk
New house 1958–62
By Claud Phillimore

Intended as a dower house in the park and used in conjunction with the castle. Planned as a tripartite 'Palladian villa' in miniature. To Claud Phillimore goes the credit for reviving the Palladian plan subsequently much used by other architects including Raymond Erith and Quinlan Terry.
See page 127.
(RIBAD: RAN 47/H/1–22;
Times 11 November 1959;
Connoisseur, June 1963 pp. 72–83)

Ashden House, Lympne, Kent
For Lord Sainsbury
New house 1964
By Sir Hugh Casson

Single-storeyed modern house in the Modern style but paying tribute to Kentish vernacular with white boarded walls, monopitch roof, black eaves and a circular brick 'oast house' bathroom at one end. Splendid views over Romney Marsh. Later additions to the original concept comprised a conservatory, nursery, guest bedrooms and a swimming pool pavilion. *See page 150*
(Casson and Conder Partnership Office Records;
(*House and Garden*, December 1966)

Ashford Water, Fordingbridge, Hampshire
For Mr and Mrs Newall
New house 1961
By Donald Insall and Partners

Mrs Newall was American and the house has an American Colonial feel. Single-storeyed and thirteen bays wide; 3–2–3–2–3. Porticoes on both fronts of slim Tuscan columns with wooden-board pediments. A slated roof and painted brickwork. Agreeably informal.
(Donald Insall and Partners Office Records)

Aske Hall, Yorkshire (NR)
For the 3rd Marquess of Zetland
Truncation and remodelling 1961–3
By Claud Phillimore (in association with Chippindale and Edmondson)

Aske had developed round a fifteen-century pele tower into a large pile of eighteenth- and nineteenth-century buildings with an incoherent plan. Claud Phillimore

demolished the Victorian ballroom, dining-room and a large area of redundant service quarters at the back of the house, reduced the projecting wings on the entrance front and entirely refaced the front of the house in stone. A new roof was built with a steel structure. The interior was rationalized, the former great hall subdivided to form a new entrance hall and library. The old library became the dining-room. Chimneypieces and other fittings were introduced from elsewhere including the splendid marble one in the new hall from Clumber.
(RIBAD: RAN 47/J/1,2,3;
Apollo, September 1967, pp. 170–3)

Aswarby Park, Sleaford, Lincolnshire
For Nicholas Playne

Conversion of stable block of the demolished seat of the Whichcotes to form a new house.

Aughentaire, Fivemiletown, County Tyrone.
For Captain John Hamilton-Stubber
New house 1956–7
By Claud Phillimore

It replaces a Victorian Italianate house demolished in 1954. Mrs Hamilton-Stubber is a Breitmeyer and this house is similar to her brother's house, Bartlow Park, in Cambridgeshire. It is Neo-Regency with bow windows, etc. Captain Hamilton-Stubber is Lord-Lieutenant of County Tyrone.
(RIBAD: RAN/47;
Mark Bence-Jones, *Burke's Guide to Country Houses, Volume I, Ireland* (1978) p. 15)

Badgewood, Henley-on-Thames,
Oxfordshire
For Mr A. A. Vlasto (sold 1950 to W. H. McAlpine)
New house 1941–50
By C. Birdwood Willcocks

The old house, dating from the eighteenth and nineteenth centuries, was partly demolished in 1939 and the large new Neo-Georgian house begun in July that year. It was held up by the war but the shell was finished by January 1941 and taken over by the army to accommodate troops. The interior was finished and the remains of the

old house demolished in 1950. The outside is of red brick with sashed windows, a pair of canted bays, and doorways with pediments of stone. The interior contains features reused from the old house, including chimneypieces and the staircase balustrade. The accommodation includes a drawing-room, library, dining-room, servants' hall, housekeeper's room, eleven bedrooms and seven bathrooms.
(*Builder*, 21 March 1952 pp. 441–4)

The Cottage, Badminton, Gloucestershire
For David and Lady Caroline Somerset (now
  11th Duke and Duchess of Beaufort)
Additions and remodelling 1960s
By Sutton, Griffin and Morgan, architects;
  Colefax and Fowler, decorators; new
  garden designed by Russell Page

A dower house developed out of a cottage in the village. The additions include a large library with French windows overlooking the garden. The exterior is plastered and painted a mellow apricot colour. Attractive interiors.

The Cottage, Badminton, Gloucestershire

Balrath Burry, County Meath
For the Nicholson family
New centre block 1942

The eighteenth-century house was damaged while in use as barracks in 1939–42. The centre block was demolished in 1942 and rebuilt in American Colonial style with a colonnaded verandah along the ground floor of the garden front and a new *porte cochère* on the entrance side made of columns brought from Rosmead. The principal rooms are arranged on either side of a large hall with a two-branched staircase.
(Mark Bence-Jones, *Burke's Guide to Country Houses, Volume I, Ireland* (1978) p. 30.)

Barnwell Manor, Northamptonshire
For HRH the Duke of Gloucester
New drawing-room *circa* 1950
By Sir Albert Richardson, PRA

Designed to incorporate a series of large eighteenth-century paintings of the 3rd Duke of Rutland hunting.

Baro House, Gifford, East Lothian
For H. J. Younger
New house. Begun 1939, completed 1955
By Reggie Fairlie (completed after his death
  by Charles Gray)

Reggie Fairlie was Lorimer's chief pupil and Baro is his last house. It is harled with a 'butterfly plan' and is an interesting late example of the early-twentieth-century Scots vernacular revival. The octagonal drawing-room repeats that at Kilmany in Fife, designed by Fairlie between the wars.
(Colin McWilliam, *Lothian* (1978), p. 210)

Bartlow Park, Cambridgeshire
For Brigadier A. W. Breitmeyer
New house 1963–4
By Claud Phillimore

The estate was bought by Brigadier Breitmeyer from Lord De Ramsey after the old house had been demolished. The new one was built on a different, more secluded site further from the village. It comprises a centre block with two flanking wings, one being a staff cottage and the other having the garages and estate office. The main block contains the drawing-room, library,

dining-room, kitchen, study, playroom and a dramatic entrance hall with screens of columns. Upstairs there are six bedrooms, two dressing-rooms, four bathrooms and a linen room. The house is built of red brick with Claud Phillimore's usual type of low pitched roof, casement windows and Neo-Regency detail. There is a semicircular bow in the centre of the park front and a Doric portico *in antis* on the entrance front.
(RIBAD: 47/L4–6)

Basing House, Privett, Hampshire
For James Langmead
New house 1968–70
By Claud Phillimore

Not to be confused with Basing House, Basingstoke. At Privett the old house was demolished and the new house built on the site. It has an interesting plan with two flanking wings at an angle on the entrance front, one containing the kitchen, the other the estate office. The main block has a Tuscan portico *in antis* and three segmental bows on the garden sides. Casement windows. Low-pitched hipped roof.
(RIBAD: RAN 48/B/4 −8)

Bayham Manor, Kent
For the 5th Marquess Camden
New house *circa* 1973
By Kenneth Bemlow of Clutton's

Red brick. Neo-Georgian.

Baro House, Gifford, East Lothian

Beamsley Hall, Bolton Abbey, Yorkshire
(WR)
For the Marquess of Hartington
Extensions and remodelling 1980–3
By Sir Martyn Beckett.

Beamsley has a seventeenth-century core with additions of the eighteenth and twentieth centuries. Sir Martyn Beckett has added a large billiard room, refenestrated the drawing-room and built new garages, etc. He has also introduced new heating and services.
(Sir Martyn Beckett office files)

Belsay House (alias Swanstead),
Northumberland
For Sir Stephen Middleton, Bt
New house 1946–7
By Claud Phillimore

The first proposal at Belsay in 1946, when the Grecian house was given up, was to build a new house on to the old castle, making it an L-shaped Georgian-Jacobean building with eleven bedrooms and five bathrooms. Building licences put an end to this and instead an old farm on the edge of the park was reconstructed as a new house. It was to have a plain five-bay centre with a hipped roof and two little flanking pavilions, all of stone. In some of the drawings the latter have a Gothick air. One was to be for staff and the other for guests with three spare bedrooms and two bathrooms. The main block contained the dining-room, library, drawing-room and hall. The scale increased while work was in progress which led to trouble over building licences. *See pages 16, 125.* Sir Stephen subsequently bought Bitchfield, an old pele tower nearby and Swanstead is now occupied by Mr Long, the heir to the Belsay estate.
(RIBAD:RAN 47/A/6 1–15)

Bessellsleigh, Berkshire
For the Lenthall family
New house *circa* 1960

The Lenthalls have been lords of the manor of Bessellsleigh for centuries. The new house in Cotswold Georgian style replaces a Victorian house, a quarter of a mile away, which has been sold to a preparatory school.

Biddick Hall, County Durham
For the 6th Earl of Durham
Neo-Georgian wing at back 1954–5
Internal alterations
By E. M. Lawson and Partners, and
    Trenwith Wills and Wills

Dining-room enlarged and decorated; fitted
china cabinets in side walls with dog baskets
underneath designed by Trenwith Wills. The
Venetian window on staircase of 1960 is also
by Trenwith Wills. From 1837 to 1932
Biddick was the agent's house. In 1932 the
Lambtons moved there from Lambton
Castle, which was part demolished in that
year, and it is now their main seat on the
estate. They have made elaborate formal
gardens round the house. There are
chinoiserie bee-hives designed by Lord
Lambton.
(*Country Life*, 28 April and 10 September
1966)

Birkhall, Aberdeenshire
For HM Queen Elizabeth, the Queen Mother
Large new wing *circa* 1955
By A. Graham Henderson (of Keppie,
    Henderson of Glasgow); Ian G. Lindsay
    (consultant)

Old house of two storeys and basement
dated 1715. New wing has bow front. Oliver
Hill hoped for the job and prepared sketches
but did not get it. Ian Lindsay was
consulted instead, but the extent of his
advice is not clear. Work actually done by
A. Graham Henderson of Keppie,
Henderson of Glasgow.

Blackhall, County Kildare
For Sir Harold Wernher, Bt and the 3rd
    Viscount Astor
New house *circa* 1950
By Philip Tilden

Built of concrete. The accommodation
included nine bedrooms. (Philip Tilden, *True
Remembrances* (1954) pp. 168–71)

Blackheath, Aldeburgh, Suffolk
For Major C. J. Vernon Wentworth
Victorian mansion Georgianized 1958–9
By Raymond Erith

The Victorian Jacobethan chimneys were
kept; they make the house look sixteenth-
century with an eighteenth-century front
added. The bay windows were shaved off,
reducing the size of the rooms. A very
lavish job, beautifully executed.
(Norman Scarfe, *Shell Guide to Suffolk*)

Bosahan, Helston, Cornwall
For the Graham-Vivian family
New house

On the site of demolished Victorian house.

Bourne Wood, Hampshire
For Colonel Kingslake Tower
New house 1956
By A. S. G. Butler

A late specimen of the Arts and Crafts
Movement on a green field site. The low
swept roof is covered with handmade tiles,
the walls faced in handmade bricks; all
meant to look 'rather 1906'. *See page 61.*
(*Country Life,* 11 December 1958)

Bowood, Wiltshire
For the 8th Marquess of Lansdowne
Demolition of Big House and conversion of
    the two courts into a new house 1954–73
By Philip Tilden, F. Sortaine Samuels, Sir
    Martyn Beckett, and Harry Graham

Bowood is the grandest stable conversion in
England. Chimneypieces and other fittings
were used from the Big House. *See page 19.*
(*Country Life,* 8 June 1972)

Brahan, Ross and Cromarty
For Captain A. A. Matheson.
Stables converted to house

A substantial job, well executed.

Bridgham Manor, Thetford, Norfolk
For the Honourable Arthur Baillie
Part demolition and rebuilding 1962–4
By Trenwith Wills and Wills

Some of the front wall of the old house was
retained but the house was otherwise rebuilt
and enlarged. The whole of the interior is
new including the semicircular staircase with
twisted balusters and mahogany handrail.
(Office records in the possession of Mrs
Dyer)

Broadleaze, Boyton, Wiltshire
For Raymond Wheatley-Hubbard
New house *circa* 1963
By Robert Bostock of Bostock and Wilkins

A green field site. Neo-Georgian, of brick
with stone plinth. Roof of clay tiles and
metal sashes in the windows. Also two
cottages, new drive, etc.

Broad House, Wroxham, Norfolk
For Edmund de Trafford
Alterations and additions 1963–4
By Trenwith Wills and Wills

(Office records in the possession of Mrs
Dyer)

Broad Oak, Carmarthen
For Viscount Emlyn (now the 7th Earl
   Cawdor)
New house 1960
By Donald Insall and Partners

Handmade red brick with a hipped Welsh
slate roof and dormers. Good lead
downpipes. The main façades of seven bays
with tall sash windows. The garden front
has a single-storey bow in the centre with
attached Tuscan columns, and the entrance
front a semicircular porch with slim Tuscan
columns. Broad Oak replaced Stackpole
Court, which has been demolished.
(Donald Insall and Partners Office Records)

Brockenhurst Park, Hampshire
For the Honourable Denis and Mrs Berry
New house 1965
By Harry Graham

Built on the site of an eighteenth/nineteenth-
century house which has been demolished.
The old garden remains with a formal canal
on the central axis. The house is of brown
brick with a shallow copper roof; a
hexagonal centre and raking flanking wings;
the first floor windows have segmental
heads. The style is traditional but without
overtly historical features. Interesting
geometrical plan. Martyn Beckett had been
commissioned to design a new house in
1960 and sent to America with Mrs Berry to
study Modern American architecture,
including Frank Lloyd Wright's Falling
Water. He prepared detailed drawings
before Mr Berry cancelled the project.
(*Country Life*, 31 August 1967)

Bruern Abbey, Oxfordshire
For the Honourable Michael Astor
Library, etc. *circa* 1956
New cottages and alterations 1966; new
   façade 1973–4
By Sir Martyn Beckett; interior decoration by
   John Fowler

Sir Martyn remodelled Bruern in three
phases. *See page 120.*
(Sir Martyn Beckett office files)

Brockenhurst Park, Hampshire

Buckhurst Park, Ascot, Berkshire
For Peter Palumbo
Reconstruction of an old house 1963
By Claud Phillimore

This scheme for remodelling the old house at Buckhurst was based on a previous proposal by D. Armstrong-Smith. Claud Phillimore's design has better proportions, a hipped roof and simpler details. An old colonnade was reused and sash windows introduced. Inside, the rooms were lavishly redecorated, a Chinese Chippendale staircase balustrade added and beautiful joinery with fretted and Greek key-pattern architraves installed in all the main rooms.
(RIBAD: 47/K/3–7)

Buckminster Park, Leicestershire
For Major Tollemache
New house 1965–6
By Trenwith Wills and Wills

A Neo-Georgian red brick house with a hipped roof and stone Tuscan porch. One of Trenwith Wills's best post-war jobs. It replaces a late-eighteenth-century house of the Tollemaches, formerly Earls of Dysart. Buckminster was retained as the family seat, and this new house built after Ham House at Twickenham, the other Tollemache house, was given to the National Trust.
See page 79.
(Office records in the possession of Mrs Dyer)

Buxted Place, Sussex
For Basil Ionides
Reconstruction and new interior 1940–7
By Basil Ionides

Originally a three-storeyed, early-Georgian house, Buxted was gutted by fire in 1940. The owner, Mr Basil Ionides, reconstructed it to his own design, removing the top storey, making a new entrance at the west end, with a new forecourt and entrance lodges. The interior had to be reconstructed entirely and is a museum of brought-in fittings, mainly from eighteenth-century London buildings demolished in the 1930s.
See page 175.
(*Country Life,* 4 and 11 August 1950; James Lees-Milne, *Caves of Ice,* 1983, p. 43)

Callernich, North Uist
For the 5th Earl Granville
Large circular house 1962
By Sir Martyn Beckett

On the model of Scottish 'round squares', influenced directly by that at Gordonstoun. It is circular with concrete two-foot-thick battered walls. Harled and whitewashed. Crow-stepped gables over central features. Double-glazed windows with teak frames. Fourteen bedrooms, eight bathrooms all on one floor. The site is only fifty yards from the Atlantic. *See page 120.*
(Sir Martyn Beckett office records)

Candacraig, Aberdeenshire
For A. P. F. Wallace
New house improvised out of ruins after a
    fire 1952
By A. G. R. Mackenzie (A. Marshall
    Mackenzie and Sons)

Old Neo-Tudor house by the Smiths of Aberdeen (cf. Balmoral) was burnt out and reconstituted as virtually a new house.

Capel Manor, Horsmonden, Kent
For John Howard, MP
New house 1970
By Michael Manser Associates

A Victorian house designed by Thomas Henry Wyatt was demolished in the 1950s, leaving only the foundations, an arcaded terrace with balustrades, and the shell of the conservatory. The new house is Modern and has a steel frame on a concrete podium clad in dark blue quarry tiles. The windows have bronze-tinted glass in aluminium frames. The underside of the steel roof is clad in pine boarding and the internal walls are of dark brown brick. The floors are blue quarry tiles. The shell of the conservatory encloses a swimming pool. Mr Howard was PPS to Edward Heath. *See pages 25, 142.*
(Richard Einzig, *Classic Modern Houses in Europe,* 1981, pp. 94–7; June Park, *Houses for Today,* 1971)

Castle Gyrn, Wales
New house 1977
Designed for himself by John Taylor (of
    Chapman Taylor, Architects)

Built of stone with a picturesquely asymmetrical layout. The decorative keystones were carved by Nicholas Wood. *See page 21.*

Caunton Manor, Nottinghamshire
For Major Hole
Substantial remodelling *circa* 1960
By Percy Houfton

The house is basically a two-storeyed four-bay early-eighteenth-century house extended in 1902. The new work consists of a complete Neo-Georgianizing with new windows, doorcases, modillion cornices, huge stone entrance porch; garden front with central five bays pedimented and two plain bays on either side.
(*Buildings of England, Nottinghamshire* (2nd ed 1979) p. 95)

Claughton Hall, Garstang, Lancashire
For Michael Fitzherbert-Brockholes JP
New house 1956
By Fulke Fitzherbert-Brockholes

The estate has passed down by descent since the Middle Ages. The previous house dating from 1816 was demolished and the present house built in 1956. It is plain Neo-Georgian, rendered, with a hipped roof of slate. The interior contains marble chimneypieces and other fittings from the old house. Mr Fitzherbert-Brockholes is Vice Lord-Lieutenant of Lancashire, a county councillor and was chairman of the education committee from 1977–81. The architect is the owner's brother.

Clock House, Sawrey, Lancashire
For Peter Naylor
Stables converted to a new house 1965
By Gordon Thompson of the Liverpool
  School of Architecture

The Victorian house, Bryerswood, by R. Knill Freeman, has been demolished. The new house is a successful conversion and has a grand entrance hall and drawing-room connected by double doors so that both can be used for formal entertaining. Mr Naylor was for a time chairman of Cumbria County Council.

Clovelly Court, Devon
For the Honourable Mrs Asquith
Reinstatement after fire damage 1952–7
By Claud Phillimore

The old house had an early Georgian block (1740 by Zachary Hamlyn) which was burnt in 1944. Claud Phillimore designed a new house, incorporating the remains of the old wing which is three storeys high with corner turrets. The ambitious preliminary proposals had to be curtailed because of building licences, and as executed the work is little more than a modest patch job.
(RIBAD: RAN 47/B/1$^{1-34}$)

Combermere Abbey, Cheshire
For Viscountess Garnock
Unexecuted scheme 1971
By Raymond Erith and Quinlan Terry

Combermere is a sixteenth-century house refaced in 1795. It was bought from the Cottons *circa* 1920 by the Crossleys and has descended to the present owner. Lady Garnock considered a scheme for rebuilding the house in the Gothick style reusing features from the old house but in the event this was not carried out and a different scheme of reconstruction was done *circa* 1975 by A. N. Brown of A. H. Brotherton and Partners of Chester.

Coniston Cold Hall, Yorkshire (WR)
For Michael Bannister
New house 1972
By Neville MacKay

Successful Neo-Georgian of stone. On the site of a demolished nineteenth-century house by the Websters of Kendal and reusing architraves, pediment and chimneystacks from the old house. Landscaping by Lanning Roper, making the most of the beautiful site overlooking a lake.

Connel, Argyllshire
For the Captain of Dunstaffnage
New house
By Leslie Grahame MacDougall

In the Scottish traditional style with harling and gables. Single-storeyed with a semi-elliptical plan.
(SNMR: Leslie Graham MacDougall's drawings)

Coniston Cold Hall, Yorkshire

Cranmer Hall Norfolk
Reconstruction 1955

A Victorianized house of 1721 was
substantially remodelled in 1955, including
the removal of the top floor and a Victorian
porch. Small-paned sashes were restored to
the windows and a new pedimented
doorcase installed. Sir Lawrence Jones, a
former owner, was the author of the
autobiographical trilogy: *Victorian Boyhood*,
Edwardian Youth, *Georgian Afternoon* which
describe the estate.
(Peter Reid, *Burke's Guide to Country Houses*,
Volume III, East Anglia (1981) p. 101)

Crathes, Kincardineshire
For Mr Burnett of Leys
New house *circa* 1970
Completed by Schomberg Scott

The old house was given to the National
Trust for Scotland. The new house was built
on the estate after the family wing was
burnt down. A plain, harled Scottish
vernacular design with gables and stone
coping. Heraldic carving over the front door.
The interior contains a drawing-room,
sitting-room, dining-room, kitchen wing,
five bedrooms and two dressing-rooms.

Crathorne House, Yorkshire (NR)
For the 2nd Lord Crathorne
New house

A Modern bungalow built in the park before
moving out of the old house, a giant
Edwardian affair by Sir Ernest George and
Yates now a hotel.

Cubberley, Herefordshire
For the 4th Lord Greville
New house 1966–7
By Claud Phillimore; garden by Brenda
  Colvin

A large plain Neo-Regency L-shaped house
overlooking the River Wye. The principal
room is the drawing-room, 36′ × 24′ and
two storeys high with a coved ceiling and
dentil cornice.
(RIBAD: RAN 47/N/3–6
            48/A/1–3)

Culross Abbey House, Fife
For the 10th Earl of Elgin
Reconstruction 1952
By Robert Hurd

The old house dated from the seventeenth
century, was enlarged in 1830 and had been
empty since the beginning of this century.

206

The derelict shell was reconstructed to form a new house close in size to the 1610 original. The top storey was removed and the corner towers reduced to single-storeyed pavilions with bell roofs. A well-proportioned hipped roof was added to the house and covered with old slates. The interior is entirely new and plainly fitted up. The staircase has a wrought iron balustrade incorporating roses and tulips inspired by the secondary staircase at Caroline Park in Edinburgh. The south front has a large central drawing-room flanked by the dining-room and library. On the north front the hall has the kitchen to the west and the cloakrooms to the east. Upstairs there are six bedrooms two dressing-rooms, three bathrooms and a linen room.

The main rooms have handsome carved stone chimneypieces of 1670 reused from the old house.
(*Country Life*, 16 May 1957)

Dalton Hall, Westmorland
For Anthony Mason-Hornby
New house, forecourt, temple and garden
    layout 1968–71
By Clough Williams-Ellis

His last work. *See page 98.*
(RIBAD: RAN 32/F/16 [1–9])

Dewlish House, Dorset
For Anthony Boyden
Conservatory 1983–4
By John Stark and Partners of Dorchester

A large Neo-Regency conservatory with a glazed dome and canted central bay added to an old house to include swimming pools and a squash court.

The Doune, Rothiemurchus, Inverness-shire
For the Grants of Rothiemurchus
Restored from ruins and de-Victorianized
    1980–3
By Mary Tindall

The house figures in Elizabeth Grant's *Memoirs of a Highland Lady.*

Druminnor, Aberdeenshire
For the Honourable Margaret Forbes-Sempill
Restoration of tower house 1958
By Ian Lindsay

Large Victorian additions were demolished and the old tower house reinstated.
(*Country Life*, 14 February 1974)

Dunwood, Yorkshire
For Mr G. Wiles
Additions and reconstruction 1963
By Clough Williams-Ellis

Culross Abbey, Fife, before reconstruction

Culross Abbey after reconstruction

Clough produced a series of grandiose schemes for transforming a three-bay villa into a mansion with a portico, formal forecourt, avenue and gardens.

In the event the scheme was carried out in a modified way by somebody else. (RIBAD: RAN 32/F/22 [1-20])

Dupplin Castle, Forteviot, Perthshire
For the 2nd Lord Forteviot
Very large new house *circa* 1970.
By W. Schomberg Scott

This large new house replaced on the same site a house by William Burn which had been reduced in size and architectural interest after a fire in the 1930s, and was in a very unsatisfactory state with extensive stone decay. The new house is white-harled with stone trim and is an exercise in Schomberg Scott's characteristic version of Scottish-Georgian. *See page 117.*
(SNMR: Schomberg Scott collection)

East Carleton Manor, Norfolk
For Colin Chapman
New house 1964
By James Fletcher-Watson

The client (a well-known racing driver) was keen on East Coast America and wanted a house in the style of the South, hence the Colonial Georgian exterior with a tall portico and balcony. *See page 116.*

Eaton Hall, Cheshire
For the 5th Duke of Westminster
New house 1971–3
By John Dennys of Farrington, Dennys, Fisher; structural engineers, Ove Arap and Partners

Large Modern house on the site of the demolished Victorian house. *See page 136.*
(*Architectural Review*, May 1975, pp. 293–8)

Edenhall, Cumberland
For Airlie Holden-Hindley
Stable conversion *circa* 1950–76
By Michael Bottomley of Kendal

The old house by Smirke was demolished in 1934. The estate was bought after the war by the Hindleys, cotton manufacturers from Burnley, Lancashire, and they have converted the stables into a house over many years, beginning as little more than one room for shooting lunches till it has become the family's main house following the sale of Read Hall, Burnley. The handsome entrance hall incorporates eighteenth-century wooden niches.

Ellel Grange, Lancashire
For Miss Betty Sandeman
Stables converted into house 1979–80

On inheriting the 1000-acre estate from her brother in 1979 Miss Sandeman sold the Victorian house and its contents and converted the stables for her own use.

Elvetham Farm House, Winchfield,
   Hampshire
For Sir Richard Anstruther-Gough-
   Calthorpe, Bt
Remodelled former farmhouse *circa* 1966
By Robert Bostock of Bostock and Wilkins

The Victorian big house, by Teulon, is let to a school, and different members of the family live in up-graded smaller houses on the estate.

Everingham Park, Yorkshire (ER)
For the 16th Duke of Norfolk
Reconstruction 1960
By Francis Johnson

See page 104.
(*Country Life*, 15 and 22 February 1968)

Exbury, Hampshire
For Lionel de Rothschild
New house 1964–5
By Law and Dunbar-Nasmith

A Modern house planned round a music room to hold fifty people. *See page 145.*
(*Architectural Review*, April 1966 pp. 295–8)

Eythorpe Pavilion, Buckinghamshire
For Mrs de Rothschild
Reconstructed and enlarged 1950s

The new house on the Waddesdon estate to replace Waddesdon Manor, given to the National Trust. A small older house of 1883 by Devey has been extended to form a proper country house. Lavish interior with French fittings and works of art.

Findhorn, Nairn, Scotland
For Madame de Rochbeau
Two houses 1979
By Sir Martyn Beckett

Two houses at right angles facing the River
Findhorn, one for her, one for her children.
Professor James Dunbar-Nasmith had
previously provided sketch plans which
were not executed.
(Sir Martyn Beckett's office records)

Foliejon Park, Windsor, Berkshire
For I. A. F. Donelly
Alterations to an existing house 1952
By Claud Phillimore
(RIBAD: RAN 47/K/1 $^{1-5}$)

Fonthill House, Tisbury, Wiltshire
For the 1st Lord Margadale
New house 1972–4
By Trenwith Wills and Wills

A Neo-Georgian house on the site of Detmar
Blow's predecessor. *See page 77.*
(Office records in the possession of Mrs
Dyer)

Fosbury Manor, Wiltshire
For C. W. Garnett
Reconstruction 1957–8
By Claud Phillimore

A later billiard-room wing was demolished
and a symmetrical front formed with a
semicircular porch. The interior was
remodelled in Regency style to provide a
drawing-room, dining-room, library, garden
room, gun room, kitchen and staff sitting-
room. A separate staff cottage was built in
the back yard with two bedrooms.
(RIBAD: RAN 47/F/5)

Freechase, Warninglid, Sussex
For Sir Gawaine Baillie, Bt
New house 1971
By Tom Hancock in association with Tony
  Swannell

Sir Gawaine first approached Claud
Phillimore who designed a Neo-Georgian
house. In the event, the client changed his
mind and decided to build a Modern house.
The result is perhaps the finest post-war

country house in the Modern style. It is L-
shaped with a flat roof and square piers clad
in Portland stone, supporting a Portland
stone fascia, a 1930s Classic-Modern effect.
The external wall surfaces are clad in
aluminium panels and large windows have
tinted glass. The main rooms include a
study, two-storeyed drawing-room,
octagonal dining-room and a family sitting-
room. A feature of the house is the lavish
circulation space in two arms with splayed
walls. All the internal finishes including
joinery and plasterwork are of a high
standard. *See page 152.*
(RIBAD: RAN 48/B/7 $^{1-3}$;
Architectural Review, May 1977, p. 314)

Gannochy Lodge, Edzell, Angus
For the Fosters
New house 1973
By W. Schomberg Scott

Scotts Georgian style with flanking pavilions
and quadrant links. The main block with
gables. The estate has subsequently been
sold. *See page 119.*
(SNMR: Schomberg Scott collection)

The Garden House, Cerne Abbas, Dorset
New house 1983–4
By John Stark and Partners of Dorchester.

A Neo-Tudor house with gables, canted
bays and mullion windows with an
assymetrical plan. The main rooms are a
drawing-room, sitting-room, dining-room
and kitchen. There is also a sauna,
swimming pool and solarium.

Garmelow Manor, Eccleshall, Staffordshire
For Arnold Machin
Eighteenth-century-style landscape gardens
  with grotto, lake, etc. 1970s (old house not
  altered)
By Arnold Machin and son Francis.

The new garden layout at Garmelow
included a Gothic tower, lake, boat house,
bowling green, raised walk and a
subterranean top-lit grotto with statues,
approached by a spiral staircase. All these
were designed by Arnold Machin (a
sculptor) himself, helped by his son who
has developed a successful commercial line

in prefabricated Gothic conservatories. *See page 188.*

Garretstown House, County Meath
For Julian Jameson
New house 1976
By Austin Dunphy of O'Neill-Flanagan and
  Partners.

A single-storeyed U-shaped Classical house, the entrance front with two projecting wings and a pedimented centre, and the garden front with a top balustrade and two semicircular bows. The drawing-room has a screen of Corinthian columns, the dining-room is octagonal with a tented ceiling and a Chinese air, the library has recessed bookcases in the Regency manner.
(Mark Bence-Jones, *Burke's Guide to Country Houses, Volume I, Ireland* (1978), pp. 131–2)

Garrowby Hall, Yorkshire (ER)
For the 3rd Earl of Halifax
New house, lodge, temple, gardens 1980–3
By Francis Johnson and Partners

Among the finest recent country houses. *See page 109.*

Garth, Perthshire
For Mr Fry
Reconstruction of tower house 1962–3

This was one of the pioneer post-war efforts in the reroofing of ruined tower houses. It was an unarchaeological reconstruction with a galleried plan and the remains of the cap house cleared off for a flat roof.

Gask, Auchterarder, Perthshire
For Mrs Jardine Patterson
Substantial remodelling 1964
By Claud Phillimore

Top floor removed. Internal remodelling. An unfortunate mutilation of a good Classical house.
(RIBAD: RAN/47/J/6 [10–23])

Girsby Manor, Lincolnshire
For Mr Varley
Unexecuted design for a new house *circa* 1980
By Rick Mather

An interesting scheme for a Post-Modern house on the site of a demolished Edwardian mansion. Unfortunately abandoned. *See page 154.*
(*Architectural Review*, September 1981, pp. 161–2)

Glen Quaich Lodge, Perthshire
For the 7th Earl Cadogan
New shooting lodge 1970s
By George West

Simple Scottish vernacular with harling, rubble stonework and a low-pitched roof. Informally grouped, with Modern windows.

Glen Tanar, Aberdeenshire
For the Honourable Jean Bruce
New house incorporating Edwardian
  ballroom 1970
By Law and Dunbar Nasmith

An ingenious Modern house on the site of the late Victorian seat of the Lords Glentanar. *See page 145.*
(*House and Garden*, April 1972, p. 66)

Glympton Park, Oxfordshire
For Alan Good
Remodelling and estate cottages 1948–9
By Trenwith Wills and Wills

The exterior of the house (mid-eighteenth-century, remodelled 1846) was re-Georgianized and the interior was replanned. It was intended to reface the garden front according to a design for Glympton by Vanbrugh, discovered by Lawrence Whistler, but Mr Good's death in 1948 and difficulties over building licences prevented this.
(Office records in the possession of Mrs Dyer; Lawrence Whistler, *The Imagination of Vanbrugh* (1948) p. 126)

The Grange (Lake House), Hampshire
For the Honourable John Baring
New house 1976
By Francis Pollen

See page 143.

Great Hundridge Manor, Buckinghamshire
For Viscount Ednam (now the 4th Earl of
  Dudley)

Extensions and stable block 1962
By Trenwith Wills and Wills

The original house is a compact
seventeenth-century design with a hipped
roof. Two large wings were added at the
back in the same style.
(Office records in the possession of Mrs
Dyer)

Greenmount, County Limerick
For the 11th Earl of Harrington
New house *circa* 1968
By Donal O'Neill-Flanagan

Lord Harrington bought the estate and
demolished the small late Georgian house to
make way for a large new one *circa* 1968. It
is externally plain with modern steel-framed
windows but inside, the rooms are of a
surprising size and grandeur. There is a
two-storeyed hall forty feet square flanked
by a drawing-room and library each forty-six
feet long, thirty feet wide and fifteen feet
high. Rich Classical decoration.
(Mark Bence-Jones, *Burke's Guide to Country
Houses, Volume I, Ireland* (1978) p. 146)

Grove Farm, Leighton Buzzard,
  Bedfordshire
For William Shand-Kidd
Enlargment and remodelling 1960s
By Ian Grant and Ashley Barker

Unique among post-war country houses in
being a Victorian rather than a Georgian
reconstruction. This was done on the advice
of the architects who told the client that the
Victorian farmhouse could never look a
convincing Georgian house, but it could be
made to look a good Victorian house. It was
doubled in size, the number of bedrooms
increased from five to eight and a games
room sixty feet long formed at the top of the
house. A conservatory and clock tower were
also added. The new entrance portico has
Tuscan columns, a balustrade and stone
balls on top. All the specialist stonework
was by Axtell and Perry of Oxford. The
general building contractors were Hinkins
and Frewin of Banbury.
(*House and Garden*, April 1972, pp. 110–11)

Fonthill House, Tisbury

Grove Farm, Leighton Buzzard, Bedfordshire,
before reconstruction

Grove Farm, Leighton Buzzard, Bedfordshire,
after reconstruction

211

Grove Park, Warwickshire
For the 15th Lord Dormer
New house 1976

The old house, an early-nineteenth-century
Tudor job, on the ancestral estate of the
Dormers, was demolished and replaced by
the present house. It is Neo-Georgian, long
and low with pyramidal roofs at either end.
The interior contains important seventeenth-
century chimneypieces from the old house,
which came originally from Eythorpe in
Buckinghamshire.
(Peter Reid, *Burke's Guide to Country Houses,
Volume II,* (1980) p. 148)

Grundisburgh Hall, Suffolk
For the 3rd Lord Cranworth
Drastic reconstruction

Lord Cranworth inherited from his
grandparents. Part of the house was
demolished, keeping the hall of *circa* 1500
and incorporating it in a new house in Neo-
Tudor style. The estate is the Akenfield of
fiction.

Hampton Lucy, Warwickshire
For Mr K. A. Hunt
Unexecuted scheme for large additions 1983
By Quinlan Terry

The enlargement of the old rectory, with
palatial-scale additions on the garden front
to contain a saloon, long gallery (eighteen
feet wide rising through two storeys) and
dining-room, behind a new stone façade
with a rusticated Tuscan order and flanking
pavilions with Venetian windows. The
scheme was abandoned when the client's
firm, 'Good Golly Products' of Birmingham,
went into liquidation.

Hasells, Bedfordshire
For the Right Honourable Francis Pym MP
New house 1970s

A Neo-Georgian house of little interest. The
old house has subsequently been converted
into flats. The park at Hasells is by Repton.

Hedsor Wharf, Bourn End,
  Buckinghamshire
For Roland 'Tiny' Rowland

Remodelling, new elevation and courtyard
  1969–71
By Trenwith Wills and Wills.

(Office records in the possession of Mrs
Dyer)

Henbury Hall, Cheshire
For Sebastian de Ferranti
New house 1984
By Felix Kelly and Julian Bicknell

The Henbury estate (formerly the property
of the Brocklehursts) was bought after the
war by Sir Vincent de Ferranti. The old
house, a Victorianized eighteenth-century
pile, was demolished in 1958 and the stables
converted into a house for the family.
Subsequently another house was made on
the estate out of a keeper's cottage to form
an eighteenth-century-style Gothick pavilion
called 'The Cave', designed by Felix Kelly;
Sir Vincent's son, Sebastian, however, now
intends to rebuild the hall itself as a version
of Palladio's Villa Rotonda. Felix Kelly
produced a painting showing the concept in
1982; Julian Bicknell was appointed to make
the detailed working drawings in April 1983.
Work on the site started in Spring 1984 and
is expected to take a year to complete. *See
page 192.*

Hereford House
For the 21st Viscount Hereford
Unexecuted scheme for a new house 1966
By Oliver Hill

See page 91.
('William Hickey', *Daily Express,* 17 February
1966)

Herriard Park, Hampshire
For J. L. Jervoise
New house 1970; estate cottages
By Sir Martyn Beckett

On the old site. Brick-built. Informal and
asymmetrical. Contains chimneypieces,
paintings and furniture from the old house.
Sir Martyn got this job because, of twenty
architects interviewed, he was the only one
who suggested designing a house to
incorporate the family possessions.
(Sir Martyn Beckett office files)

High Beeches, Handcross, Sussex
For the Honourable Edward Boscawen
New house 1966
By Claud Phillimore

New house on the site of the old one which was destroyed by fire. A Y-shaped plan was abandoned and a more ordinary rectangular scheme adopted. Sussex vernacular.
(RIBAD: RAN/48/A4 1–22
                    5 1–51)

Hinton Ampner House, Hampshire
For Ralph Dutton (now 8th Lord Sherborne)
Rebuilding interior after fire 1962–4
By Trenwith Wills and Wills

See page 78.
(Ralph Dutton, *A Hampshire Manor* (1968);
Country Life, 10 June and 9 September 1965)

Hockering Hall, Norfolk
For John Verel
New house 1968
By Cecil Smith

Built on an estate owned by Mr Verel's family since 1655. The new house is Neo-Georgian of brick, two storeys high, the north front of seven bays and the south of nine, both with pediments.

The Holt, Upham, Hampshire
For Mr and Mrs Leavett-Shenley
Internal remodelling 1962
By Trenwith Wills and Wills

The Holt is a late-seventeenth-century house. It was left alone outside, apart from some small extensions and general tidying-up. The interior is largely by Trenwith Wills in the Georgian taste with Gothick cornices in the dining-room and drawing-room, scaled down from William Kent's at Rousham. An attic bedroom and bathroom were painted in *trompe l'oeil* by Mr Willetts. Trenwith Wills's work also included a games room and garden pavilion.
(*Country Life*, 4 and 11 June 1964;
Office records in the possession of Mrs Dyer)

Hornby Castle, Yorkshire (NR)
For the Clutterbucks

Additions to remnant of old castle to form a new country house. The greater portion of

the old castle had been demolished in the 1930s.

Horsted Keynes, Sussex
For Julian Faber
New house 1971
By Claud Phillimore

A large Neo-Regency house with four segmental bow windows, two on each front, repeating the Tusmore plan. The main feature of the interior is the grand Imperial staircase in the hall. The other main rooms are a drawing-room, study, office, dining-room and playroom. Upstairs are seven bedrooms, five bathrooms, linen room and one dressing-room.
(RIBAD: RAN 48/C/2)

Houghton Hall, Yorkshire (ER)
Countess Fitzwilliam for her nephew Lord Manton
Reconstruction 1957–60
By Francis Johnson

See page 102.
(*Country Life*, 23 December 1965)

Howick Hall, Northumberland
For the Honourable Charles Baring (now 2nd Lord Howick of Glendale)
Conversion of kitchen wing to new house *circa* 1970
By Philip Jebb

Howick is a large late-eighteenth-century house remodelled after a fire in the late 1920s by Sir Herbert Baker. The kitchen wing was derelict. Philip Jebb's work consisted of external restoration and total internal reconstruction to make a new family house. The main block has dry rot and is empty.

Hungerhill House, Sussex
For the 7th Earl of Cottenham
Additions, alteration, forecourt, cottages 1945–54
By A. S. G. Butler

See page 59.
(RIBAD: Butler album)

Hunters Hill, East Godstone, Kent
For the late Lord Byers

New house *circa* 1973
By Sir Martyn Beckett

Small Neo-Georgian house of five bays with pediment. Red brick. Fibreglass detail. It was intended to have applied pilasters but these were scrapped by the client who was the Liberal Leader in the House of Lords.
(Sir Martyn Beckett office files)

Hunton Manor, Hampshire
For Angus MacKinnon
Alterations 1960
By Raymond Erith; interior decoration by
  John Fowler

Erith added the cupolas on the wings, the horseshoe staircase and a large new room to one side. He also built the home farm in Georgian style in 1959.

Hyning Hall, Lancashire
For the 2nd Earl Peel
Remodelling and enlargement 1952

The work in 1952 was done in preparation for a proposed visit of the Queen to Lancashire, Lord Peel being the Lord Lieutenant of the county. He created the forecourt with wrought iron railings, added the Georgian-style porch and made a grand new drawing-room with a marble chimneypiece bought in London. The work infringed the building licences then in force and led to Lord Peel being fined and resigning as Lord Lieutenant.

Inchdrewer Castle, Banff
Tower house restoration *circa* 1965
By Oliver Hill
Part of the castle was left as a ruined shell and the tower reconstructed as a new house with a vaulted kitchen on the ground floor, great hall on the first floor, state room and bedroom on the second floor and more bedrooms and an oratory on the third floor.
(RIBAD: RAN 16/K/8)

**Jenkyn Place (formerly Bentley House),
  Bentley,** Hampshire
For Lieutenant Colonel Gerald Coke
Interior remodelling, garden layout,
  swimming pool 1963–7
By Trenwith Wills and Wills

(Office records in the possession of Mrs Dyer)

Kenmare, Killarney, County Kerry
For Mrs Beatrice Grosvenor
New house 1956
Another new house 1974
By Francis Pollen

Mrs Grosvenor inherited the Kenmare estate from her uncle the 7th and last Earl of Kenmare. She sold part of it including her uncle's house and built a new one on the site of the Victorian house (burnt in 1913). It comprises a seven-bay block with recessed centre and two square flanking wings.
  In 1974 Mrs Grosvenor moved to the other end of the estate and built another new house with a square central block, screen walls and single-storeyed wings. Francis Pollen, the architect, is her cousin.
(Mark Bence-Jones, *Burke's Guide to Country Houses, Volume I, Ireland* (1978) pp. 162–3)

Kenwick Hall, Lincolnshire
For the Dixon family
New house 1960
By Eric Houfe of Richardson and Houfe

Neo-Georgian on the site of the demolished Georgian house and incorporating its cellars. Faced in fawn Stamford brick with two segmental bays and a verandah on the garden front, and a Tuscan porch on the entrance. Interior with fine joinery designed by the architects. *See page 65.*
(Bedford Record office: Richardson and Houfe papers)

Kesworth House, Dorset
For Harry Clark
New house 1979
By Anthony Jaggard (John Stark and
  Partners of Dorchester)

A new house on a new estate. 800 acres, forming an outlying portion of the Drax estates, were bought by the present owner and he has built a proper house there. It is Neo-Georgian and the commission followed from the new house at Lulworth. The house is built of brick with two main fronts of five bays. It has an unusual plan whereby the library, estate office, dining-room and kitchen occupy the ground floor and the drawing-room the first floor in order to take advantage of the views. The interior demonstrates an unusually high level of craftsmanship with a central circular staircase of timber and carved panelling in the drawing-room which could easily be mistaken for Edwardian work.

Kings Walden Bury, Hertfordshire
For Sir Thomas Milburne-Swinnerton-
  Pilkington, Bt
New house 1967–71
By Raymond Erith and Quinlan Terry

See page 161.
(*Country Life*, 27 September and 4 October 1973)

Kinmount, Dumfriesshire
For the Birkbeck family
Stables converted to house 1982–3
By H. Anthony Wheeler

The old house by Smirke has been sold after consent to demolish it was refused.

Kirkdale, Yorkshire (NR)
For Sir Martyn Beckett, Bt
New house 1952.
By himself.

Sir Martyn sold his father's large Edwardian house after the war for a school and built himself a new house on the estate. It is informal, with a low-pitched roof, partly of stone and partly white stuccoed. It has six bedrooms, three bathrooms and a self-contained two-bedroomed staff flat.
(H. Dalton Clifford, *Houses for Today* (1963) pp. 22–4)

Knowsley, Lancashire
For the 17th Earl of Derby
Reconstructed old house 1953–4
New house in park 1963
By Claud Phillimore

See page 126.
(RIBAD: RAN 47/D/1
                        J/5 and 6)

Langton Hall, Yorkshire
Substantial remodelling 1960
By Sir Martyn Beckett

The Victorian front and flanking turrets were demolished, the Georgian core was refaced in the Georgian style and linked by quadrant walls to symmetrical wings containing staff cottages.
(Sir Martyn Beckett office files)

Kesworth House, Dorset

215

Kirkdale Farm, Yorkshire

Leagram Hall, Lancashire
For Charles Weld-Blundell
New house *circa* 1960
By Fulke Fitzherbert-Brockholes

A Neo-Georgian house of stone with a slate
roof on the site of the old house demolished
after the war. Splendid views.

Lessingham Manor, Norfolk
For W. Neave
New house 1945
By A. S. G. Butler

(RIBAD: Butler album)

Dower House, Letcombe Regis, Berkshire
For Major Carlton-Crosse
New house, 1958
By Thomas Rayson

The old house at Letcombe Regis was let to
the Agricultural Research Council and the
new house built on the site of the dower
house. It is Neo-Georgian, brick, of five bays
with a hipped tiled roof. The interior was
designed round the furniture and pictures
from the old house.
(H. Dalton Clifford, *Houses for Today*, (1963)
pp. 104–6)

Leuchie, East Lothian
For Major Sir Hew Hamilton-Dalrymple, Bt
New house built in walled garden 1960
By Law and Dunbar-Nasmith

Informal and flat-roofed with large
windows. The interior has in-built family
portraits. The big house is let to a convent.
(*Country Life*, 26 October 1961)

Llangoed, Breconshire
For the Chichester family
New house 1977–8
By Nicholas Johnston

It replaces Clough's castle of 1912/13 which
has been sold. The new house is simple
Welsh vernacular.

Llanstephan House, Radnorshire
For the Honourable Hugo Philipps
New house 1974–6
By Nicholas Johnston

A large but manageable new house with
something of the air of a border castle on
the site of the previous house inherited from
Lord Milford, an amorphous building of
little interest. The new house is single-
storeyed, of local brown brick, and has a
tower at one end to give it presence. There
are ten bedrooms. Some of the floors and
the staircase are of Welsh slate. The interior
decoration is by David Mlinaric.

Llysdinam, Radnorshire
For Sir Michael Dillwyn-Venables-Llewelyn,
  Bt
Reconstruction *circa* 1954
By Claud Phillimore

216

Llysdinam was a rambling Victorian house with additions of different dates, the latest stage being by S. W. Williams. Sir Michael Dillwyn-Venables-Llewelyn began to reconstruct it *circa* 1934 to the design of Guy Elwes, but the project was interrupted by the war and only completed in the 1950s when Claud Phillimore was called in as architect. Phillimore swept away the remains of the Victorian house and also some of Guy Elwes's work. The exterior is now a characteristic example of Claud Phillimore's Neo-Regency style with a low pitched roof and segmental bows. The main fronts are nine bays wide, that overlooking the park with a central bow, and that round the corner with two flanking bows. The interior contains a bedroom with complete decoration of *circa* 1820 transported intact from Penllergaer, Glamorgan.
(Richard Haslam, *The Buildings of Wales: Powys* (1979), p. 357)

Lockinge, Berkshire
For Christopher Loyd
Unexecuted scheme for a new house 1948
Betterton House (aggrandizement of a farm-house) 1948–55
By Claud Phillimore

The eighteenth/nineteenth-century house of the Loyds of Lockinge was demolished after the war. A scheme to replace it was abandoned because of building licences. The work at Betterton in 1950 was a small-scale Georgian-style conversion to provide a living-room, estate office, dining-room and staff flat. It was all that could be done at that time because of building licences. In 1955 a large new wing was added with a drawing-room (32' × 25'), library, and ante-room which enabled the house to be used for formal entertaining and provided a setting for the famous picture collection. It is a pity that the scheme to build a decent house on the site of the old one at Lockinge fell through because Claud Phillimore's proposals for a thirteen-bay house were among his most ambitious and full-blooded Georgian designs.
(RIBAD: RAN 47/L/1)

Langton Hall, Yorkshire

Logan House, Wigtownshire

Lofts Hall, Essex
For the Graham-Watson family
Large new house 1950s

The old house at Lofts, a very fine sixteenth-century manor house, was burnt in 1938. The war interrupted schemes for replacement and the present large Neo-Georgian house of seven bays and two storeys with a hipped roof, sash windows and a staff wing was not built until after 1945. The interior is elaborately fitted out, the entrance hall with a semicircular staircase and onyx-clad columns.
(NMR)

217

Logan House, Wigtownshire
For Olaf Hambro
Reduced and refronted 1950s
By David Style

David Bryce's Baronial house was
demolished and the Georgian house was
excised and refronted. The original robust
Scots Georgian design was not reinstated
but a more refined English treatment. The
owner had strong say in the design. In
Christopher Hussey's view, Logan was 'an
architectural miracle, admirably performed'.
David Style was an amateur decorator rather
than a professional architect.
(*Country Life*, 5 August 1954)

Long Newnton Priory, Gloucestershire
For Major Morris Keating
New house 1963
By Oliver Hill

See page 89.
(*Country Life*, 25 September 1969)

Lowther Castle, Westmorland
For the 7th Earl of Lonsdale
Unexecuted proposal for a new house in the
  ruins of the castle 1956
By Sir Albert Richardson PRA

A whimsical proposal for a new house
inside the shell of Smirke's castle, probably
never intended to be taken seriously. Since
the removal of the roof of Lowther, Lord
Lonsdale has lived at Askham Hall, another
old house on the estate.
(Sketch drawing in the Lonsdale archives)

Lulworth Castle, Dorset
Sir Joseph Weld for his son
New house 1975
By Anthony Jaggard (John Stark and
  Partners, Dorchester)

Large Neo-Georgian house of pale red brick
with sash windows and segmental bow
windows at either end. The main rooms
have eighteenth-century marble
chimneypieces from Ince Blundell in
Lancashire. The original intention was to
rebuild the Jacobean castle which had been
gutted by fire in 1929, but after encountering
historic buildings problems and faced with
rapidly mounting costs, it was decided to

place the shell of the castle in guardianship
to secure its restoration as a romantic ruin in
the park and to build a new house nearby.
Part of the stable block had already been
converted into a special art gallery for the
display of the pictures from Ince Blundell
which Sir Joseph inherited from cousins.

The new house is cleverly planned in two
halves so that part can be used by the family
when on their own, or the whole opened up
for grand entertaining. On the central axis
are the entrance hall and the monumental
two-storeyed staircase hall with scagliola
columns from the Grange and a segmental
ceiling. To the east are the formal rooms
comprising drawing-room, library and
dining-room, and on the west the family
rooms comprising garden room (opening
onto the swimming pool), sitting-room and
the kitchen-eating room.

Lupton Park, Devon
For the 4th Lord Churston
New house 1954
By Oswald Milne

After the war the Churstons let their old
house at Lupton to a preparatory school and
when building restrictions were lifted built a
new house in the park with a splendid
panoramic view across Tor Bay. Their
architect was Oswald Milne, Lutyens's chief
pupil, and the house was intended to be
economical to run and comfortable to live in.
It is Neo-Georgian of white-painted stucco
with a Delabole slate roof and contains a
drawing-room, dining-room, library, four
bedrooms, two dressing-rooms and three
luxuriously equipped bathrooms. *See page 59.*
(*Country Life*, 26 March 1959)

Luttrellstown, County Dublin
For the Honourable Mrs Brinsley Plunkett
Internal remodelling 1950–63
By Felix Harbord

Luttrellstown was given to Mrs Plunkett by
her father, Ernest Guinness, as a wedding
present in 1927. After the Second World
War, many alterations were carried out. The
Victorian banqueting hall was demolished
and replaced by an early-eighteenth-century-
style dining-room with rich plasterwork,
marble chimneypiece and an eighteenth-

century ceiling painting in 1950. The Grisaille Room was created by Felix Harbord at the same time to take a series of nine *grisaille* paintings by Peter de Gree representing Irish trade and commerce. The staircase was formed in 1963 when a ceiling painting attributed to Thornhill from a demolished house in Suffolk was inserted. Other rooms were embellished with new chimneypieces, doorcases, marble floors, etc.
See page 179.
(Desmond Guinness and William Ryan, *Irish Houses and Castles* (1971) pp. 139–43)

Lulworth Castle, Dorset

Lulworth Castle—stair hall

The Manor House, Hambleden, Oxfordshire
For the 4th Viscount Hambleden
Conservatory 1961; swimming pool pavilion
    1971; billiard room 1980
By Sir Martyn Beckett

The pavilion is a symmetrical design with some applied trelliswork decoration and was not shown at the Royal Academy because Sir Hugh Casson thought it was 'scenery'. The billiard room was done up as a Moorish tent.
    The conservatory was intended for shooting lunches in winter and has a warm and exotic atmosphere in contrast to the outside. It is octagonal with a dome twenty-six feet in diameter and subtropical planting. *See pages 33, 120.*
(Sir Martyn Beckett office files)

Matson Ground, Windermere, Westmorland
For Peter Scott
New house 1961
By Basil Wood

Mr Peter Francis Scott, Chairman of Provincial Insurance, built this large Modern-style house in the grounds of his father's house in 1961.

Membland, Haddington, East Lothian
For Admiral Sir Peter Reid (3rd Sea Lord)
New house 1966
By W. Schomberg Scott

In the Scots domestic tradition. L-shaped with a projecting stair turret in the re-entrant angle. White-harled with a slated roof.
(SNMR: Schomberg Scott collection)

Meols Hall, Southport, Lancashire
For Roger Hesketh
Reconstruction and new east front 1960–4
By Roger Hesketh

A remodelling and expansion of a seventeenth-century house by the owner himself to form one of the most successful country houses built in England since the Second World War. *See page 179.*
(*Country Life*, 25 January, 1 and 8 February 1973)

Milford Lake House, Highclere, Hampshire
For Lord Porchester
Additions and alterations and two staff
    cottages 1964
By Sir Martyn Beckett

Milford Lake House is a charming Victorian
folly by Sir Charles Barry in the park of
Highclere Castle and has been taken over
and converted into his house by Lord
Porchester while his father, the 6th Earl of
Carnarvon, continues to live in the castle.
Sir Martyn's additions are in the same
materials and same style as the original.
(Sir Martyn Beckett office files)

Millearne House, Perthshire
New house
By T. Toms of Dundee

The new house, which is plain and gabled,
was built in front of the old house by R.
Dickson which was demolished when the
new house was completed.

Moncreiffe, Bridge of Earn, Perthshire
For Miss Elizabeth Moncreiffe
New house *circa* 1960
By Sir William Kinimonth PRSA

Old house burnt (with the baronet). It was
by Sir William Bruce. New house echoes its
shape—harled with hipped roof.
Incorporates old doorpiece.

Monteviot, Roxburghshire
For the 12th Marquess of Lothian
New entrance front and picture gallery
    1962–3
By W. Schomberg Scott

The old house, part Georgian with a large
wing by Blore, was refronted and internally
replanned. Scottish Georgian-style interiors.
See page 117.
(SNMR: Schomberg Scott collection)

Mount Edgcumbe, Cornwall
For the 6th Earl of Mount Edgcumbe
Interior rebuilt after war damage 1958–60
By Adrian Gilbert Scott

Mount Edgcumbe was gutted by incendiary
bombs in 1941, destroying the eighteenth-
century interior and leaving only the shell,
dating from 1555. The War Damage

Commission, on the recommendation of the
Ancient Monuments Department of the
Ministry of Works, agreed to rebuild the
house. The outside walls were stripped of
nineteenth-century plaster and the
battlements rebuilt, but are otherwise largely
original. Internally the house was
completely rebuilt with a steel frame and
concrete floors. The rooms are arranged
round a top-lit hall decorated in a Neo-
Georgian style with pedimental doorcases
and a grand balustraded staircase. Along the
east front are the large drawing-room and
library with the morning room and boudoir
in the octagonal corner towers. The dining-
room is on the south side near the kitchen.
All these rooms have simple Georgian
decoration with moulded cornices, Classical
doorcases and brought-in chimneypieces.
(*Country Life*, 22 December 1960)

Nantclwyd Hall, Denbighshire
For Sir Vivyan Naylor-Leyland, Bt
Reconstruction of house and park, follies
    1957–74
By Clough Williams-Ellis
See page 96.
(RIBAD: RAN 33/A/9 [1–40];
Clough Williams-Ellis, *Round the World in
Ninety Years* (1978) pp. 45–7)

Neasham Hall, County Durham
For Sir John Wrightson, Bt
New house 1971
By Sir Martyn Beckett

The old house by Dobson (Tudorish) was
demolished in 1970 and the new house built
on the same site. *See page 122.*
(Sir Martyn Beckett office files)

Newfield, Yorkshire (NR)
For Mr Michael Abrahams
New house 1980
By Quinlan Terry

See page 168.

Newsells Park, Hertfordshire
For Sir Humphrey de Trafford, Bt
New house 1954
By Victor Heal

Entrance front, Membland, East Lothian

Newsells Park, Hertfordshire

This very large Neo-Georgian house was built on the old site to replace the mainly eighteenth-century house burnt down during the war while occupied by the army. *See page 66.*

North Port, Haddington, East Lothian
For Elizabeth, Duchess of Hamilton
Dower House 1978–9
By Philip Jebb

Built on the Lennoxlove estate in Neo-Regency style inspired by a Nash villa.

Bishop's House, Norwich, Norfolk
For the Bishop of Norwich
New house 1959
By James Fletcher-Watson

Neo-Georgian of brick and cobbles with a sprocketed tiled roof. The entrance front has a semicircular pediment containing the episcopal arms under a mitre. The garden front is flanked by two segmental bows. The interior contains a handsome semicircular staircase. Described by Pevsner as 'agreeable Neo-Georgian'! *See page 114.*
(James Fletcher-Watson's office files)

Ockham Park, Surrey
For Felix Fenston
Reconstruction *circa* 1966
By Felix Harbord

Mr Fenston was a successful property developer who bought the Ockham estate. Ockham was a Jacobean house, remodelled

in 1727 by Hawksmoor and again in the nineteenth century when it was stuccoed and a tower added to the kitchen wing. The house was gutted by fire in 1948 leaving only the shell of the kitchen wing. This was reconstructed by Felix Harbord in the Hawksmoor manner, demolishing the tower, stripping the stucco, inserting new sash windows and adding an idiosyncratic clock turret/chimney stack to the centre of the roof, based on a sketch by Hawksmoor dated 1727. Felix Harbord moved into the lodge while working on the reconstruction of the house, and produced a model as well as plans. *See page 179.*

Odell Castle, Bedfordshire
For the 2nd Lord Luke
New house 1962
By Gerald Banks of Bicester

A large square stone house with a low-pitched roof concealed by a parapet. It stands on a substantial revetted terrace surviving from the previous castle.

Okeover Hall, Staffordshire
For Sir Ian Walker-Okeover, Bt
Reconstruction and additions 1957–60
By Marshall Sisson

Perhaps the most successful new country house built in England in the 1950s.
See page 68.
(RIABAD: RAN 23/H/4;
Exhibited Royal Academy 1959;
Country Life, 23 January and 12 March 1964)

221

Old Court, Strangford, County Down
For the 27th Baroness de Ros
New house 1976
By Robert McKinstrey of Belfast

The estate was brought to the de Ros family from the Fitzgeralds by the marriage of Charlotte, Baroness de Ros. Old Court was built in 1976 on a superb site overlooking Strangford Lough close to the foundations of an earlier house burnt down in the 1920s. However, the design of the new house, by the Belfast architect Robert McKinstry, is entirely different to what was there before and with a total floor area of some 5000 square feet the plan of three linked blocks allows for the closing off of one wing and a first floor. Generally traditional building materials have been used but the pillars to the colonnades are of simulated stone and the proprietary plaster wall finish is a brick-purple colour.

   The owner of Old Court, the Baroness de Ros, and her husband Commander David Maxwell supervised all the building work which was carried out by a local firm of contractors.

Oving House, Buckinghamshire
For Lord Hartwell
Interior remodelling and swimming pool
   1954–5
By Felix Harbord

Oving dates from the seventeenth and eighteenth centuries. Most of the interior was re-Georgianized by Felix Harbord 'with great skill and swagger', keeping the best original features and supplementing the theme with new work in the same style. The hall, library, dining-room and drawing-room all have splendid rococo-style plasterwork designed by Felix Harbord. The interior of the swimming pool pavilion has painted decoration carried out in 1957 by Robert Morris. One of the bedrooms is treated as a print room.
(*Country Life*, 20 and 27 November 1958)

Parracombe, Devon
For Major Lindsay MP
Ballroom addition *circa* 1960
By Trenwith Wills and Wills

Neo-Regency to match the old house. Exterior stuccoed and painted white.
(Office records in the possession of Mrs Dyer)

The Pavilion, Little Horkseley, Essex
For Reginald Duthy
New house 1969–70
By Raymond Erith and Quinlan Terry

A miniature French *château* for a client with a strong love of France. Five-bay centre with mansard roof and two little pyramid-roofed wings. The end product was the result of a careful and enjoyable study of French vernacular detail by the architects on frequent visits to France.
(Frank Russell, Ed., *Quinlan Terry* (1981) p. 43)

Penn's Rocks, Sussex
For Lord Gibson
Alterations 1957–9
By Guy Elwes

The Gibsons bought Penn's Rocks in 1957 and immediately commissioned Colonel Guy Elwes to reconstruct the centre of the house to form a new dining-room, pantry, cloakroom and remodelled staircase. The new dining-room is a handsome Soanic design with a segmental arched recess for the sideboard. Pendentives in the corners of the room convert the ceiling to a circle and the mullions of the tripartite Wyatt window have inset strips of looking glass reminiscent of 14 Lincoln's Inn Fields.
(*Country Life*, 30 March 1961)

Pentillie Castle, Cornwall
For Major Coryton
Part demolition and remodelling 1968–71
By Trenwith Wills and Wills

The demolished part comprised an early-nineteenth-century Gothic house attributed to William Wilkins Senior. The seventeenth-century wing was retained as the core of the new house.
(Office records in the possession of Mrs Dyer)

Peverey House, Shropshire
For Sir David Wakeman, Bt
New house *circa* 1960

222

Old Court, Strangford, County Down

A Neo-Georgian red brick house of five bays and two storeys built in the walled garden of the former Wakeman Seat, Yeaton Peverey. The latter is a large Edwardian Jacobethan pile by Aston Webb and is currently empty.

Philiphaugh, Selkirk
For Sir William Strang-Steel, Bt
New house *circa* 1965
By Sir William Kinimonth PRAS

The nineteenth-century Baronial house has been demolished and replaced by a new Neo-Georgian one. The interior has a grand circular staircase and three reception rooms.

Pitcorthie, Fife
For Lord Balniel (now the 29th Earl of Crawford)
New house 1960s
By Trevor Dannatt

On the site of an eighteenth-century house destroyed by fire. It is Modern and informal, intended as a 'versatile holiday home'. The walls are of stone reused from the ruin and are carried on a concrete raft over the old foundations. The roof is a shallow monopitch. Interior with a compact and ingenious plan divided into three sections: at the west end a secluded drawing-room and study, in the centre the living-room and service core with the children's bedrooms at the east end. Strip boarded or quarry tile floors. Large glazed windows with views.
(*Country Life*, 30 May 1968)

Plas Brondanw, Merioneth
For Sir Clough Williams-Ellis
Reconstruction after the fire 1951–3
By himself

See pages 15, 93.
(*Country Life*, 5 September 1957)

Ranston, Iwerne Minster, Dorset
For the Gibson-Fleming family
Reconstruction and reorientation, 1961–3
By Louis Osman

The house, seat of the Baker baronets (ancestors of Mrs Gibson-Fleming), dated from 1753 but had been altered later when flanking wings were added. It was rebuilt to its original form of a square block with three new façades and one resited old façade. The new elevations are stuccoed with stone quoins and, on the entrance front, a central stone doorway with a Venetian window over. On the park front, the twin wrought iron balustraded steps originally intended but never carried out have been built. The interior has also been reconstructed and paintings by Andrea Casali reset.
Louis Osman is better known as a goldsmith and was responsible for the design of Prince Charles's crown for the investiture at Caernarvon. *See page 188.*
(*Buildings of England, Dorset* (1972) p. 237)

Rawfleet, Roxburghshire
Small new house 1960s
By W. Schomberg Scott

223

Ranston, Dorset

A handsome Georgian-style house developed out of a single-storeyed farmhouse in a deeply rural situation three miles west of Monteviot. It has white harled walls and slated roof, and a symmetrical front of simple traditional design with a central porch between two slightly projecting wings.
(SNMR: Schomberg Scott albums)

Revesby Abbey, Lincolnshire
For Mrs A. Lee
New house *circa* 1970

A large Neo-Georgian house on a new site in the park intended to replace Burn's house, consent for the demolition of which has subsequently been refused, leaving Revesby with two large houses near to each other.

Rhiwlas, Merioneth
For the Lloyd-Price family
New house 1954
By Clough Williams-Ellis

A plain stone house with sash windows replacing an older house. The interior contains inscribed beams from the previous house and the staircase has a good wrought iron balustrade. *See page 95.*
(RIBAD: RAN 33/E/17 [1–5])

Ribblesdale Park, Ascot, Berkshire
For J. R. Hindley
New house 1961–4
By Claud Phillimore; garden by Lanning Roper

Claud Phillimore produced five different variants for a large Neo-Georgian house after part of the Buckhurst estate was sold

and made into an independent stud farm. The first proposal was his most interesting geometrical plan and comprised a large irregular octagon, possibly inspired by Goodwood. As built, the house was L-shaped, rendered, with a low-pitched roof and Claud Phillimore's usual detail. Lavishly decorated interior comprising hall, dining-room, study, drawing-room, garden room and office. The hall has a marble floor and the staircase, with a wrought iron balustrade, rises behind a screen of Tuscan columns. The three main reception rooms all have dentil cornices and brought-in chimneypieces.
(RIBAD: RAN 47/K/1 [1–30])

Rossie Priory, Perthshire
For the 13th Lord Kinnaird
Truncation and remodelling *circa* 1958
By Sir Basil Spence

William Atkinson's main block, a wild early-nineteenth-century Gothic design, was demolished apart from the main stair and library. The new house was created by patching up the service wing and adding a new wing of red sandstone containing the drawing-room at one end with a large bay window in a sort of inter-war Tudor manner.

Round Oak, Ascot, Berkshire
For the Schroder family
New entrance front and stable block 1961
By Eric Houfe of Richardson and Houfe

The new front has a Corinthian porch and Wyatt windows.
(Bedford Record Office, Richardson and Houfe office records)

Saighton Grange, Cheshire
For the 4th Duke of Westminster
Interior remodelling 1957
By John Dennys

Saighton is a subsidiary house on the Eaton estate and for a short time in the 1960s was the seat of the Dukes of Westminster following the demolition of Eaton Hall. Saighton comprises a fifteenth-century gatehouse of the abbots of Chester and a large Victorian wing. John Dennys completely altered the interior in a grand Neo-Georgian manner with a central hall containing a balustraded gallery and Wyatt doorcases brought from Dauntsey Park in Wiltshire.

Sandringham, Norfolk
For HM the Queen
Unexecuted scheme for a new house 1960s
By David Roberts of Cambridge

The idea was to demolish the late-nineteenth-century house by Humbert and Edis and to build a new house on the site. In the event, this scheme was abandoned as too drastic and the existing house modernized under the direction of Sir Hugh Casson.

Saxonbury House, Frant, Kent
For Lord Roderic Pratt
New house 1970s
By Kenneth Bemlow of Chittons

Red brick. Neo-Georgian. Lord Roderic Pratt is a younger son of the 4th Marquess Camden, and employed the architect of the new Bayham and the Somerley Dower House for this house.

Scarisbrick, Lancashire
New house 1960s
By Nelson and Park

The Scarisbrick estate was sold up from 1947 onwards. A portion, including the old home farm, was bought by the present owner who built a new house on the site of some of the farm buildings. It forms two sides of the courtyard and is built of old brick. The style is Modern but a spiky silhouette consciously echoes the Gothic of Pugin's masterpiece. (June Park, *Houses for Today* (1971) pp. 72–5)

Scriven Park, Yorkshire (NR)
New house 1962

Neo-Georgian, brick, single-storeyed. Eleven bays wide. Reused stone balustrade round the roof. Illiterate Ionic portico.
(Sale particulars in NMR)

Settrington House, Yorkshire (NR)
For Lord Buckton
Centre block rebuilt after fire 1963
By Francis Johnson

Successful Palladian-style remodelling after fire damage. Now belongs to Lord Buckton's son Sir Samuel Storey, Bt. *See page 106.*

Sevenhampton Place, Wiltshire
For Ian Fleming
Reconstruction and additions 1963
By Pinckney and Gott

A stone Neo-Georgian house on the site of a larger eighteenth-century and nineteenth-century house called Warneford Place. The Flemings bought the property in 1960 and demolished the old house apart from one wing, which was incorporated into the new L-shaped house. The old wing was remodelled internally to form a high-ceilinged drawing-room and dining-room. The new wing contains the entrance hall, staircase and bedrooms. Additional guest accommodation was provided in 1975 when the adjoining stable block was rebuilt with a replica Georgian façade, to the design of Nicholas Johnston. Sevenhampton is a well-arranged and convenient house but failed to impress Evelyn Waugh. *See page 9.*
(Michael Davie, Ed., *The Diaries of Evelyn Waugh* (1976) p. 791)

Shane's Castle, County Antrim
For the 4th Lord O'Neill
New house 1958
By Lord O'Neill and Arthur Drury of Belfast

This good and convincing Neo-Regency design is the third house of the name on this estate. The intermediate house by Sir Charles Lanyon and Henry Lynn was burnt in the Troubles, 1922. The earlier house, remodelled by Nash in 1815, was believed to have been burnt by the family banshee in 1816. Its ruins survive on the estate as a romantic folly overlooking Antrim Bay.
  The estate, on the north-east coast of Lough Neagh, is one of the oldest in Ireland, because the O'Neills (descended from the ancient Irish Royal house) were allowed to keep their land after the Plantation of Ulster. The Georgian stables survive next to the new house. *See page 185.*
(Mark Bence-Jones, *Burke's Guide to Country Houses, Volume I, Ireland* (1978) p. 257)

Sevenhampton Place, Wiltshire

Sheshoon, County Kildare
For the Aga Khan
New house and stud farm 1982
By Casson and Conder Partnership

A large complex of buildings in traditional style with whitewashed walls, pitched, slated roof and tall chimneystacks. They are arranged round a hilltop courtyard and comprise the manager's house, guest rooms, three staff cottages and forty-eight loose boxes. The race horse Shergar was kidnapped from Sheshoon by the IRA in 1982.
(Casson and Conder Partnership Office records)

Snaigow, Dunkeld, Perthshire
For the 7th Earl Cadogan
New house 1960–1
By Basil Hughes

A Neo-Georgian house, informally planned. The main rooms have magnificent Classical marble chimneypieces from Arundel Castle, bought by Lord Cadogan's grandfather for the Edwardian part of Culford, Suffolk, and given to the present Lord Cadogan after the last war by Culford School; while the Victorian timber staircase came from the

previous house at Snaigow. The late Basil Hughes was the architect to the Cadogan Estate in London.

The new Snaigow is on the old site (the previous house by Burn was demolished because of dry rot) and uses the old foundations, thus perpetuating the plan of the previous house.

Dower House, Somerley, Hampshire
For Fiona, Countess of Normanton
New house *circa* 1970
By Kenneth Bemlow of Clutton's

Red brick. Neo-Georgian. Lady Normanton is the sister of Marquess Camden who employed the same architect to do the new house at Bayham (qv).

Southfield House, Chawton, Hampshire
For Sir Richard Sharples
New house 1956
By Sir Martyn Beckett

Sir Martyn's first major country house job. It is Neo-Georgian of seven bays and red brick with a pediment. Sir Richard Sharples was subsequently murdered while Governor of Bermuda.

226

Southwold House, Warter, Yorkshire (ER)
For the 4th Marquess of Normanby
Reconstruction *circa* 1976
By Francis Johnson

The large Warter Priory estate was bought by a family trust of Lord and Lady Normanby's and the Victorian house demolished. The new house was developed out of one of the farmhouses and has a Jacobean front with shaped gables and two wings in late Georgian style with a pretty forecourt in between. The main rooms contain chimneypieces from Warter Priory. *See page 108.*

Stainsby Hall, Derbyshire
New house 1972–4
By David Shelley

An amazing Modern house with Hispano-American touches on the site of a demolished eighteenth-century house.

Stanton Harcourt, Oxfordshire
For the 2nd Viscount Harcourt
New drawing-room added 1953

When Nuneham was sold in 1948 to Oxford University, Stanton Harcourt was restored as the Harcourt family seat and the fragments of the great medieval house stitched together and planted about to form an agreeable new house and garden. The drawing-room was designed to contain the best French furniture in the Harcourt collection.

Stoke Albany, Northamptonshire
For Major R. Chaplin
Alterations to house 1955–6
By Claud Phillimore

The office wing was demolished and the interior remodelled. Outside a new front porch was added with 'Phillimore Tuscan' columns and a pretty segmental fanlight. (RIBAD: RAN 47/F/6 [1–21])

Stone Hall, Balcombe, Sussex
For Mrs P. H. Greenwood
Alterations 1966–7
By Claud Phillimore

A vernacular house, rambling with gables and tile hanging.
(RIBAD: RAN 47/M/1 [1–35])

Stratton Park, Hampshire
For the Honourable John Baring
New house 1963–5
By Stephen Gardiner and Christopher Knight

See page 142.

Studley Royal, Yorkshire (WR)
For Henry Vyner
Stables conversion 1947
By himself

The big house was burnt in 1945 and the family moved to the stables. Good interior, incorporating fittings and furniture salvaged from the big house. *See page 18.*

Snaigow, Perthshire

Southfield House, Chawton, Hampshire

227

Sudbury House, Derbyshire
For the 10th Lord Vernon
New house 1965
By Sir Martyn Beckett

New house of brick overlooking lake to replace the big house which was transferred to the National Trust. Five-bay Neo-Georgian. The sprocketed roof with cedar shingles gives it a Chinese air. *See page 122.* (Sir Martyn Beckett office files)

Sunderlandwick Hall, Yorkshire (ER)
For Sir Thomas Ferens
New house circa 1963
Designed by Francis Johnson

This well planned and beautifully executed Neo-Georgian house replaces a Victorianized eighteenth-century house of no great merit, which had been burnt in 1945. *See page 108.*

Sunningdale, Berkshire
For Mr and Mrs Andrews
New house 1962
By Oliver Hill

Large Neo-Georgian house showing Lutyens influence, of brick with stone trim and flanked by little conical-roofed pavilions. *See page 89.*
(RIBAD: RAN 16/K/3)

Swarcliffe Hall, Yorkshire (WR)
For Colonel B. C. Greenwood
New house *circa* 1970
By Sir Martyn Beckett

The new house is on the site of the kitchen garden and replaces the Victorian house

which was sold to a school. It is of stone and somewhat indeterminate character with modern windows yet a pitched roof. (Sir Martyn Beckett office files)

Swinton Grange, Yorkshire (NR)
For Colonel W. E. Behrens
Partial demolition and remodelling
By Trenwith Wills and Wills

(Office records in the possession of Mrs Dyer)

Swyncombe House, Oxfordshire
For the Christie-Miller family
New house *circa* 1980
By David Hicks and Jeffery Ruddell

A new Neo-Georgian house in a beautiful park to replace a nineteenth-century Neo-Jacobean one which was demolished in 1978.

Tancreds Ford, Farnham, Surrey
Additions and alterations, 1981–2
By Roderick Gradidge

The old house, built in 1913 to the design of Faulkner, has been ingeniously and sensitively enlarged in the same Arts and Crafts Georgian style by Roderick Gradidge. His improvements include the enlargement of the hall, the conversion of the servants' hall to a breakfast room, the creation of a new library in the attic, and a fascinating suite of bedroom, dressing-room and bathroom, all with segmental arches and lavish use of looking glass (combining Soane and Oliver Hill). Much of the furniture was specially made for the house and Roderick

Stainsby Hall, Derbyshire

Gradidge has even designed a Georgian-style dolls' house for the owner's daughter. (*Country Life*, 17 and 24 March 1983)

Thames House, Newbury, Berkshire
For Timothy Sainsbury
New house 1960s
By Denys Lasdun

A very large Modern house of concrete with long, low lines on a dramatic site on the crest of a low hill. It is one of the few post-war country houses by a leading Modern British architect and looks strikingly incongruous in its setting, just like encountering the National Theatre in the middle of a field.

Thenford House, Northamptonshire
For Michael Heseltine MP
Garden pavilion 1982
By Quinlan Terry

See pages 8, 170.

The Dower House, Tillmouth Park,
 Northumberland
For Sir Michael Blake, Bt
Remodelling and enlargement 1976
By Felix Kelly

The Dower House is the fourth house on the Blake estate in Northumberland and succeeds the monstrous eighteenth-century Twizell Castle (demolished 1880), the even more monstrous eighteenth-century Tillmouth Park (demolished 1880) and the Victorian Tillmouth Park (let as a hotel). The new house was formed out of a farmhouse and is Gothic with a five-bay single-storeyed porch on the entrance front and three canted and embattled bay windows on the garden front. This was Felix Kelly's first excursion into architectural design from painting and is a very successful, light-hearted design. The builder was local, Peter Young of Coldstream. *See page 191.*
(*House and Garden*, February 1979, p. 59)

Torry Hill, Lenham, Kent
For Robin Leigh-Pemberton
New house 1956–8
Own design with the assistance of H. G.
 Freemantle

Sudbury House, Derbyshire

Swarcliffe Hall, Yorkshire

Replaces an old house of 1865 in a good park on an estate of 2,400 acres which was inherited. Robin Leigh-Pemberton, formerly chairman of National Westminster Bank, was appointed Governor of the Bank of England by Mrs Thatcher from June 1983.
 The new house is late-seventeenth-century in style, of seven bays by five, red brick with a hipped roof, dormers and prominent panelled chimneystacks. The builder was local, M. Butcher and Sons of Sittingbourne. *See page 186.*
(John Newman, *North-East and East Kent* (1969) p. 317)

Torry House, Fife
For the Wemyss family, of Wemyss
Reconstruction of surviving wing of old
 house to make new one *circa* 1960
By Stewart Todd.

The old house was monastic Gothic and

huge. The new house is much smaller but ingeniously converted.

Towns End Springs, Thriplow,
  Cambridgeshire
For Lord Walston.
New house 1970
By Sir Leslie Martin

This replaces a Neo-Georgian house built by Lord Walston's father which has been sold. The new house is compact and situated in the village. From it Lord Walston farms the 3000-acre estate, all of which is in hand.

Tusmore Park, Oxfordshire
For the 2nd Lord Bicester
New house 1961–2
By Claud Phillimore

On the site of a demolished house by Robert Mylne. Many Edwardian outbuildings including lodges and formal terraces were retained as the setting of the new house, which is of stone with a stone-flagged roof, and segmental bows at either end of each front. The clients had great taste and the interior of Tusmore is beautiful, with a marble-floored hall, excellent Regency-style joinery and reused chimneypieces by Robert Mylne. *See page 131.*
(RIBAD: RAN 47/I/2 1–31)
                3 1–21)

Udny, Aberdeenshire
For the Honourable Margaret Udny-
  Hamilton (Mrs Keith Schellenberg)
Restoration of tower house 1962–4
By John Lamb

The Victorian house by J. M. Wardrop was demolished and the exterior of the tower restored, its harling painted pale pink. The interior was converted into a comfortable modern house. The ground floor has a segmental vaulted dining-room. Wardrop's great hall on the first floor has become the drawing-room and is cleverly fitted with built-in drinks cupboards, etc.
(*Country Life*, 24 February 1974)

Uffington House, Lincolnshire
For Lady Muriel Barclay-Harvey
Unexecuted scheme for new house 1948
By Marshall Sisson

The old house (dating from 1681) had been burnt in 1904. Marshall Sisson's design took its cue from the vanished mansion and had a hipped roof, façade of nine bays, pediment, and a replanned interior. The scheme had to be abandoned because of trouble over building licences.
(RIBAD: RAN 23/G/2)

Ulva House, Ulva, Argyllshire
For Edith, Lady Congleton
New house *circa* 1953
By Leslie Grahame MacDougall

The old house was burnt five years after Lady Congleton bought it. The new house on a nearby site is smaller but has a round drawing-room and good eighteenth-century marble chimneypieces bought in Edinburgh.
(SNMR Leslie Grahame MacDougall's drawings)

Vaynol, Carnarvonshire
For Sir Michael Duff, Bt
Remodelling 1960s

Half the old house was demolished and the retained part considerably adapted. The chief alteration was the creation of an oval hall with mural decoration by Martin Newall.

Voelas, Denbighshire
For Lieutenant Colonel J. C. Wynne-Finch
New house 1958
By Clough Williams-Ellis

It replaces a demolished Victorian Gothic house by John Hungerford Pollen. Neo-Georgian with a nine-bay façade, the garden front with a central pediment. The exterior is painted white and has sash windows. The interior is spaciously planned with a gallery forty-nine feet long for the family pictures as well as a drawing-room, library, dining-room. There are ten bedrooms and three bathrooms. *See page 94.*
(RIBAD: RAN 33/C/14 1–4)

Wakefield Lodge, Northamptonshire
For Norman Gee
Conversion of stables to staff flats;
  remodelling of house with new façade and
  interiors 1947

By A. S. G. Butler

See page 60.
(RIBAD: Butler album)

Walton Castle, Clevedon, Somerset
For M. H. Sessions Hodge
Restored from ruin 1980–2
By Stuart Lennox

Walton was built in 1615 by the 1st Lord Poulet but was abandoned after the Civil War and fell into ruin. It has an octagonal 'Keep' standing within an octagonal curtain wall with eight angle turrets. The keep has been partly rebuilt, a second storey added and a new roof. The interior is entirely new, the architectural detail is copied from authentic examples or brought in from other buildings. The principal room is the octagonal drawing-room with a diameter of twenty-three feet and a plaster frieze copied from Barrow Court. There are five bedrooms and three bathrooms, and one of the turrets in the curtain wall has been made into a separate guests' cottage.

Warham House, Norfolk
For Lady Mary Harvey
Reconstruction 1957
By James Fletcher-Watson

The façade of a farmhouse was kept for the centre block of the new house but all the rest was rebuilt, and two flanking pavilions with pyramidal roofs of red pantiles were added, doubling the overall size.
See page 113.

Warnham Park, Horsham, Sussex
For Charles Lucas
New house *circa* 1960

The old house on the estate, Warnham Court, is now a GLC school, but the land is retained by the family and they have built a new house in the park in a simple vernacular style with a Horsham stone roof. The builder was J. J. Stanford.

Warren House, Beaulieu, Hampshire
For the 2nd Lord Montagu of Beaulieu
New house 1956
By Casson and Conder Partnership

A small beach house in the Modern style on a remote corner of the estate overlooking the Solent. It has a flat roof and boarded walls.
See page 134.
(*Architectural Review*, October 1957)

Wasing Place, Berkshire
For Sir William Mount, Bt
New house 1957
By Alan Gotelee

The old house was burnt in 1945. The new house is built from the same materials, retaining part of the outer walls. It has a five-bay pediment on both fronts, an unusual feature. Before the fire the house was larger with a top storey and servants' wing which have both been demolished. It looks and works well.

Watlington Hall, Norfolk
For John Pope
New house 1965
By James Fletcher-Watson

The new house is Neo-Georgian of brick and occupies the site of a Donthorn house burnt in 1943. The main front is of seven bays and two storeys with a central pediment, prominent hipped roof and flanking single-storeyed colonnaded loggias. *See page 114.*

Waverton House, Gloucestershire
For Jocelyn Hambro
New house 1977–80
By Quinlan Terry

A completely new house of stone on a stud farm and 'an excellent demonstration of the architect's belief in the relevance of the Classical language today'. *See page 166.*
(*Architectural Review*, September 1981, pp. 157–60; *Country Life*, 6 August 1981)

Wellingham House, Sussex
For Ian Askew
Remodelled and extended 1954–71
By Raymond Erith

Erith added a new south-west front and two wings to an older house and remodelled the interior, including an attractive octagonal Chinese Room with wallpaper from Panshanger and the library with fitted shelves in alcoves designed by Erith.
(*House and Garden*, November 1958, p. 64)

Wasing Place, Berkshire

Wemyss Castle, Fife
For Captain Michael and Lady Victoria
  Wemyss
Reconstructed in phases 1945–65
By Stewart Todd

Victorian additions to the house were
demolished and a new single-storeyed block
built on the north side, linking the old castle
with the seventeenth-century wing. A new
entrance was formed in a bell-roofed turret
copied by Stewart Todd from the tollbooth
at West Wemyss. All the stucco was
stripped from the external walls, plate glass
replaced by sashes in the windows, and the
castellation removed and replaced with a
simple parapet giving the exterior a new
unity. The interior was remodelled, a
dining-room constructed out of the old
billiard room, a new staircase built with a
wrought-iron balustrade and other rooms
restored and redecorated.

  Oliver Hill designed a new entrance
portico for Wemyss in 1954 which was not
executed. *See page 87.*
(*Country Life*, 10 June 1971, 6 and 13 January
1966)

West Woodhay, Berkshire
For John Henderson
Remodelling 1948–51
Designed by Claud Phillimore

West Woodhay was a late-nineteenth-
century asymmetrical Queen Anne style
house. Claud Phillimore demolished bits
and created a new symmetrical Neo-
Georgian front.
(RIBAD: RAN/47/B/2 [1–24])

Whitwell, Yorkshire (NR)
For David Brotherton
New house *circa* 1966
By Francis Johnson

David Brotherton bought part of the
Whitwell estate and built a new house on a
new site. It is like a Regency villa of pink
brick with a Tuscan porch *in antis* flanked by
two segmental bows. An early-nineteenth-
century Tudor-style lodge was restored from
ruin to serve the new house.

Wichwood House, Hethersett, Norfolk
For Michael Watt
New house 1956
By James Fletcher-Watson

A Neo-Georgian house of red brick with a
central pediment similar to Watlington. The
interior contains an elegant semicircular
staircase and the architect designed some of
the fittings himself, including chandeliers.

The Wicken House, Castle Acre, Norfolk
For Sir Kenneth Keith (now Lord Keith of
  Castle Acre)
Remodelling of old farmhouse, and new
  stable block 1955
By James Fletcher-Watson

This is a new estate of 3000 acres formed out
of an outlying part of the Holkham estate
sold for death duties. An old farmhouse was
used as the basis of the new house. To it
was added a pediment, Tuscan doorcase,
black pantiled roof, formal forecourt, and a
stable block. Since then the house has been
further enlarged and altered by a London
architect and has lost its original freshness.
There is an indoor swimming pool with
decoration by David Hicks. Interior of the
house itself was furnished and decorated
with the help of Francis Egerton of Mallets.
See page 113.

Wiseton Hall, Nottinghamshire
For Major-General Sir Robert Laycock
New house 1962

A neat rectangular brick house of seven bays
and two storeys, with a low-pitched tiled
roof. It was built on the site of the old
Laycock family house by Sir Robert on his
return from the governorship of Malta. The

232

Watlington Hall, Norfolk.

drawing-room and dining-room have handsome marble chimneypieces and the library has fitted Adamesque bookcases.

Witley Park, Surrey
For Gerald Bentall
New house 1961–2
By Patrick Gwynne

An ambitious Modern house with a plan based on interlocking hexagons on a new site in an Edwardian park. The interior is remarkable for its electric gadgetry.
See page 146.
(*Architectural Review*, March 1963;
Country Life, 19 December 1963)

Wivenhoe New Park, Essex
For Charles Gooch
New house 1962–4
By Raymond Erith

A Palladian villa in modern terms built on the Wivenhoe estate after the big house was acquired for the University of Essex.
See page 158.
(*Country Life*, 22 July 1965)

Woodcote House, Fala, Midlothian
For Mr and Mrs James Morris
New house 1977
By James Morris

This large Modern house replaces a decayed house by Bryce and was intended as a modern version of the country house

Wichwood House, Hethersett, Norfolk

'endowed with traditional amenities but incorporating labour-saving equipment and providing protection from the rigours of the Scottish climate'. The site is in the middle of an eighteenth-century estate. The house has two floors, the ground floor with bedrooms, bathrooms, kitchen, laundry, dining-room, play room; while upstairs is one large living area divided into library, gallery, drawing-room and billiard room. At one end is a double height conservatory with a swimming pool. Both floors are completely enclosed in an envelope of glass. The roof

233

Wivenhoe New Park, Essex

rests on laminated timber beams, supported by eight brick columns. The windows have bronze-tinted double glazing throughout, except for the conservatory which has clear glass and a plastic vaulted roof.
(Peter Willis, *New Architecture in Scotland* (1977) pp. 24–7)

Wormington Grange, Gloucestershire
For Lord Ismay
Reduction and alterations 1947
By A. S. G. Butler

More a restoration than a new house.
(RIBAD: Butler album)

The Worthies, King's Worthy, Hampshire
For Barney Bishof
Remodelled old house *circa* 1966
By Robert Bostock of Bostock and Wilkins

Worthy Park, the old house by Smirke, was sold to the TUC and a smaller old house remodelled and regularized (straightened out) with a new Doric porch, to replace it.

Wynyard Park, County Durham
For the 9th Marquess of Londonderry
Reconstruction and alterations 1963 and 1983
By David Hicks; Gordon Thompson

When Lord Londonderry inherited Wynyard and decided to restore it as a family house, he concentrated on the former office wing at the east side and reconstructed it as a new house with a lavish interior by David Hicks. A new phase of work has just begun under the direction of Gordon Thompson aimed at providing a grand new private entrance hall and converting the orangery into a swimming pool. *See page 32.*
(*Vogue*, 1 August 1964, p. 115;
Royal Academy Summer Exhibition 1983 designs by Gordon Thompson)

234

PHOTOGRAPHIC ACKNOWLEDGEMENTS

Thanks are due to the following for permission to reproduce colour photographs: Mark Fiennes, opposite pages 16, 33 (bottom), 64 (top and bottom), 128, 129 (top), 176 (bottom), 192, 193 (top); Roderick Gradidge, opposite pages 17 and 32; Sir Martyn Beckett, opposite 33 (top) and 129 (bottom); the Marquess of Hertford, opposite page 65; Lord Howard of Henderskelfe, opposite page 80; Lord Sherborne, opposite page 81; A. F. Kersting, opposite page 144 (bottom); Kathryn Gammon, opposite page 144 (top); Gavin Stamp, opposite pages 145 (top), 193 (bottom); Charles Hall, opposite pages 145 (bottom), 176 (top); Christie's, opposite page 177.

Thanks are due to the following for permission to reproduce black and white photographs: *Architectural Review*, frontispiece and pages 25, 39, 135 (top and bottom), 136, 137, 139 (top and bottom), 140 (top and bottom), 142, 143, 144(3), 146, 147, 148 (top and bottom), 153; Quinlan Terry, page 8; *Country Life*, pages 10, 15, 17, 18, 19, 20 (top and bottom), 37, 52 (top and bottom), 54, 55, 63, 81 (top and bottom), 82 (top and bottom), 88, 90(3), 102, 103, 104 (top and bottom), 105 (top and bottom), 157, 158, 159, 160 (top and bottom), 161, 163 (top and bottom), 164, 176, 178 (top and bottom), 181, 183 (top and bottom), 185 (top and bottom); John Taylor, page 21; RIBA, pages 23 (top and bottom), 60 (top and bottom), 71 (top), 89, 125; the Duke of Norfolk, page 28; Lavinia, Duchess of Norfolk, page 128; Gavin Stamp, pages 30(2), 162; the Greater London Council, pages 44, 46 (left), 48, 50; A. F. Kersting, pages 46 (right), 48, 128, 130 (top and bottom); Martin Andrews, page 58; NMR, pages 62 (top and bottom), 69 (top), 89, 103 (top), 107 (top), 180 (left); Simon Houfe, page 66; *Derbyshire Life*, pages 69 (bottom), 71 (bottom), 72 (top and bottom), 75 (top and bottom); Mrs Simonne Dyer, pages 76(3), 78, 79, 80; G. Livingstone Evans, pages 94 (top and bottom), 95; Edward Diestelkamp, page 96; Mark Fiennes, pages 99 (left and right), 168, 169(3); Francis Johnson, pages 107, 109; Sir Samuel Storey, page 107 (bottom); James Fletcher-Watson, pages 113 (left and right), 114, 115 (top and bottom), 116 (left and right); W. Schomberg Scott, pages 118(3), 120; Earl Granville, page 121; Sir Martyn Beckett, page 123; *Lancashire Life*, page 126; Aerofilms Ltd, page 131; Casson and Conder Partnership, pages 150, 151; Ian Leith, page 157; Charles Hall, pages 167(3), 170 (left and right), 171 (top and bottom); Harry Graham, page 172; Surrey County Council, page 180 (right); Lord O'Neill, pages 186, 187 (top and bottom); Robin Leigh-Pemberton, page 189 (left and right); Peter Reid, page 190 (left and right); Sir Michael Blake, page 191; Sebastian de Ferranti, page 193.

For photographs in the Gazetteer thanks are due to: *Country Life*, pages 198, 200, 234; SNMR, pages 201, 207, 217; Harry Graham, page 203; William Bell, page 206; Martin Andrews, page 211 (top); Ian Grant, page 211(2); Anthony Jaggard, pages 215, 219(2); Sir Martyn Beckett, pages 216, 217 (top), 227 (bottom), 229(2); W. Schomberg Scott, page 221 (left); Louis Osman, page 221 (right); Roger White, page 227 (top); *Derbyshire Life*, page 228; Robert McKinstrey, page 223; Peter Reid, page 232; James Fletcher-Watson, page 233 (top and bottom).

In addition, thanks are due to the following authors and publishers for permission to quote copyright material in the text: Michael Davie and Weidenfeld and Nicolson for an extract from *The Diaries of Evelyn Waugh*; 'Jennifer's Diary' of *Harpers and Queen* Magazine for an extract from September 1983; Portmeirion Limited for extracts from the works of Clough Williams-Ellis.

INDEX

*Numbers in italics refer to captions
of illustrations*